Banking in Transition Economies

Developing Market Oriented Banking Sectors in Eastern Europe

John Bonin

*Professor of Economics, Wesleyan University, United States
and Editor, Journal of Comparative Economics*

Kálmán Mizsei

*Chairman, Hungarian Export Credit Insurance Company
and President, Hungarian Export–Import Bank, Hungary*

István Székely

*General Manager, Economics and Research Department,
National Bank of Hungary and Senior Lecturer, Budapest
University of Economics, Hungary*

Paul Wachtel

*Research Professor of Economics, Stern School of Business,
New York University, United States and Senior Economic
Advisor, Institute for EastWest Studies, United States*

Edward Elgar

Cheltenham, UK • Northampton, MA, USA

Published by
Edward Elgar Publishing Limited
8 Lansdown Place
Cheltenham
Glos GL50 2HU
UK

Edward Elgar Publishing, Inc.
6 Market Street
Northampton
Massachusetts 01060
USA

A catalogue record for this book
is available from the British Library

Library of Congress Cataloguing in Publication Data

Banking in transition economies: developing market oriented banking
    sectors in Eastern Europe / John P. Bonin . . . [et al.].
        Includes bibliographical references.
        1. Banks and banking—Europe, Eastern. 2. Banks and banking—
    Europe, Central. 3. Europe, Eastern—Economic policy—1989–
    4. Europe, Central—Economic policy. 5. Post-communism—Europe,
    Eastern. 6. Post-communism—Europe, Central. I. Bonin, John.
    HG2980.7.A6B346   1998
    332.1'0947—dc21   97–41480
                                                                  CIP

ISBN 1 85898 604 4
Printed and bound in Great Britain by
MPG Books Ltd, Bodmin, Cornwall

Banking in Transition Economies

Contents

List of Tables   *vii*
About the Authors   *ix*
Preface   *xi*

1. Towards Market-Oriented Banking
    for the Economies in Transition:
    A Summary of Policy Recommendations   1

2. Bank Privatization in Hungary, Poland
    and the Czech Republic   19

3. The Role of Foreign Banks in Economies in Transition   57

4. Regulation of Bank Failures   101

5. Retail Banking in Central and Eastern Europe   141

References   *187*
Index   *191*

Tables

3.1	Distribution of Ownership of Total Banking Sector Assets, 1988	60
3.2	Number of Banks by Type	77
3.3	Major Foreign Banking Activities in Poland	79
3.4	Structure of Banking in Hungary, 1994	82
3.5	Large Banks and Foreign Shares of Banking Activity in Hungary	85
3.6	Foreign Banking Activities in Hungary	86
3.7	Structure of Banking in the Czech Republic, 1994	87
3.8	Foreign Banking Activities in the Czech Republic	89
3.9	Distribution of Bank Lending in the Czech Republic	91
5.1	The Shares of Retail Deposits and Loans in Five CEE Countries	145
5.2	The Shares of Forex Deposits and Loans in Five CEE Countries	146
5.3	Market Position of SBs in CEE (in percent)	151
5.4	Net Credits to Households, Corporate Sector, and Government in the Czech Republic	162
5.5	The Shares of Retail Deposits and Credits in the Czech Republic, 1990–94	163
5.6	Maturity Structures of Credits and Deposits in the Czech Republic, 1991–94	164
5.7	Net Credits to Households, Corporate Sector, and Government in Hungary, 1989–94	169
5.8	The Shares of Retail Deposits and Credits in Hungary, 1989–94	171
5.9	Household Savings and Portfolio Structures in Hungary, 1990–94	172
5.10	The Asset Side of the Balance Sheet of OTP	178
5.11	The Liability Side of the Balance Sheet of OTP	179

About the Authors

JOHN BONIN is Professor of Economics at Wesleyan University in Middletown, Connecticut, US, and was the co-director (with Kálmán Mizsei) of the Institute for EastWest Studies project on state withdrawal from the banking system. He has published extensively on the theory of the labor-managed firm, including a recent survey on producer cooperatives in the *Journal of Economic Literature*. He is the editor of the *Journal of Comparative Economics* and the past-President of the Association for Comparative Economics. He received his PhD from the University of Rochester.

KÁLMÁN MIZSEI is President of both the Hungarian Export–Import Bank and the Export Credit Insurance Corporation. From 1992 to 1995 he was the Vice-President for Economic Programs at the Institute for EastWest Studies, where he conducted studies of enterprise bankruptcy, corporate governance, and banking reform. He is the editor of *Developing Public Finance in the Emerging Market Economies* and of *From Association to Accession* (with Andrzej Rudka). In 1993, at the request of the Hungarian Minister of Finance, he and an international group of experts helped to revise the country's bankruptcy law. Dr Mizsei has a PhD in economics from Budapest University.

ISTVÁN SZÉKELY is a general manager in the Economics and Research Department of the National Bank of Hungary and a senior lecturer in the Department of Mathematical Economics and Econometrics of the Budapest University. He has also worked previously at the United Nations, Bonn University, the University of Cambridge, and was a visiting scholar at Wesleyan University. An associate editor of the *Journal of Structural Change and Economic Dynamics*, he was co-editor of the books *Industrial Restructuring and Trade Reorientation in Eastern Europe, Development and Reform of the Financial System in Central and Eastern Europe, and Hungary: An Economy in Transition*, and co-author of the book *Practical Econometrics*, as well as a contributor to numerous journals. He took his PhD at the University of Cambridge and his MA at Budapest University of Economics, where he lectured until 1989.

PAUL WACHTEL is the Senior Economic Advisor for Economic Programs at the Institute for EastWest Studies and Research Professor of Economics at the Stern School of Business at New York University. He has also been a consultant on banking and financial sector issues to the World Bank, the International Monetary Fund, and the Bank of Israel. He is the author of *Macroeconomics: From Theory to Practice* and many journal articles on inflation, saving behavior, and financial markets. He received a PhD from the University of Rochester and has been at the Stern School since 1972, serving as chairman of the Department of Economics from 1983 to 1990.

Preface

This volume is the finale of an Institute for EastWest Studies project on Comparative Privatization which was established in 1994 with the support of the European Bank for Reconstruction and Development, the World Bank and the United Nations Development Program under the direction of Dr Kálmán Mizsei, then the Institute's Vice President for Economics. The final phase of the project focused on creating market-oriented banking sectors and this volume presents the findings and conclusions of the project team.

Our findings were presented at task force meeting in London in December 1995. We are grateful to the European Bank for Reconstruction and Development, and in particular to Deputy Vice President Guy de Selliers, for hosting the meeting and to the British Know-How fund for its support.

Chapter 1 – the summary of policy recommendations – was published in March 1996 as an Institute for EastWest Studies task force report by John Bonin, Kálmán Mizsei and Paul Wachtel.

Portions of the manuscript were presented at the first forum of the Economic Policy Initiative, a joint project of the IEWS and the Centre for Economic Policy Research (London), held in Warsaw in January 1996. In addition, the policy recommendations (Chapter 1) were presented by Paul Wachtel to central bank and other groups in Sofia and Talinn in May 1996. Finally, a paper drawing on Chapters 2 and 3 was presented by John Bonin and Paul Wachtel to the Second Dubrovnik Conference on Transition Economies, June 1996.

Country researchers provided information on banking sector developments in five key transition economies. The authors would like to express their gratitude to Ervin Apathy (Hungary), Roman Kramarík (Czech Republic), Nikolay Markov (Bulgaria), Marten Ross (Estonia) and Jan Solarz (Poland).

Additionally, we would like to thank a number of individuals at the IEWS and elsewhere for various and always competent help throughout the project: Jeffrey Davis, Rumen Dobrinsky, Arjun Jayaraman, Kaja Kell, Gunnar Kraft, Mitch Mitchell, Radoslav Petkov, Erki Raasuke, Mike Reagan, Tammy Smith, Tamara Trayler and Dean Wilson. In addition, we would like to acknowledge the intellectual contributions of Istvan Abel on Chapter 5, Bozena Leven and Roman Kramarick on Chapter 2 and Lorand Ambrus, Ervin Apathy and Stan Bereza on Chapter 4.

A number of individuals provided valuable comments on all or part of the manuscript. We are grateful to Jack Sustman for his thorough editorial review of the whole book and to Ami Barnea and Richard Grossman, for helpful comments. Finally, the support of John Mroz, President of the IEWS, and Anthony Solomon, chairman of the Economics Program, are gratefully appreciated.

1. Towards Market-Oriented Banking for the Economies in Transition: A Summary of Policy Recommendations

Privatizing the banking sector in the economies in transition (EITs) requires the state to disengage from direct governance of financial institutions and to assume its rightful arms-length role as bank regulator and supervisor. Although substantial strides toward privatization have been taken, several significant problems are still pervasive. First, the state is still excessively involved in the business of the banks (especially those created from the old financial structure). This is a problem that the EITs share with many Western countries, both developed and developing. Second, the infrastructure for bank supervision and regulation has not developed as quickly as it should. Third, economic growth is inhibited by the lagging development of banking sectors that are able to support and promote real sector growth.

The first issue indicates that the banks created from the state are both too big and too politicized to change. Hence, privatization as practiced to date in EITs often fails to insure independent governance. Rather, it often entrenches state/insider control. Lessons learned from experiences to date can be applied in the EITs where privatization efforts are just getting underway. Privatization should be designed in a way that (i) fosters a competitive environment so that the financial sector is not dominated by just a few institutions and (ii) leads to privatized institutions whose governance is independent of the government.

An important lesson from financial sector developments so far in the EITs is that the infrastructure for bank supervision must be developed very quickly. The privatization process is only meaningful if state ownership is replaced by a transparent relationship between the privatized banks and the government. There are several aspects of this relationship which ought to be put in place as privatization occurs: (i) a responsible and independent bank examiner must be in place; (ii) capital adequacy standards should be defined; (iii) strategy for dealing with banks that do not satisfy regulatory requirements should be in place.

In general, the privatization process will have accomplished very little if the regulators have no effective means of influencing bank behavior.

1

Furthermore, if all banks are viewed as being too big to fail, the government has not effectively disengaged itself from the banking sector.

The failure to establish a functioning independent banking sector has serious macroeconomic implications. Banks in the EITs have tended to restructure their asset portfolios away from lending to the business sector and toward safer high-yield government securities. In effect, banks are financing government spending and not intermediating between savers and borrowers in the real sector due to the perceived excessive riskiness of the latter activity. The challenge is to induce banks to take on the roles played by healthy banks in vibrant, growing economies.

The challenges faced by banking officials in the EITs are formidable, but not ones that we believe are insurmountable. The essential problem is that three tasks, each one difficult in its own right, must be taken on at the same time.

First, the state-owned banks must be restructured so that their balance sheets are healthy. This involves removing or writing off worthless assets and providing adequate capital. Moreover, the banks must stop extending credit to non-viable business enterprises which leads to the further accumulation of worthless assets.

Second, the banking sector should be privatized. The central role of banks makes privatization of this sector much more compelling than the privatization of any other industry. The failure to privatize the steel industry, for example, can lead to some misallocation of capital and labor that could be more productively deployed elsewhere; the failure to privatize the banks inhibits the development of any means for the efficient allocation of capital throughout the economy. Moreover, effective privatization goes beyond a formal change in ownership structure. It must be accompanied by a change in control as well.

Third, the regulatory structure must be organized and operational. That is, the structure for bank examination and supervision should be put in place as soon as the privatization process starts.

In addition to the operational issues faced by central bank and other authorities, policymakers need to discuss strategic issues. The process of change in the EITs started very quickly and dramatically as political changes unfolded. Thus, there was little opportunity to think strategically about the ultimate outcomes that are sought. Strategic issues are particularly important with respect to the banking sector.

The strategy for the banking sector should involve objectives with respect to the desired competitive structure and the appropriate regulatory framework. For example, there should be some planning about the role of savings banks or the role of commercial banks that have a dominant market role. Will these banks be allowed to wither in size as competitive pressures dictate? Will there be political pressures to preserve their market shares?

Strategy for bank failure should also be a matter of discussion among policy makers. Is every financial institution too big to fail? Is the threat to close a bank or force a merger sufficiently credible to influence the risk taking behavior of owners? Effective regulation requires a clear understanding of the kinds of regulatory responses that will occur. Capital, liquidity and other requirements are important, but it is also necessary to specify the sanctions that will be imposed when violations occur and such sanctions should be credible. Finally, there will inevitably be instances where the government will consider extraordinary and even extralegal interventions in the banking sector. Such interventions may be warranted in very rare circumstances and should not be expected as part of the normal sequence of events.

Our policy recommendations are divided into three sections. First, the issues of privatization are discussed. Second, we discuss broader issues that relate to the transformation of the existing financial institutions into viable banking institutions that can contribute to macroeconomic development. Finally, we discuss the development of an appropriate regulatory structure.

1. PRIVATIZATION OF STATE-OWNED BANKS

In the financial sector reform of EITs, state-owned commercial banks (SOCBs) were created as joint stock companies by hiving off the commercial portfolios of the national banks and dividing the clients along regional (for example, Poland) or sectoral (for example, Hungary) lines. Savings banks, one each in Hungary and the Czech Republic and two in Poland, and the commercial foreign trade bank in each country also became joint stock companies with almost full state ownership. The objective of privatization is to leave these banks independent of direct state governance with the state assuming its proper role of regulatory control. A coherent plan for financial liberalization requires effective coordination between bank privatization and regulation.

Bank privatization policy in EITs refers to the partial or complete divestiture of state-held ownership shares in the existing joint-stock banks. One of the goals of privatization is to strengthen the financial capability of the bank by augmenting its capital base. This has not always been the case in the transactions to date, as revenues from privatization have usually gone to the government privatization agency (Treasury). However, public funds have often been used to recapitalize banks, usually by substituting government securities for nonperforming loans, prior to privatization.[1]

When created as part of the two-tier banking system, the state-owned commercial banks (SOCBs) were sources of revenue for the state budget. At just the time when the SOCBs needed to become financially stronger, governments tended to drain liquidity from the banks through tax and dividend policies. According to domestic accounting practice, accrued interest was part of the tax base so that nonperforming loans provided taxable income but no cash flow. This philosophy carried over to the privatization process as selling state-owned bank shares was expected to bring in significant government revenues. The future financial strength of the bank was in many instances not of primary concern. Dividend policy often reflected the desire of the state-owner to draw liquidity from the banks. As the actual poor quality of the portfolios of the banks began to be recognized, rapid provisioning and state recapitalization were needed for banks' own capital to meet the newly adopted regulatory requirements.

The financial needs of the newly born banks and the fiscal needs of the state were often at odds in the early period of economic transition. In fact, the banking sector needs additional capital in order to develop adequate lending capabilities in a business environment that has both great growth potential and high risks. Therefore,

- *When created as joint stock companies, the SOCBs must be viewed as independent financial entities in need of internal accumulation of capital in order to strengthen their lending capacity and not as sources of revenue for the fiscal budget.*

Privatization is a natural source of such capital but the legacies of the government's perception of banks as sources of revenue negatively impacts policies. Furthermore, recapitalizing the SOCBs without changing significantly governance, and consequently bank behavior, invites continued bad lending as the expectation of future bailouts prevails. Privatization should lead to improvement in the quality of management and to improvements in the efficiency of operations. Government support of banks should be conditioned on improved behavior. Hence,

- *To change the expectation that future government support (bailout) is likely, recapitalization should be linked directly to the privatization process by levering state funds with an infusion of new capital from the sale of government shares to augment each bank's own capital.*

The governance and business strategy of the banks will depend crucially on the ownership structure that results from privatization. The different methods of divestiture used include initial public offering (IPO), private placement with a strategic foreign financial investor (SFFI), voucher distribution, or some combination of the above. Of these, IPOs and vouchers result in dispersed ownership, leaving the state (as it usually retains a significant share) and bank management (insiders) locked in a struggle over bank governance. An independent core investor must then rely on thin and somewhat non-transparent secondary markets to accumulate the necessary stake. In cases where ownership is dispersed after partial state divestiture, the transfer of governance to an independent body awaits the 'second' round of privatization. Hence,

- *The privatization method chosen should maximize the likelihood that the governance of the bank will be independent of the state and of existing bank management. This is most likely to occur when a core investor obtains a significant stake in the bank.*

As corollaries,

- *A strong bank CEO can influence significantly the privatization process so as to prevent independent governance and to continue with 'business as usual.' The practice of negotiating bank policy with the state will often be to the detriment of future management efficiency.*

- *Non-state core investors who can exercise managerial control should be encouraged. In particular, strategic foreign investors are a positive means of introducing independent management.*

Although some legitimate concerns about foreign dominance of a country's banking system exist, foreign investment represents the best source of strategic investors who can augment the bank's capital position and bring about independent governance quickly. Thus, policies that limit significantly foreign participation in bank privatization in EITs unduly insulate the domestic sector and preclude the most fruitful and least costly avenues for banking sector development.

The country most open to foreign banking, Hungary, also chose the strategy of searching for SFFIs to privatize SOCBs. Given the existence of a large number of SOCBs of questionable franchise value in the region, this search takes time and resources. Such a strategy not only allows the augmentation of the bank's own capital but also results in an increase in its franchise value due to the reputational capital supplied by the foreign investor.

The difficulty in pursuing this policy lies not only in the excess supply of seekers but also in the need to determine a selling price for the transaction. From the perspective of the potential buyer, there may be a substantial option value to waiting (for example, Allied Irish and WBK in Poland).[2] Uncertainty and weak demand may lead to administrative pricing that fails to capture fully the future expectations of the market and result in the perception that a bank was 'given away' to foreigners (for example, Bank Slaski to ING in Poland). Despite the potential political problems and the transaction costs involved, successful searches for SFFIs are likely to pay off in improved performance and enhanced franchise value. Hence,

- *Attempts to find a SFFI are worth the time and resources because they promise to achieve an independent counterbalance to state/insider control. Furthermore, there should be no barrier to the strategic foreign investor exercising control and obtaining majority ownership.*

Experience with IPOs in Poland indicate difficulties with using nascent developing stock markets to privatize SOCBs. In addition to the pricing problem mentioned above and the dispersed ownership resulting, the IPO depends for its success on substantial absorption capacity of the market and an appropriate institutional infrastructure for registering and trading. To the extent that IPOs result in dispersed non-state ownership, state and insider control continue (for example, BPH in Poland and the recent effort by the Finance Ministry to include its almost majority stake in this privatized bank in the Bank Handlowy group). Voucher distribution avoids many of the problems of an IPO, although it too is likely to result in dispersed ownership. Experience in the Czech Republic indicates an ability to use the mass privatization infrastructure to effectuate ownership transfer of SOCBs to the public without any pricing or absorption capacity problems. The emergence of investment funds consolidated some of the ownership shares, leaving a potential governance role for the funds. The possibility of an independent investor accumulating a core stake may be improved because funds can exchange larger blocks of shares. Secondary markets may allow the accumulation of core-investor stakes more rapidly so that the second wave of privatization may promote independent governance more quickly. Hence,

- *If speed of state divestiture is a primary goal, the voucher method of distribution is preferred to the IPO because of lower transaction costs.*

As a corollary,

- *Combining voucher distribution with a tender designed to attract an SFFI would both lead to independent governance and avoid the problems associated with IPOs.*

Finding a SFFI requires that the proper conditions for privatization be achieved. For many of the SOCBs in the region, these conditions may not be obtainable in the first wave of privatization. Alternatives that move in the direction of independent control include seeking institutional investors – both domestic and foreign – and encouraging domestic banks to take core investor stakes. However, there is an unfortunate tendency to encourage outside investors but to balk when they attempt to exercise any independent control, particularly when the core investors are foreign.[3]

The international financial institutions have been actively involved in financial sector reform and bank privatization in the EITs. Regarding privatization, the European Bank for Reconstruction and Development (EBRD) has played a catalyst role by taking significant ownership stakes in SOCBs (for example, WBK, BPH). As a temporary owner and caretaker, EBRD has a strong interest in not only the independent governance of the bank but also in the overall development of the financial sector. To protect its investment, EBRD can align with minority shareholders to exert independent governance. However, the large residual state stake held in the privatized banks can interfere with this attempt (for example, the BPH account above). A coherent and integrated strategy involving not only the EBRD but the other international institutions is necessary to prevent inappropriate state intervention in the evolution of proper bank governance. Hence,

- *The international finance institutions should pursue a coherent policy regarding financial sector reform, for example, by relating conditionality for structural adjustment loans from the World Bank to independent bank governance.*

The dual objective of state disengagement from direct control over bank business and state assumption of its proper regulatory function requires that any remaining state ownership stake in the SOCBs be administered in a passive way. That the state will hold some significant ownership stake in the SOCBs in the medium term is likely so as to not 'rush' the first stage of privatization and to establish the proper conditions for independent governance in the second stage of privatization. The conflict between the bank's need to use its cash flow to strengthen its own capital base and the state's desire for fiscal support must be resolved. Hence,

- *The agent responsible for holding and representing the state's ownership stake must not be the fiscal authority; in particular, government ministries should not have representation on the governing board of the bank.*

2. TRANSITION POLICY

Financial sector reform involves the transformation of a virtually passive banking structure of a centrally planned economy into an active financial sector supporting the development of the real sector. In addition to the restructuring and privatization of existing banking entities, reform strategy focuses on 'privatizing' the banking sector. Specifically, entry and exit policies must be designed to promote the financial health and competitiveness of a banking sector independent from direct state control but subject to state regulation intended to insure prudent and sound banking practices.

The fast-reforming EITs both established regulations based on international standards and encouraged entry of 'de novo' banks with low initial capital requirements. The resulting banking sectors consisted of a few large SOCBs and many small new banks.

Relatively easy entry was viewed as a means of quickly introducing competition into the banking sector. However, many of these institutions in Poland, Hungary, and the Czech Republic encountered difficulties. The new entrants were often ill-prepared for the banking business, and bank supervisory agencies were not prepared to monitor their activities. Thus, easy entry created many problems and largely failed in its stated aim of increasing competition in banking.

Both the large domestic SOCBs, with their dominant market share but the burden of nonperforming loans to their inherited clients, and the small new entrants find themselves undercapitalized and unable to meet the needs of the developing real sectors in all EITs. Thus, efforts should be made to create and enforce appropriate standards for capital adequacy.

- *Capital requirements should be increased for both new bank licenses and for existing banks that were created under the laxer regime to encourage mergers and takeovers of undercapitalized small private banks.*

In the expansion of the banking sectors in the initial stages of the transition process, regulators often failed to impose the standards applied in developed countries. Bank regulators should have the discretion to allocate bank licenses only to individuals deemed 'fit and proper.' Both the political climate, in which such discretion would be viewed as more of the old cronyism, and the lack of credible regulators explain why such policies were not applied. However, the resulting proliferation of small banks, some of which are of dubious origin, indicates a need for stricter supervision of licensing. Hence, regarding entry policies,

- *The supervisory structure must be strengthened to the point where it is competent to effectively exercise discretion over who should be allowed to set up a bank. The supervisory agency must offer adequate compensation to attract capable and competent personnel.*

It is important that the regulatory discretion over bank entry and bank mergers should not be distorted so as to protect the existing industry from competition. Competition is introduced most effectively by foreign participation in the banking sector (for example, Hungary). However, many countries seek to protect and strengthen domestic banks by requiring foreign banks to buy into the existing banks (that is, takeover of smaller banks or the purchase of stakes in privatizing SOCBs). Hence,

- *There should be no special restrictions on the entry of foreign banks (that is, greenfield operations) or the purchase of existing banks by foreigners.*

> *Foreign entrants should be subject to the same capital adequacy and exam ination standards that would apply to any domestic entrant or purchaser. Moreover, foreign banks should be expected to buy or absorb existing domestic banks as a cost of entry.*

National governments likely will be concerned with significant foreign ownership of total bank assets. Widespread foreign ownership of the banking sector may eventually lead regulators to take a harsher view of foreign entrants or purchasers. However, such concerns should not be used as a means of defending existing state ownership and management structures. In the transition process, a search for a SFFI should not be inhibited by additional review procedures being placed on foreign investors.

Exit policy is complex in the transition phase due to the excessively risky nature of traditional lending operations. On the one hand, many of the traditional clients of the banks are in need of extensive restructuring to meet the demands of the new market conditions. On the other hand, much of the growth of the real sector comes from new start-up firms without much of a financial or business history. The well-run banks are trying to extricate themselves from traditional clients who are unable to meet even their existing financial obligations (that is, bad loans). Providing the financing necessary for restructuring or growth of small new firms is risky in any economy. The transition exacerbates this risk. Exit policy must take account of both the bad loans problem due to the legacies of the past burdening of SOCBs and the inevitable failure of some of the small undercapitalized new banks.

Country experiences in dealing with the bad loans problem differ, but the basic principles apply throughout. The central issue is to avoid creating expectations that state banks are 'too big to fail' or 'too political to fail.' As we argue above, linking recapitalization to privatization when an independent core investor is found is one way to achieve this goal. In many cases, this is not immediately possible so that an interim policy must be designed. Any recapitalization policy should take into account the incentive problem of signalling to the management that the state stands prepared to bail out the bank when imprudent actions are the cause of its financial distress. The scarce supply of competent personnel in the bank should also not be overly burdened with the mistakes of the past. Loan workout divisions can be breeding grounds for competent loan officers, but focusing the 'best and the brightest' on the past rather than on evaluating the profitability of future, often new, clients is inappropriate. Hence, regarding recapitalization,

- *The asset portfolio of the bank must be 'marked to market' as quickly as possible and the entire balance sheet should be downsized in the process.*

- *Additional resources must be provided to the workout of problem loans, either by establishing a hospital bank or by providing financial support using recovery contracts with the proper incentives.*

- *The 'hole' (or negative net worth) arising from marking to market the asset portfolio should not be filled solely by public funds without strong assurances that management practices and personnel will behave prudently in the future (for example, removal of current management and provision of proper incentive contracts).*

- *Additional capital from non-public sources, especially an infusion of new capital from shareholders and/or new owners, should be used in conjunction with public funds.*

- *Bank management should not have any explicit or implicit obligation to continue lending to enterprises that are not appropriate credit risks. If necessary, subsidies to firms should be provided directly by the government and not channeled through the banking system.*

The inevitable failures of small undercapitalized banks must be dealt with expeditiously to contain and isolate problems and avoid systemic failure. The supervisory framework must be sufficiently developed to prevent runs of the banks by uninformed depositors. The safety net must not be so extensive as to allow informed agents to shirk their responsibilities of prudent behavior. Intervention should occur before the net worth of the bank becomes zero and closure is in order. Hence, regarding bank failures,

- *A transparent sequence of graduated intervention should be in place to signal potential problems with banks and trigger responses designed to preclude failure.*

- *Within this framework, individualized treatment based on the bank's characteristics is preferable to general bailouts.*

- *Financial obligation for the situation must be shared among the responsible parties, namely, the bank's management, its shareholders, and the informed depositors. Specifically, commercial clients on both sides of the balance sheet should share in the write-off (that is, their deposits should not be fully insured).*

- *Any bailout, full or partial, using public funds should involve conditionalty. Management should be replaced or, at least, sanctioned.*

During the transition, increased competition will provide additional market discipline. The competitiveness of a banking sector is a two-edged sword. On the one hand, competition promotes both product development and enhanced services to clients while ensuring that interest spreads represent a reasonable return for risk taken. On the other hand, unbridled competition can lead to excessive risk-taking as the possibility of systemic failure is not included in the individual bank's decision to increase the risk of its loan portfolio on the margin. The artful balance of these two forces makes a banking sector both vibrant and healthy. Banking sectors in EITs tend to be both moribund and unhealthy during the transition. Hence,

- *Pro-active policies should be undertaken to promote competition in the financial sector and to encourage the downsizing of banks created from the traditional financial apparatus. Specifically, non-bank domestic financial institutions should be encouraged to develop and foreign participation on equal terms should be espoused.*

- *The tax code should be 'merger-friendly' to encourage market-driven consolidation of the banking sector (in contrast to the orchestrated consolidation underway in Poland).*

Bank regulators who will have to approve mergers and acquisitions should be concerned with influencing the competitive structure of the banking system.

- *Regulatory policy should foster a competitive market structure. Bank consolidations should be encouraged when they will form viable institutions and discouraged when concentration is likely to choke competition. Moreover, anti-trust (competition) agencies need to be more assertive in the banking industry than they generally have been.*

Savings institutions often require special attention. Regulation of the thrift industry depends on which model is chosen for the development of the industry. Two possibilities exist: a narrow bank model and a universal banking model. A narrow bank is a deposit-taking institution that restricts itself to assets with very little risk and provides limited banking activities, basically the provision of payments services. Such a bank would have a very restricted range of activities and would also have extensive deposit guarantees. There are examples of such institutions in many large countries, for example Japan and Germany, and the savings banks could develop in this way. However, the speed of product innovation in the financial sector suggests that narrow saving banks may not be viable in the long run. In both the economies in transition and elsewhere, the commercial banks have been expanding into the retail deposit-taking sector.

An alternative and more likely model is to allow the state-owned savings banks to simply evolve into universal banks. The sheer size of the state savings banks in many EITs is worrisome. However, the rapid development of competition from commercial banks expanding into the retail sector and from foreign banks indicate that the dominant market share of the state savings banks will erode quickly. Thus, it may be unnecessary to consider the break-up of monopoly savings banks.

Savings banks that evolve as universal banks would compete with existing commercial banks, develop new products and innovate. This is a perfectly satisfactory development if several conditions are satisfied. First, there must be an agency for rigorous bank examination. Second, the regulator must have powers to enforce capital adequacy standards. A significant danger in the evolution of monopoly banks into privatized universal banks is that the institutions are viewed as being too big to fail and therefore are largely immune from regulatory oversight. The high levels of concentration are likely to lead to bank bailouts and recapitalizations by the government, which will create inefficiency in the industry. On the other hand, breaking up the large monopoly deposit banks into many undercapitalized, small institutions with little managerial experience is not a good alternative.

- *Policy makers should develop a clear view of the evolving role of savings institutions. A single savings institution with monopoly powers should be avoided. The savings industry should not be insulated from competitive forces by excessive deposit insurance guarantees.*

3. DESIGNING THE REGULATORY STRUCTURE

The appropriate design of bank regulatory structure is not a problem that is restricted to the economies in transition. In the wake of recent banking crises, both large and small countries around the world are, once again, grappling with the issues. Authorities have come to realize the importance of a well designed structure for bank regulation. Moreover, it is clear that no matter how well intentioned, the regulatory framework must also be managed in ways that make regulatory discipline credible. The challenge for the economies in transition is designing a structure for bank regulation that can also be quickly and effectively implemented.

Large country experiences have illustrated the importance of these issues. For example, in the United States, although an inadequate regulatory structure was not, in all likelihood, responsible for the crisis in the thrift industry in the 1980s, the inadequacies of the regulatory response probably made the crisis more severe than it needed to be. A similar argument can be made regarding the ongoing crisis in Japanese banking. Although a regulatory structure is in place, it has not responded in as timely a fashion as it should. A design of a regulatory structure that insures a timely and well-informed response to problems as they develop is a topic of international interest. These experiences in major countries suggest that conventional forms of bank supervision may not be able to stem bank failures in all situations. Perhaps the implicit understanding that authorities will rescue any bank in collapse and, at the very least, make the depositors whole creates an insurmountable moral hazard problem.

Although an effective regulatory structure is extremely important, it should be understood that legislation that establishes a regulatory framework is not a simple panacea for all potential problems. That is, the regulatory structure is a necessary but not a sufficient condition for a sound banking system. Moreover, the staffing and training of the bank regulatory structure is both a difficult and expensive task. An effective regulatory agency evolves; it cannot be put in place instantaneously.

Furthermore, a regulatory framework is not a substitute for the salutary effects of market discipline but should complement it. The regulatory authorities in New Zealand have come to this realization and are introducing a system where conventional bank regulation will be augmented by market discipline; no deposit insurance will be provided and there will be extensive requirements for banks to regularly publish information on their condition.

The first issue to consider is simply where bank regulatory powers should be located. There are three possibilities – in the government (for example, Ministry of Finance), in the central bank, or in an independent bank regulatory authority. The disadvantages of placing bank regulatory authority (including the power to close banks) under the authority of a cabinet member are obvious.

- *Bank regulatory agencies should be independent of the government and protected from political pressures.*

The central bank, especially when its independence has been firmly established, is a logical agency for bank regulation. The principal function of a central bank is to act as the source of liquidity for the financial sector, which is both a macroeconomic monetary function and a bank regulatory one. The macroeconomic function relates to the aggregate amount of liquidity that is provided. The regulatory function relates to how much liquidity is provided to particular financial institutions. The central bank can determine whether to provide liquidity to a particular bank and what the terms of such loans should be. The central bank will often have a broader supervisory role as well because it is more able to attract and pay capable staff than other government agencies.

The existence of a liquidity facility implies that the central bank, as a lender, will want to have the information any lender would require. Thus, the central bank's role as bank examiner follows from the existence of the central bank lending facility. However, central bank lending should not be distorted into a means of providing government support to the banking system.

- *The central bank should provide a lender of last resort facility and also monitor the quality of such lending. That is, central bank lending should provide liquidity or discounting of banks' assets. Such lending should be made only after an appropriate assessment of the bank's creditworthiness.*

- *Central bank lending should not be used to provide government assistance to failed or failing banks. Furthermore, it should not be used to augment bank capital. Separate and distinct facilities should be utilized for the recapitalization of banks.*

- *As a result, the central bank should not bear sole responsibility for bank regulation.*

Regulatory oversight should not be the responsibility of the central bank alone for at least two reasons. First, macroeconomic credit goals of the central bank and the liquidity needs of individual banking institutions may be in conflict. For example, the central bank may well be reluctant to take regulatory actions that might lead to increased demand for central bank loans if, at the same time, macroeconomic policy dictates that credit expansion be constrained.[4]

Second, in the event that the central bank does not provide liquidity to a troubled banking institution, another regulatory structure to monitor and deal with the troubled institution needs to be in place. That is, there needs to be an independent regulatory agency that can either close down or sustain failed banks.

- *A two-tiered regulatory structure is preferable. The first tier is the central bank, which provides a liquidity facility and a supervisory and monitoring function in order to judge when liquidity should be provided. The second tier should be provided by an independent agency that licenses banking activity and provides guarantees of banking operations.*

The division of regulatory responsibilities between the central bank and the independent bank regulatory agency will vary from situation to situation. The responsibilities of the independent agency can include: (i) granting and removing bank licenses, (ii) determining the range of acceptable banking activities, and (iii) maintaining a scheme for deposit insurance. In some instances, the first two functions are preformed by the central bank and in some instances the deposit insurance function is independent of other regulatory structures.

- *The deposit insurance agency should also have regulatory powers that enable it to restrict bank activity and/or remove a banking license. Thus, the insurer should be able to act before there is a need to call on the limited insurance funds.*

Since it is almost impossible (in the EITs or elsewhere) to envision a deposit insurance fund that is sufficiently well capitalized to provide insurance against all risks, the deposit insurance agency should have sufficient power to minimize the calls on the insurance funds. Thus, the deposit insurance agency should also have extensive regulatory powers over banks.

In order to make the deposit insurance scheme credible, the rules regarding the deposit insurance scheme should be as transparent as possible and should be uniformly and consistently applied. Any deviation from specified rules will create the expectation that the government is willing to guarantee the continued existence of banks, which simply encourages moral hazard problems.

- *Any deposit insurance scheme should have transparent rules that are consistently applied. The government should not create the expectation that it will extend guarantees beyond the specified insurance scheme.*

With respect to all aspects of bank regulation, it is important that there be a credible commitment to the structure and the rules. In both large countries and small, the efficacy of bank regulation is undercut when all the players – bankers, governments, and so on – believe that, in the event of any bank failure, there will be some provision of liquidity or government-financed recapitalization that guarantees the continued operation of the bank in trouble. Bank regulation is only effective if a fear exists of the consequences of non-compliance.

Another aspect of bank regulation requires mention. As long as some state ownership of the banks continues (as is likely), the state's ownership role must not be confused with its regulatory functions.

- *The ownership role of the state should not be exercised by the agencies responsible for bank supervision.*

The specific design of the structure for bank regulation should reflect international standards for bank regulation. There are several specific implications of this:

- *Banks should adopt international accounting standards and standards for the classification of loans. In addition, auditing standards should be established that create an environment where accounting reports are viewed as credible.*

- *Bank regulators should make every effort to satisfy the conditions of the European Union association agreements.*

- *All banks should comply with the Basel minimum capital standards. Moreover, regulators should understand that the minimum capital standards are based on risk levels inherent in developed countries. Higher overall*

> *riskiness argues for higher capital asset ratios in the EITs than in the major industrial economies.*

The minimum risk-based capital requirements in the Basel agreements are often taken as an appropriate standard for banks in the region. However, these standards were designed for well-run banks in a rather stable macroeconomic environment and apply risk adjustments that are appropriate for such an environment. In fact, the 8 percent minimum requirement is far too low for banks in the economies in transition.

Appropriate bank regulation goes beyond simply structuring the regulatory organizations. Important issues of implementation also can be very difficult to solve. In fact, the banking crises that have occurred in major Western countries are usually due to errors in implementation and not to the inadequacies of the regulatory structure.

The implementation of the deposit insurance scheme has already been discussed. A related issue is the coordination of the different regulatory powers. For example, the lender of last resort function of the central bank can provide liquidity that removes the appearances of a weak balance sheet. However, the bank regulators should not be complacent in such instances. The regulatory powers should be used to rectify the underlying balance sheet weakness.

> •   *Bank regulators should act promptly to change bank behavior before a crisis emerges.*

Coordination of regulatory authority is particularly important when banks may be viewed as being too big to fail. In such instances, which are very common, regulatory action must be timely because closing the bank with or without deposit insurance guarantees may be impossible for any of several reasons. Bank closure may be politically unfeasible or systemic consequences on the economy may be feared and closure may often impose costs that are beyond the capabilities of the deposit insurance scheme. If closure is precluded, then effective regulation takes the form of examining and disciplining the bank's activities. The regulators should have a clear understanding of the types of sanctions that can be imposed on a bank prior to closure. There should be a plan of action for dealing with failing banks that enable the regulators to forestall bank activity prior to failure.

> •   *Regulatory authorities must provide diligent examination of banks and respond promptly to any inadequacy, particularly when the bank is viewed as too big to fail. The failure to do so will lead to a loss of regulatory credibility.*

The failure of the regulators to respond promptly to poor banking practice when the banks are too big to fail will lead inevitably to re-nationalization of the banking sector. In all likelihood, situations will arise where governments decide that extraordinary interventions are warranted. Any such interventions should be limited to very rare circumstances and should not be accepted as part of the normal sequence of regulatory responses.

- *Regulators should have the tools to deal with failed or failing banks. They should be able to arrange the sale, merger, or recapitalization of banks without forcing bankruptcy or resorting to the re-nationalization of banks.*

Public policy in the transition economies should have a long-range view of the structure of the banking industry and how a competitive environment can be fostered. Competition in the banking industry can be fostered in many ways. In fact, the proliferation of many small, undercapitalized and inexperienced banks is not a good way to create a competitive environment. A small country can have a competitive financial system even with just a few banks. Competitive practices follow when the capital markets are open and there are no barriers to entry. Thus, the ability of customers to take all or part of their banking business abroad and the ability of foreign banks to enter can combine to make a concentrated small country banking system highly competitive.

- *Public policy should develop a long-run view of the structure of the banking industry that fosters the development of a competitive environment with healthy banking institutions.*

- *Supervisory and regulatory agencies should have a clear mandate to apply established policies. They should have an arms-length relationship from the government and from the banks themselves.*

CONCLUSION

The mandate for change in public policy towards banking in the economies in transition is very broad and very demanding. In fact, a look around the world indicates that many developed and developing countries with much more extensive private sector experience would measure up poorly against these tasks. However, that does not imply that the tasks faced in the EITs are impossible ones. Quite the contrary, we believe that public sector officials who remain keenly aware of the potential difficulties will be able to avoid many of the pitfalls and help build a functioning financial system throughout the region.

NOTES

1. In Hungary, the securities are serviced from general revenues and the Ministry of Finance acquired a substantial ownership stake from the recapitalization. In Poland, funds made available by donor countries and international financial institutions are available to service the securities once the SOCBs have been privatized. In the Czech Republic, ownership transfer of the large banks occurred through the mass voucher privatization program that generated no new capital for the banks involved in this first round.
2. This is illustrated by the example of Allied Irish and WBK in Poland.
3. Developments in the privatization of banks in Poland illustrate some of these problems. When BPH was privatized, Bank Slaski and ING each acquired about a 5 percent stake and the duo was negotiating the purchase of additional shares indicating a desire to take a core-investor stake. However in late 1995, the government announced its intention to place its substantial ownership stake (around 45 percent) with the Bank Handlowy group, which is itself being formed by government directive. This signals a desire to prevent an SFFI from consolidating its position. On the other hand, the privatization of Bank Gdanski resulted in the acquisition of a core-investor stake (24 percent) by a Polish bank BIG, a widely held private bank established in 1989 and quoted on the Warsaw Stock Exchange. These events suggest that the Polish Finance Ministry understands the advantages of privatization with a core investor but has a clear preference for domestic core investors (see also Chapter 2)
4. Perhaps a more likely and less desirable scenario occurs when the central bank is adding liquidity to the economy in order to finance or monetize the government's debt. In such situations, the central bank is unlikely to refuse bank demand for liquidity and may well be less than diligent in fulfilling its regulatory functions.

2. Bank Privatization in Hungary, Poland and the Czech Republic

1. INTRODUCTION: FROM STATE-OWNED TO PRIVATE(?) BANKS

Somewhat different approaches have been taken in the economies in transition (EITS) to the creation of a two-tier banking system. All involve the hiving off of commercial banking activities from the former state monobank, leaving an independent central bank to pursue monetary policy and exchange rate strategy. SOCBs have been born as joint-stock entities with predominant and often exclusive ownership of the shares by a state agency or agencies. In Hungary, the commercial portfolio of the National Bank of Hungary (NBH) was divided along sectoral lines to create three SOCBs. In Poland, the commercial portfolio of the National Bank of Poland (NBP) was divided on a regional basis to create nine SOCBs. Existing specialized banks, that is, the foreign trade (merchant) bank and the state savings bank(s), were granted universal charters and restructured as joint-stock companies. In Hungary, the foreign trade bank, the savings bank, and one of the three large SOCBs have been privatized. In Poland, the focus has been on privatizing the SOCBs with four completed to date; the large specialty banks, one foreign trade bank, two state savings banks (one for zloty deposits and one for foreign currency deposits) and an umbrella bank for local (agricultural) cooperative banks, have not yet been included in the bank privatization program.

In the Czech Republic, the commercial portfolio was separated from the socialist monobank, the Czechoslovak State Bank (ČSB), in 1990. Three new universal state-owned banks were born; two were SOCBs, one consisting of the Czech part of the commercial portfolio of the ČSB and one of the Slovak part, and one was an investment bank. Prior to this in 1969, the Czechoslovak Savings Bank had already been divided into a Czech and a Slovak Savings Bank controlled by their respective MoFs. The foreign trade bank established in 1964 has combined Czech and Slovak participation currently. These three specialized banks were granted universal charters in 1990. After its separation from Slovakia at the beginning of 1993, the big four banks in the Czech Republic consisted of one large SOCB, one large state savings bank, joint ownership in the state foreign trade bank, and an investment bank that had

19

been divided into two joint-stock companies (a Czech and a Slovak entity) prior to the first wave of voucher privatization in 1992.

In Bulgaria, the creation of the two-tier banking system occurred in two steps. In 1987, the Bulgarian National Bank (BNB) created seven specialized development banks to join an eighth that had been established independently in 1981. The purpose of these banks was to provide long-term investment credit to specific sectors of the economy. Full separation of all commercial activities from BNB occurred in 1990. At that time, any of the 145 branch offices of the commercial division of BNB were allowed to undertake commercial business either as an individual entity or in combination with other branches. The result was the formation of 59 universal SOCBs in addition to the eight specialized banks. Like the other countries, Bulgaria has a large state savings bank. The state's intent in creating so many small SOCBs was to stimulate competition by encouraging a large number of universal banks. The foreign trade bank, the largest bank in Bulgaria, in partnership with the BNB founded the Bank Consolidation Company (BCC) in 1992 to oversee and orchestrate the eventual consolidation of the banking sector.

In Estonia, the two-tier banking system began under Soviet rule in accord with the Soviet banking legislation of the perestroika period. In 1989, a Soviet decree granted the Baltic states the right to organize independent banking systems. Initially five specialized banks and the state savings bank were separated from the Tallinn branch of Gosbank and the five sectoral banks were restructured as SOCBs. Simultaneously new commercial banks were established and an independent Estonian central bank (Bank of Estonia, BoE) was created. The foreign trade bank was separated from its Moscow head office in late 1990 and was taken over by the BoE. However, the final separation from the former Soviet banking system occurred only in 1992 when Estonia introduced its own currency. Banking crises rather than managed consolidations and orchestrated privatizations have dominated the evolution of the Estonian banking sector. In addition, the establishment of a currency board to govern monetary policy and the ease with which Estonians can access Finnish bank facilities make Estonia significantly different from the other four countries.

Bank privatization in EITs refers to the divestiture of state ownership in an existing joint-stock bank. As such, bank privatization of SOCBs should be distinguished from the creation of new (zero) private banks. The newly conceived private banks have no significant state ownership stake while the state retains a core-investor-size stake in the privatized SOCBs. For specificity, we shall consider a stake to be of 'core-investor size' if it is larger than 25 percent of the total equity in a bank. Government policy that encourages (or discourages) the entry of either new private banks or foreign banks as greenfield operations corresponds to the privatization of the banking sector.

The orchestrated transfer of some ownership shares in existing banks from the hands of the state to private hands is our conception of bank privatization. Although both types of privatization are related in establishing a market-based, private banking sector, the two topics are treated with separate and distinct conceptual frameworks in Chapters 2 and 3.

Government policy toward bank privatization involves choosing the method of divestiture, that is, initial public offering (IPO), private placement with a strategic foreign financial investor (SFFI), or voucher distribution (or some combination of these). Related to the method adopted is a determination of the maximum stake any single investor, foreign or domestic, can take. Due to an ingrained sense of the importance of maintaining a predominantly domestic-controlled banking sector, most countries in the world limit foreign ownership of banks. For our purposes, a foreign-owned bank is defined as one in which more than fifty percent of the shares are held by a foreign owner(s). However, policies that are restrictive of foreign participation may insulate unduly the domestic sector and discourage competition (see Chapter 3). Hence, for any EIT, the government's strategy for bank privatization involves the choice of both a policy on foreign ownership and a method of divestiture consistent with this policy. The chosen strategy influences significantly the speed with which the banking sector moves toward becoming a market-based efficient allocator of credit. However, 'privatization of the credit market' and privatization of existing SOCBs are not equivalent. In promoting efficient credit allocation, policies that encourage competition and entry by foreign banks may prove to be more important than privatizing SOCBs. Competition, especially from international banks, constrains the ability of the SOCBs to act inefficiently and induces the rapid development of the domestic banking industry to meet the foreign invasion.

In this chapter, we focus primarily on the privatization of SOCBs by examining the experiences of the three countries that have taken the greatest strides to date, namely Hungary, Poland, and the Czech Republic. These three Visegrad countries provide an interesting laboratory for all EITs as each has used a method of bank privatization that is broadly representative of one of the prototypes presented above. Two of the three bank privatizations to date in Hungary involves a SFFI. After experimenting with an eclectic approach that combined a search for a SFFI with an IPO, the Polish government has settled on the IPO as its preferred strategy for recent privatizations. In the Czech Republic, the banks were included in the voucher mass privatization program. Hence, the lessons drawn from a careful analysis of the experiences of these three countries will be useful for providing policy advice to EITs choosing among the three prototypical bank privatization strategies. Furthermore, as can be seen most prominently from the Polish experience, analysis of past privatizations provides useful guidance for policy makers embarking on subsequent bank privatizations in the same country.

In Bulgaria, the bank privatization plan proposed in July 1995 involves the state divesting itself of all but a 34 percent share in the banks. As the state is virtually the sole owner of all the banks, this is a significant transfer. The banks are proposed to be included in the mass privatization program. The news led to an increase in the price of Bulgarian Brady bonds by 25 basis points. Bulgarian Brady bonds can be used at face value to 'purchase' shares in the mass privatization program. Recently however, a financial crisis and the failure of two moderately-sized banks (one of which is a private bank) has put bank privatization plans on hold in Bulgaria.

The next section examines the governance structure of the joint-stock state-owned banks in the three Visegrad countries with an eye toward drawing implications for the feasibility of independent action by non-state outsiders. The three subsequent sections provide detailed descriptions of the experiences with bank privatization in Poland, Hungary, and the Czech Republic, in turn. Section 4 discusses the relationship between the privatization method chosen and the structure of the banking sector, in particular, the extent to which foreign entry is allowed. Here we also link the likely evolution of competition in the credit market to the privatization strategy. Section 7 presents the evidence to date on the financial performance and internal governance changes of the newly privatized banks. In the final section, tentative policy conclusions are drawn from the experiences of these countries linking the method of divestiture to the likelihood of better bank governance and to the competitiveness of the market structure. Ultimately, both will have crucial effects on individual bank performance.

2. BANK GOVERNANCE AND STATE WITHDRAWAL FROM THE BANKING SECTOR

Since privatization of the state-owned banks involves only a partial divestiture of state holdings, we take the standard definition of a 'privatized' former-state-owned bank to be a bank with less than 50 percent direct state holdings. However, it is important to distinguish the state's ownership stake from its influence on governance. Bank governance statutes often afford more control to the state than might appear from only a consideration of its remaining stake. In the Czech Republic, state holdings in the largest banks are sufficient to block anything requiring more than two-thirds of the votes at the annual general shareholders' meeting (AGM). In Hungary, one method discussed for maintaining state control in banks while, at the same time, allowing a SFFI to take a majority stake is the retention by the state of a 'golden' share. Such a stake would permit the state to block any fundamental changes in governance and bank policy. Furthermore, in all bank privatizations in the region to date, the state maintains a core-investor-size stake.

The prototypical structure of bank governance is a two-tier hierarchy consisting of a Supervisory Board and a Management Board. Although each country uses different terms to characterize these tiers, the Czech Republic and Poland conform closely to this model.[1] The Supervisory Board functions as a Board of Directors meeting as frequently as once a month with the responsibility for determining overall bank strategy and overseeing large financial transactions (for example, ratifying loans over a threshold amount). The Management Board is in charge of the daily operations of the bank and proposes actions to both the Supervisory Board and the AGM (for example, recommended dividend policy). The Supervisory Board has the authority to dismiss some (in the Czech Republic) or all (in Poland) members of the Management Board and replace them with new appointees. The bank governance structure in Hungary is somewhat more complex and currently in flux. In all countries, owners are not represented on the Supervisory Board in exact proportion to their holdings. Rather many or all of the members of the Supervisory Board are elected at the AGM.

In the Czech Republic, the commercial code mandates two management bodies, the Supervisory Board (so named) and the Board of Directors which operates as a Management Board. Both are elected by the shareholders with a minimum of three members in each. In companies with more than 50 employees, one-third of the Supervisory Board must be elected by the employees. The large banks have Supervisory Boards with 12 members having four-year terms. Of these, eight are elected at the AGM and four are nominated by the employees of the bank. The Board of Directors consists of seven people, each of whom is elected at the AGM for a four-year term with the possibility of re-election for consecutive terms. The Board of Directors has extensive rights and responsibilities in not only day-to-day management but also in planning the long-term strategy of the bank. Under certain conditions, the Supervisory Board may appoint and recall a maximum of two members of the Board of Directors. In practice, the governance relationship between the Supervisory Board and the Board of Directors is evolving. For example, in the largest commercial bank in the Czech Republic, the same person held the positions of chairman of the Supervisory Board, director of the Board of Directors, and chief executive officer (CEO) of the bank until the end of 1993. In 1994, this person relinquished his position as chairman of the Supervisory Board but continued as chair of the Board of Directors and as CEO of the bank.

In Poland, the Supervisory Board, named the Bank Council, consists of between five and ten members elected for three-year terms at the AGM. The

Bank Council is mandated to influence profound changes in the bank but not monitor daily operations; hence, it discusses and reviews equity investments and loans over a certain threshold. The Bank Council appoints and dismisses the President of the Management Board (so named) and by his motion or on his acceptance the other members. The Management Board consists of between three and eight people having three-year terms and is responsible for the daily operations of the bank. The President of the Management Board thus functions as the CEO of the bank. The Supervisory Board is the elected body and appoints the Management Board. In Poland, the governance structure seems to conform closely to the two-tier prototype with a relatively clear division of responsibility between the Supervisory Board and the Management Board.

In Hungary, bank governance is more difficult to characterize partly because of recent government policy. Each bank has a Board of Directors that consists of between six and eight members and meets monthly to develop the bank's medium-term strategy. Until recently, the chairman of the Board of Directors was also the CEO of the bank. In November 1994, the government decided to separate these two positions in state-owned banks. Using its voting power in AGMs when necessary, the government was successful in separating these functions in all but one case, the state savings bank. In Hungary, banks also have a Board of Supervisors of between four and ten members. The Board of Supervisors is charged with the obligation to exercise the owners' control and oversight. The CEO presides over an executive board that is responsible for the daily management of the bank. Hence, the Hungarian situation may be characterized as a three-tier governance structure consisting of a Board of Supervisors, a Board of Directors, and an executive board. The positions of CEO and chairman of the Board of Directors are now separated. Hence, an independent chair gives the Board of Directors a more meaningful role in overseeing the operations of the executive board.

Of the three countries, Hungary has taken the greatest strides toward creating independent governance bodies within the SOCBs. The Polish structure is the simplest with an elected body responsible for appointing a managing body. In the Czech Republic, both governing bodies are elected at the AGM but the CEO of the bank has a strong role to play in both. In all three countries despite the organizational structure, a forceful personality in the CEO position can exercise significant influence over the governance and long-term strategies of the bank. Hence, the feasibility of insider control and the preponderance of state dominance as the core investor remain important issues for privatized SOCBs in the region. Are they truly private banks?

3. POLAND: PRIVATIZING SOCBS – A CHANGE IN STRATEGY

The Polish privatization strategy for the nine regional SOCBs began with the engagement of a Western 'twin' to provide technical improvements prior to privatization.[2] However, the Western twin incurred no explicit or implicit obligation to take an ownership stake at a future date. Poland's original bank privatization strategy was an eclectic one as it included searching for an SFFI to take at least a 25 percent ownership stake, using an IPO to sell another stake larger than 25 percent, allocating to the bank employees up to 15 percent of the shares at preferential rates and terms, and retaining approximately 30 percent of the shares by the Treasury. Using 1994 balance sheet totals to measure size, the nine regional banks divide roughly into two tiers.

Wielkopolski Bank Kredytowy in Poznan (WBK), the first of the nine Polish SOCBs to be privatized in March 1993, belongs to the second, smaller-size tier and has sixty-four branches. One reason for choosing a second-tier bank as the first to privatize was a desire on the part of the MoF to test the absorption capacity of the Warsaw Stock Exchange (WSE).[3] Prior to the public offering, the share capital of WBK was increased by an issue of 1,826,000 new shares at a face value of PLZ 4,100,000 per share for a total of PLZ 183 billion ($11 million). Although the government sought a SFFI to purchase the new shares, none was initially attracted to WBK. Rather the European Bank for Reconstruction and Development (EBRD) agreed to purchase the entire amount of new shares at a price of PLZ 115,000 ($6.89) per share for a total contribution of PLZ 209.99 billion (about $12.58 million). Hence, EBRD acquired 28.5 percent of the augmented share capital of WBK as a medium-term caretaker continuing the search for a SFFI.

The public offering consisted of 1,740,000 shares to be sold in two tranches (a large and a small investor tranche). The total IPO amounted to a 27.2 percent stake in the augmented capital of WBK. The offer price was again PLZ 115,000 resulting in total revenues of PLZ 200.1 billion ($11.89 million). Both the small and large tranche were oversubscribed, with demand outstripping supply tenfold. Adding the monies from the employee tranche, the total budget revenues from the privatization of WBK amounted to PLZ 252.69 billion or $15.13 million. Adding the new capital that went to the bank, the privatization of WBK yielded PLZ 462.68 billion ($27.7 million). At the end of 1993, employees owned 14.3 percent of the shares, leaving the Treasury with a 30 percent holding.

On the first day of trading on the WSE (June 22, 1993), the transaction price was PLZ 350,000 ($19.66) which was about three times the IPO selling price of PLZ 115,000. Through the fall of 1993, the share price of WBK stabilized at around PLZ 700,000 ($35), about six times its issue price. As of

January 26, 1996, WBK was selling at PLN 6.4 ($2.50) per share or slightly more than half of its zloty issue price but only about 36 percent of its dollar issue price. Furthermore, the price-to-earnings ratio of WBK is 3.8 which is the lowest of any listed and traded company on the WSE with the exception of BPH. In March 1995, Allied Irish Banks (AIB), the previous twinning partner of WBK, acquired an ownership stake of 16.26 percent for $20 million when WBK raised new capital. EBRD continues to hold a 23.9 percent stake in the augmented capital of WBK although AIB has signed an agreement to take over EBRD shares and acquire majority interest in WBK in the future. Recently, Miroslaw Bojanczyk, deputy head of the finance ministry's banking department, announced the intention to sell 20 percent of the shares in WBK by tender rather than on the bourse to avoid depressing market prices.[5] AIB indicated it was interested in increasing its stake to become WBK's strategic investor. After the planned sale, the Treasury stake in WBK would be only 10 percent.

The privatization of Bank Slaski (BSK) in Katowice in December 1993 was, in most ways, a success as a SFFI was attracted at the last minute. Having 59 branches and belonging to the first (larger) tier of state-owned commercial banks, BSK is almost twice the size of WBK. Hence, the privatization of BSK was to be an even truer test of the absorption capacity of the Warsaw Stock Exchange.

The preparations for BSK's privatization were finalized at the annual shareholders meeting in June 1993. Two Paris-based advisors, Banque PARIBAS (financial) and Jeantet et Associes (legal) were involved. At the time, BSK had outstanding a major loan to FSM SA, the Polish auto maker about to be acquired by Fiat Italy. The conditional contract between Fiat and the Polish government committed both to restructure this (and other) loans. However, as of June 8, 1993, the arrangement with Fiat had not been finalized, so that BSK provided from its own funds an amount equal to 50 percent of its exposure to FSM. The final resolution involved a writing off of the loan and recapitalization of BSK with long-term government securities serviced jointly by the Polish government and Fiat. As part of this solution, BSK agreed to remit 55 percent of its net profits to the MoF to 'decapitalize' it to a projected capital adequacy ratio (CAR) of 15 percent by the end of 1993.

Hence, unlike WBK, the privatization of BSK involved no new share issue. Rather, the 9.26 million outstanding shares with a face value of PLZ 100,000 (approximately $5 at the prevailing exchange rate) created at the time of incorporation were divided initially into three pieces. Similar to the arrangements in the privatization of WBK, approximately 30 percent of the shares were to remain with the Treasury and up to 10 percent of the shares were reserved for employees on special terms.[6] This left 5.556 million shares (exactly 60 percent) to be sold. These shares were split into two tranches, 1.389 million in a small investor tranche (15 percent) and 4.167 million in a large investor tranche (45 percent). The latter were to be sold by tender to large institutional investors and strategic foreign investors while the former were sold by IPO.

According to the prospectus dated August 31, 1993, bids for the large investor tender were accepted from September 14 to October 15, 1993. The minimum bid was 185,000 and the maximum was 2.4 million shares. In the tender, a bidder submitted two envelopes. The first envelope contained information about the bidder and a statement of the time period during which the bidder would commit to hold the shares. Bidders were invited to provide other pertinent information like financial statements, a brief description of strategic interests, information about individuals that the bidder would propose for the Bank Council. The second envelope contained the number of shares requested and the price proposed per share. Bidders were pre-selected based on the information provided in the first envelope at the sole discretion of the Treasury.

Pricing the shares of BSK was an important issue. The first Polish bank to be privatized, Bank Rozwoju Eksportu (BRE), was priced so that its valuation was about 50 percent of book value. The issue price for WBK shares was set in March 1993 at approximately 75 percent of book value. The exchange index, the WIG, increased by 260 percent between March and June when WBK opened for trading at 350 percent of its issue price. During the fall of 1993, WBK was trading on the WSE at about PLZ 700,000 ($35) or about six times its issue price. Due to the upward market index trend and BSK's relatively cleansed loan portfolio, the minimum price of a share in the BSK tender was set at PLZ 230,000 ($11.50). Using this price, the total value of the shares outstanding would be approximately equal to BSK's book value. Even at this minimum purchase price, the smallest purchase in the tender would have required an expenditure of PLZ 42.55 billion ($2.1 million), an amount that some argued was too large for a Polish investor.

The strike price (price actually paid by all bidders receiving shares) in the tender was to be determined from among the group of bidders submitting envelopes by first ranking them according to proposed price and then allocating the total available shares in descending order of price for requested shares. The strike price is the lowest price bid by any bidder receiving shares so long as it is above the minimum price set in the prospectus. It should be noted that the offer price for the subsequent small investor IPO was to be announced based on the strike price in the tender. The proposed prices in the tender ranged from the minimum of PLZ 230,000 ($11.50) to PLZ 750,000 ($37.50). As it turned out, the MoF was unable to attract a significant SFFI in the bidding process as demand was generally low. It appeared that the strike price from the exercise would have been around PLZ 250,000 ($12.50). Because the WIG had continued to rise after the minimum price had been set, the strike price was substantially below what the MoF believed to be consistent with market expectations. Due to these factors, the MoF canceled the tender in October 1993.

Applications for the small investor IPO were to be accepted from November 3 to November 17, 1993. Prior to the beginning of the application period, the MoF announced that the search for a strategic investor would continue, but if it was not successful the shares from the large investor tranche would be sold in the market at a later date. For the small investor tranche, the minimum request was ten shares and the maximum was 5,000. Pre-payment by the close of the IPO was required to validate an order. In view of the WBK experience, allocation rules in the event of oversubscription were detailed in the prospectus. Any excess payment that resulted from reallocations of shares in numbers less than the amount subscribed was reimbursed.

The MoF was now faced with the problem of setting an offer price for the IPO because the tender had been canceled. A price of PLZ 500,000 (about $25) per share was set, making BSK shares worth about twice book value. The ratio of offer price to book value for BSK was higher than the market to book ratio prevailing at the time for WBK on the WSE. Furthermore, the total value of the issue was about six times higher than the biggest issue floated on the market to that date. However, the offer price-to-earnings ratio (PE) for BSK (about 4) was significantly below the actual multiple for WBK and other stocks trading on the exchange. Indeed, the price of PLZ 500,000 turned out to be significantly below market clearing.[7]

According to the prospectus, bank employees were to receive their shares, some of which were purchased on preferential terms in accord with the privatization law, between November 22 and December 3, while the shares in the IPO were to be allocated by the State Treasury on December 7. The IPO timing was affected by the canceled tender; the application period was extended to December 1 and the allocation date delayed to December 20. Demand far exceeded supply in the IPO. In the December 20 allocation to the public, over 817,000 buyers received three shares each.[8] Employees purchasing shares received their allocations (with a much higher limit) on December 3 and could register them immediately in investment accounts at BSK brokerage houses.[9]

To be eligible for trading shares on the WSE, a holder must set up an investment account at a brokerage house, of which there were about 400 in the country, and register ownership of the shares. Prior to the BSK offer, there were about 150,000 individual investment accounts in the country. The late allocation date coming just before Christmas and the number of people allocated shares who did not already have investment accounts overwhelmed the limited capacity of the system. For example, in Gdansk, BG had the only brokering operation in the city prepared to open accounts for the estimated 50,000 residents who had received shares in BSK. This office was processing about 500 new accounts per business day.[10] At such a rate, it would take twenty weeks to open accounts for all the residents of Gdansk holding shares in BSK! But the opening of trading in BSK shares on the WSE was set for January 25, 1994.

On December 15, 1993, representatives of the MoF, BSK and ING signed an agreement according to which ING would purchase 2.4 million shares (the maximum allowed in the prospectus for the tender) and hold these shares for at least three years. ING had been a participant in the earlier canceled tender. The price was the same as the IPO price so that ING paid about PLZ 1.2 trillion (about $60 million) for a 25.92 percent stake in BSK.[11] From the time line, it is clear that ING possessed information about the excess demand in IPO prior to committing to its own purchase, which was executed on January 13, 1994. After all of these transactions had been consummated, the remaining stake held by the State Treasury in BSK was 33.2 percent.

On January 25, 1994, the first day of trading for BSK stock on the Warsaw Exchange, the price reached PLZ 6,750,000 ($337.50), a staggering 13.5 times the IPO issue price. The volume of trading on that day amounted to 32,410 shares or 0.35 percent of the total shares outstanding. Very few of the general shareholders were able to trade at this price due to the delayed distribution of shares and the required registration procedures at brokerage houses. The preferential treatment of employees allowed them to take advantage of the information about excess demand from the IPO and sell on the opening day. The employees who paid PLZ 250,000 ($12.50, half the issue price) per share stood to make a profit of PLZ 6.5 million per share (about $325) sold on the first day of trading. This situation caused a public outcry.

On January 28, 1995, Prime Minister Waldemar Pawlak dismissed Stefan Kawalek, the deputy finance minister responsible for bank privatization, in response to the public reaction to the so-called 'Slaski affair.' Subsequently Marek Borowski, the finance minister, quit in protest over the dismissal and Marian Rajczyk resigned as BSK president. The Sejm privatization committee recently finished its investigation into the incident and concluded that there were no major charges to answer. The committee determined that the agreement reached with ING had been properly conducted. However, the committee did find that BSK's brokerage house had wrongly favored the bank's employees while processing the shares and thus violated the principle of treating all shareholders equally. Hence, its license was suspended. On July 14, 1995, BSK shares were trading at PLN 135 ($57.20 or PLZ 1.35 million) which is more than two times the issue price but substantially lower than the price on the first day of trading. On January 26, 1996, the price of a share of

BSK was quoted at PLN 185 ($73.12), a 52-week high and almost three times the issue price.

The privatization of BPH, a Krakow-based SOCB, in January 1995 marked a change in basic privatization strategy in Poland. The BPH privatization was conducted solely through an IPO with the strike (initial sale) price determined at a special bourse session of the WSE on January 14 (Saturday), 1995 rather than set by the MoF in advance. Whether or not the change in strategy was due primarily to the public's reaction to the BSK affair is difficult to assess. In the preparatory stage of BPH privatization beginning in 1993, a SFFI was considered desirable. Credit Suisse First Boston (CSFB) was engaged to supervise the privatization and search for a foreign investor. The response was less than enthusiastic although both CSFB and ABN-AMRO (BPH's twinning partner) expressed interest. However, each considered the offer price set, at about twice book value, to be too high.

Contributing factors to the change in strategy include the lack of enthusiasm for a SFFI expressed by BPH's president, Janusz Quandt, and the political change in September 1993 bringing into office a new ruling coalition. The Peasant Party, an influential partner in this coalition, takes a populist approach to bank privatization. A prominent member of this party would argue vehemently in Parliament for an investigation of the Bank Slaski affair. Over a six-month period from November 1993 to May 1994 (spanning the BSK privatization), the privatization of BPH was in limbo. Quandt took the initiative by engaging Deloitte and Touche, who assisted in designing a plan to bring to the AGM in May. The new strategy involved selling 57 percent of the bank's share capital by IPO with no attempt to attract a SFFI. Portfolio investors, both domestic and foreign, were welcome. The restrictions put on the number of shares that could be purchased by any one investor was raised from 500,000 shares (a 5 percent ownership stake) to 1 million shares (a 10 percent stake) prior to the sale.

A member of the first tier and approximately equal in size to BSK, BPH (with one hundred and twelve branches) had a book value of PLN 51.8 million ($21.95 million) and offered 50.2 percent (5,200,000) of its shares with a par value of PLN 5 ($2.12) to the market at a price not lower than PLN 70 ($29.66). Another 6.8 percent (700,000) were reserved for 'sale' at a discount of 20 percent for holders of Exchange Treasury Bonds. Up to 20 percent of the bank's shares can be purchased by employees on preferential terms between February 1, 1995 and January 31, 1996, at which time any unsold shares will revert to the MoF for disposal. A prospectus dated November 9, 1994 invited purchase orders specifying the number of shares and upper limit on offer price (but at least as great as the minimum price) from December 12, 1994 to January 12, 1995. The basic strategy was to let the market determine the strike price based on demand to avoid a recurrence of the BSK problem. The timing was unfortunate as the WIG had fallen sharply by the end of 1994 closing at 7,473.1 down from its March 1994 high of 20,760.3.[12]

At the beginning of December, in an effort to raise interest among investors, the MoF announced that individuals subscribing to BPH shares by the end of the year would receive a deduction of up to PLN 1,600 ($678) from 1994 personal income taxes. Forty percent of the offer was subscribed by the EBRD and a consortium led by Daiwa Europe Ltd. Even with this attempt to increase demand among individual investors and the substantial guarantee from the above institutions, the minimum price of PLN 70 ($29.66) prevailed at the special bourse session. The resulting budget revenues from the sale totaled PLN 363,862,663.08 or about $153.5 million at the prevailing exchange rate. Original estimates of expected revenues had been between 400 and PLN 450 million although skeptics pointed out that such a figure exceeded by more than ten times the average daily volume on the WSE.

At the beginning of March 1995, the supervisory board of BPH dismissed president Quandt. One of the reasons given for this management change was that the advertising campaign orchestrated by BPH ahead of the IPO had been ineffective. The largest shareholders in BPH with their respective current stakes are: Treasury (43 percent), EBRD (15.06 percent), ING (5.3 percent), BPH's sister bank BSK (4.8 percent), Daiwa Europe (4.56 percent), an investment consortium (4.1 percent), BPH employees (3.5 percent) and WBK (2.5 percent). Recently ING expressed interest in acquiring Daiwa's stake so that its consolidated ownership position (including the stake held by BSK in which it is a SFFI) would be about 15 percent. BPH is currently the fourth largest capitalization on the WSE and was trading at PLN 81 ($32) per share on January 26, 1996. However, BPH had the lowest PE of any of the 51 stocks listed and traded in the primary market at less than four to one.

The privatization of Bank Gdanski (Gdansk), a member of the second tier having 55 branches and about equivalent in size to WBK, occurred in December 1995 using a two-tier IPO. In preparation for the privatization of BG, the bank's president, Edmund Tolwinski, announced a strategy to make BG a universal bank concentrating on four broad areas of activity, namely, investment banking, retail operations, insurance, and capital markets. BG has been active in the capital market acquiring control of Sopot Bank (a small, failing private bank) and purchasing a 5.7 percent stake in Espebebe, a construction company listed on the WSE. After privatization, BG intends to play an active role in accelerating further privatization of SOEs in Poland with a strategy of restructuring them prior to their privatization. With respect to its own growth, BG intends to explore consolidation with other Polish banks rather than open new branches.

The original plan for the two-tier IPO envisioned selling 33 percent of the shares on the WSE and 33 percent on international markets using global depository receipts or American depository receipts.[13] The employee offer is 4 percent and the MoF plans to retain a 30 percent stake. Three institutions, HSBC Investment Bank Limited, Daiwa Europe Limited and the Bank of New York, agreed to manage and underwrite an issue totalling 4.8 million GDRs (only 25 percent of the shares) at an issue price of PLN 24 ($9.48) per share. James Capel trades the GDRs on the Stock Exchange Automated Quotation (SEAQ) International market in London.

The domestic issue drew considerable attention as 6.98 million shares (35.8 percent stake) were sold at PLN 24 ($9.48) per share. Bank Inicjatyw Gospodarczych (BIG), a private Polish bank established in 1989 by a group of state enterprises and private persons, and two subsidiaries acquired a 24.1 percent stake in BG taking more than two-thirds of the domestic offering. BG's shares entered the WSE on December 21, 1995 and BIG upped its stake to 26.75 percent with a block purchase in January. BIG is seeking the approval of the NBP[14] to up its stake to 32.99 percent which it could accomplish by buying the approximate 6 percent of the shares left over from the international offer or buying more shares on the WSE. Currently the MoF holds about 39 percent of the shares. The shares of BG were trading on the WSE at PLN 26 ($10.30) per share on January 26, 1996. The GDRs are trading at about $9.70 per share.

Two other regional banks are scheduled for privatization in 1996, namely, Powszechny Bank Kredytowy (PBK), the Warsaw-based SOCB in the first tier of comparable size to BSK and BPH, and Bank Zachodni (BZ) in Wroclaw, a second-tier SOCB. Prior to its privatization, PBK had sixty branches concentrated in Warsaw and the Silesian region and plans to expand its network through acquisitions. In the summer of 1994, PBK and Kredyt Bank (Warsaw) with 17 branches announced a cooperative agreement involving mutual purchases of each other's shares to attain a 25 percent stake of cross-shareholdings; however, subsequent negotiations have hit a snag.[15] The method of privatization for PBK remains to be finalized but discussions are underway with several foreign banks. BZ is expected to be privatized late in 1996.

In early 1996, ten bank stocks[16] accounted for almost 40 percent of the market capitalization on the WSE (53 companies). Hence, the absorption capacity of the domestic market for placing more bank equity seems limited in the near term. Furthermore, the privatization of the remaining three SOCBs namely, Pomorski Bank Kredytowy (PBKS) in Szczecin, Bank Depozytowo-Kredytowy (BDK) in Lublin, and Powszechny Bank Gospardarczy (PBG) in Lodz, is currently uncertain due to consolidation plans. These three banks (along with BZ) had signed a letter of intent in October 1994 to consolidate prior to privatization but the group did not receive the approval of the MoF to pursue their plan. Now orchestrated bank consolidation prior to privatization has become the MoF's policy agenda for the banking sector.

Figuring prominently in the consolidation proposal are two of the four state-owned specialty banks, which are the largest four banks in Poland. Each of the two, namely, Bank Handlowy (BH), the foreign trade merchant bank, and Bank Polska Kasa Opieki SA (PeKaO SA), the state savings bank specializing in collecting retail deposits in foreign currency, are considered as an apex bank in a consolidated group. BH has recently been assigned an A+/A1 rating, the highest of any bank in the region, by the Thomson Bank Watch-BREE agency. The other two specialty banks – namely, Powszechny Kasa Oszczednosci-Bank Panstwowy (PKO BP), the state savings bank specializing in zloty household deposit-taking and financing housing construction, and Bank Gospodarki Zywnosciowej (BGZ), the national umbrella bank for local cooperative banks charged with financing agriculture and food processing and currently consisting of 1206 LCBs – have balance sheet problems and require restructuring prior to privatization.

The MoF's bank consolidation proposal links BDK (a tier II SOCB with 99 branches in south-eastern Poland) and PBKS (a tier II SOCB with 57 branches in Western Poland) with BH and PBG (a tier I SOCB) and PBR (the Polish development bank) with PeKaO.[17] Curiously, the MoF recently turned down PBG's request to tender for an adviser to assist in preparing its privatization claiming that PBG had overstepped its authority in mapping out a privatization plan.[18] PBKS has already engaged a privatization consultant, Morgan Grenfell, and is currently looking for a SFFI to take 30 percent of its shares. BDK is the only SOCB that has explicitly attempted to expand operations in the former USSR, especially Ukraine. It has received a good rating from Moody's and has attracted the attention of several foreign investors. BDK has already signed an agreement with Daewoo Corporation to form a joint leasing company. The future of bank privatization in Poland is uncertain. The current dance seems to involve an attempt by the SOCBs to determine their own partner before the MoF assigns them to a troupe.

4. HUNGARY: TWO SUCCESSES, MORE TO COME?

Hungary's strategy for privatizing the state-owned banks was articulated by the government on April 8, 1992. A bank privatization committee was formed consisting of one representative from each of the MoF, the NBH, the State Property Agency (SPA; Hungarian AVU),[19] and the State Banking Supervision (SBS), in addition to two ministers (or their representatives). The stated goal is to achieve an ownership structure in which the state's stake is less than 25 percent in each bank by the end of the nineties.[20] The strategy calls for cleaning up a bank's portfolio prior to privatization and encouraging foreign financial institutions to become SFFIs. However, dominance of the banking sector by foreign capital is not desired. Domestic and foreign institutions are to be sought as portfolio investors and the participation of small domestic investors is particularly desired.

By the end of 1995, Hungary had privatized three formerly state-owned banks of which two are controlled independently by outside non-state investors. The first successful bank privatization was Magyar Kulkereskedelmi Bank (MKB), the Hungarian Foreign Trade Bank and the third largest bank in Hungary, in July 1994. MKB is a full-service Budapest-based bank with 7 branches offering a wide range of products but specializing in foreign business transactions. In 1993 it was the first commercial bank in the region to tap the international capital markets without a state guarantee when it successfully floated a DM 100 million Eurobond issue. Discussions with Bayerische Landesbank Girozentrale Bank (BLB), a German state-owned bank having long-standing business relations with MKB, began in 1991 but progress was stalled in 1992 when the State Holding Company (SHC: Hungarian AV Rt.) took over MKB's ownership rights from the SPA. Then the Hungarian government's debtor and bank consolidation programs further delayed the process. In the end, the government required MKB to abide by the procedure established in 1992 for bank privatization.

This procedure requires that, first, internal due diligence be performed and the management, in consultation with the owners, decide on the desirable characteristics that a potential SFFI will possess. Second, a list of potential investors is to be drawn up and an investment consultant chosen to seek SFFIs. Those expressing interest are provided with the internal informational memorandum. Third, purchase terms are to be discussed based upon which the managers and major owners are to draw up a short list. Each investor on the short list is then invited to perform its own due diligence, after which a firm offer is expected. Fourth, the SFFI is chosen on the basis of the firm offer, and the conditions for purchase are prepared. Finally, after having obtained the consent of the state and the major shareholders, the transaction is consummated.

In 1993, MKB enlisted J.P. Morgan as its investment counselor and 25 financial institutions were approached. Six expressed serious interest in buying shares in MKB. At the end of 1993, MKB had a balance sheet total of HUF 238 billion ($2.4 billion),[21] the third largest Hungarian bank with a 9.1 percent market share, equity of HUF 16 billion ($160 million) a capital adequacy ratio of 13.9 percent, a deposit-to-lending ratio of 1.57, a commercial-credit market share of 4.8 percent, and a ratio of overdue to total commercial credit of 18.6 percent. In July 1994, BLB and the EBRD purchased shares and subscribed new capital paying $54 million. The new share issue increased MKB's capital by HUF 1.937 billion ($19 million[22] bringing the total share capital to HUF 9.1 billion ($89 million), 95.73 percent of which are ordinary shares. The resulting ownership structure of MKB at the time was BLB 25.01 percent, EBRD 16.68 percent, SHC 26.99 percent, Hungarian private and legal entities 21.32 percent, other foreign private and legal entities 8.22 percent, and MKB own shares 1.78 percent. Consequently, non-Hungarian owners hold 49.91 percent of the shares in MKB.

The purchase price per share for BLB and EBRD was $122.55 but the sale involved an equity-based, price-adjustment clause.[23] If the pre-tax profits for MKB in the last half of 1994 and the first half of 1995 exceeded respective hurdle figures, the price would be adjusted upward by 30 percent and 25 percent respectively. The hurdles were set rather low by historical standards. The first required MKB's earnings in 1994 to be more than about two-thirds of its 1993 earnings. The second proscribed first-half earnings in 1995 on an annualized basis to be about one-half of 1993 earnings. Both performance hurdles were met so that the final price paid turned out to be close to $190 per share. Given the conservative nature of the hurdles, the contract suggests that EBRD and BLB were concerned about prompting MKB to avoid a bad-case outcome in the period immediately following the privatization. By negotiating a performance-based price adjustment, the participants on both sides reduced the risks from not getting the transaction price 'right.'

After privatization, the president of the Board of Directors Gabor Erdely was retained. Other members of the six-person Board of Directors include A.H. Lerner, vice-president of BLB and P. Mellinger, a chief executive of the EBRD's Financial Institutions Directorate. The Board of Directors meets once a month to develop the bank's medium-term strategy. The owners also exercise control through the Board of Supervisors which meets less frequently.

In February 1995, the German Investment and Development Corporation (GIDC) bought 8.33 percent of the shares in MKB from its treasury portfolio. Both BLB and GIDC agreed to vote together their combined stake of 33.34 percent at MKB's AGM which is sufficient to block major policy changes requiring a two-thirds majority vote. Recently the AVP Rt (the merged Hungarian State Privatization and Holding Company) sold its remaining stake to BLB to bring the latter to majority shareholder status with a stake of 51 percent. Hence, BLB by any measures can now control governance, and the Hungarian state has divested itself fully of its ownership stake in MKB.

The first planned privatization of the three SOCBs created from the NBH's commercial portfolio was Budapest Bank (BB) with 74 branches and an expanding line of retail products. At the end of 1993, BB had a balance sheet total of HUF 157 billion ($1.6 billion), the sixth largest Hungarian bank by this measure with a 6 percent market share, equity adjusted for qualified assets of HUF 1.5 billion ($15 million), a capital adequacy ratio (CAR) of minus 0.7 percent, a deposit-to-lending ratio of 0.75, a commercial-credit market share of 11.3 percent, and a ratio of overdue to total commercial credit of 19.5 percent. As a participant in the second major government recapitalization of the banking system, the 1993 bank consolidation scheme, BB received HUF 9.6 billion in government securities. The bank had previously been granted HUF 11.8 billion in state securities as a participant in the 1992 credit consolidation scheme, the first major government recapitalization of the banking sector. The negative CAR reported above includes the securities issued in the first of two tranches in the 1993 scheme amounting to HUF 5 billion.[24] By mid-1994, BB had registered capital of HUF 17.25 billion ($167 million), shareholders' equity of HUF 7.1 billion ($69 million), trading profit of HUF 8.9 billion ($8.6 million), and pre-tax profit of HUF 1.1 billion ($1.07 million) after providing for qualified assets. BB's balance sheet grew to HUF 169 billion ($1.6 billion). However, because banks involved in the consolidation program are required to account fully for risk provisions from profit reserves, BB had accumulated losses of HUF 13.4 billion ($130 million) in profit reserves (obligations). According to a government decree, the registered capital of these banks can be no larger than their shareholders' equity; hence, BB's registered capital had to be reduced by some or all of the obligations against profit reserves when the books were settled for 1994 in time for the shareholders' meeting in May1995.

By the fall of 1994, the proposed privatization of BB had attracted the attention of four Western banks: CSFB, ING, AIB, and Credit Agricole which had already conducted its own due diligence.[25] In December, the government announced that CSFB was the preferred bidder; CSFB immediately began its own external due diligence. As a result of the 1993 consolidation program, the MoF was the majority owner and, as such, designated Lajos Bokros the sitting CEO of BB as the government's representative in the negotiations. The government approved a plan for CSFB to take a majority stake in BB financed mainly through an increase in share capital of about HUF 10 billion while agreeing on its part to provide a non-cash contribution of the bank's Budapest headquarters estimated at HUF 2 billion. Shortly after Laszlo Bekesi resigned as Minister of Finance in February 1995, Bokros assumed that post. In March 1995, CSFB decided to discontinue its negotiations to purchase BB. Both ING and AIB were invited to re-enter negotiations and both declined. In the interim, ING had acquired Barings, the failed British merchant bank, and AIB had purchased a substantial stake in Poland's WBK.

The final results for 1994 showed BB with a 6.3 percent share of total bank assets in Hungary and a 9.4 percent share of own capital (equity) for an own-capital-to-asset ratio of 10.16 percent, the highest such ratio among the big six

Hungarian banks in 1994 (next highest of this group is MKB with 6.93 percent). Profit after taxes (PAT) in 1994 equaled HUF 1.628 billion for a PAT-to-own-capital ratio of 9.44 percent. Total PAT in the banking sector amounted to only HUF 4.093 billion in 1994 as a significant number of banks made losses on an after-tax base. Not surprisingly, therefore, foreign financial institutions began showing renewed interest in BB. GE Capital, the financial services division of General Electric, has expressed a desire to purchase a stake in BB. ING purchased CSFB's due diligence analysis of BB, and EBRD considered taking between 15 percent and 30 percent of BB shares. Its strong performance in 1994 and the quality of its new management team (several of whom worked previously in Citibank-Budapest) put BB back on the block.

In December 1995, GE Capital and EBRD paid $87 million to BB, which the bank used to pay a short-term capitalization loan coming due on December 15.[26] GE Capital received a 27.5 percent ownership stake and a contract giving it full management control. EBRD took a 32.5 percent stake with the state retaining 22 percent of its shares. Another 18 percent are widely held mainly by domestic investors. In addition to the state agreeing contractually to be only a passive investor, GE Capital and EBRD were protected against downside loss with a put option for their entire 60 percent stake at a pre-determined price. GE Capital, as the bank's management, was also given the option to turn over to the government certain bad loans during a three to five year period. Finally, GE Capital was given a call option to purchase both the EBRD's and the state's stake at a pre-determined price within some time frame.[27] Hence, GE Capital is in a position to reap all the upside gain of its management decisions without incurring the risk of any downside loss. As a result, BB has independent governance and GE Capital has its reputation on the line. If BB's performance over the near term is sufficiently strong, the naysayers who complain about the government having 'given the bank away' may be quieted.

The privatization of Orszagos Takarekpenztar es Kereskedelmi Bank (OTP), the national savings bank founded in 1949 and the largest bank in Hungary with 430 branches, was the second completed major bank privatization in Hungary. Schroders, the UK merchant bank, and Creditanstalt Securities Budapest were advisors to the privatization. Originally OTP held a virtual monopoly in both retail and regional banking by collecting household deposits, financing both home construction and real-estate sales, and providing banking services to local governments. Beginning in the eighties, OTP began handling commercial activities and is well on its way to becoming a full-service universal bank having a loan portfolio consisting of both household (home mortgages) and commercial clients and an increasing market share of foreign currency transactions.

On January 1, 1991, OTP was transformed into a joint-stock company and began to consolidate its banking operations. In 1991, the home mortgage portfolio was rationalized by a special government program offering either to buy out individuals who held low-interest, long-term mortgages or forcing those who kept their mortgages to convert the contract to one bearing interest at market rates on the outstanding debt. In 1992, OTP participated in the credit consolidation program swapping HUF 8.5 billion of bad loans for HUF 6.5 billion of government securities. By the end of 1993, OTP had a total balance sheet of HUF 831 billion ($8.3 billion), the largest Hungarian bank by this measure with a 31.6 percent market share, equity adjusted for qualified assets of HUF 30 billion ($300 million), a capital adequacy ratio (CAR) of 16.5 percent, and a deposit-to-lending ratio of 2.31. Total personal deposits at OTP at the end of 1993 stood at HUF 532 billion ($5.2 billion). Although still focused on retail and regional banking with a 60 percent share of household savings deposits and a 90 percent share of local government accounts, OTP had a commercial-credit market share of 7.6 percent in 1993 with a corresponding ratio of overdue to total commercial credit of 27 percent. OTP did not participate in the 1993/94 consolidation program because of its relatively strong portfolio.

At the beginning of 1994, 20 percent of the existing share capital of OTP was offered to holders of compensation vouchers in accordance with settling general restitution claims in Hungary. Subsequently, a new offering of 5 billion shares was fully subscribed by the MoF. The government's privatization plan for OTP gave preference to institutional investors and did not seek a SFFI to inject new capital. Expatriate financier George Soros had expressed interest in acquiring a large stake in OTP, but the government declined his offer.[28] The state planned to retain a direct ownership stake of 25 percent of OTP's stock plus one vote. Towards the end of 1994, 2 percent of OTP's shares were transferred to municipalities. The final results for 1994 showed OTP with a 30.6 percent share of total assets in Hungarian banks and a 19.3 percent share of own capital for an own-capital-to-asset ratio of 4.28 percent. PAT in 1994 equaled HUF 6.575 billion for a PAT-to-own-capital ratio of 23.48 percent.

In May 1995, 20 percent of the OTP share capital was transferred to the two state social security funds.[29] Prior to its privatization, the ownership structure of OTP was as follows (with voting shares in parentheses): APV Rt 58.4 percent (60.9 percent), the social security funds 20 percent (19.9 percent), OTP 2.8 percent (2.9 percent), municipalities 2 percent (2 percent), and other investors 16.8 percent (14.2 percent). The privatization offering involved selling 28.4 percent (29.6 percent) of OTP's shares plus allocating an additional 5 percent (5.2 percent) to the employees at preferential rates for a total of 33.4 percent (34.8 percent) bringing the state's share, which will be held by the APV Rt, to the targeted 25 percent (26.1 percent). Of the shares sold (34 percent), a 20 percent stake was purchased by foreign portfolio (mainly institutional) investors and the remaining 14 percent stake was purchased by domestic portfolio investors and the employees.

The privatization of OTP follows somewhat the revised Polish strategy for SOCBs. The IPO yielded a disperse group of new owners and the state retained a 25 percent direct stake. Adding to the state's holdings the shares allocated to the two social security funds results in a strong controlling block of 45 percent. On the other hand, the two social security funds could align themselves with the management and employees of OTP and create a 25 percent voting block in which insider control could counterbalance the state's position. It is likely that the monopoly position enjoyed by OTP in retail banking convinced the government to limit foreign ownership in OTP to portfolio investors only, at least for the present time. Consequently, OTP remains in the hands of a strong CEO and governance will depend on negotiations between the state and the insiders.

As the privatization of BB at the end of 1995 indicates, the Hungarian government did not abandon the policy of searching for a SFFI. The already strong presence of foreign banks in Hungary makes it imperative that the government continue its courting of foreign investors as the privatization of the remaining two SOCBs continues in 1996. Magyar Hitel Bank (MHB), specializing in industrial clients, has been separated into two divisions based on the qualification of the loan portfolio. The 'good' bank with the bad assets removed can be privatized with a SFFI during the year. The 'bad' bank can continue to operate as a hospital bank specializing in loan workout. Kereskedelmi Bank (K&H), specializing in agrobusiness, is currently scheduled to be privatized for redemption coupons due to its poor-quality loan portfolio and heavy exposure to agriculture. When these two SOCBs are privatized, the Hungarian banking sector will have only one major bank, OTP, with strong government ties while foreign banks will have a large share of the commercial business.

5. THE CZECH REPUBLIC: VOUCHERS FOR BANKS – BANK FUNDS FOR VOUCHERS

The Czech banking sector is highly concentrated with two major players, Komerční Banka (KB) and Česká Spořitelna (ČS). A large commercial bank, KB inherited the Czech part of the commercial portfolio of the ČSTB in 1990 while ČS is the Czech savings bank created in 1969. Both participated in the first wave of voucher privatization which concluded in December 1992. ČS and KB are universal banks attempting to diversify their portfolios and develop new products. Rounding out the 'big four' banks in the Czech Republic are Československá Obchodní Banka (ČSOB) and Investiční a Poštovní Banka (IPB). Established in 1964, ČSOB is a merchant bank jointly-owned with the Slovak Republic and specializing in foreign exchange business. ČSOB is state-owned and was not included in either of the two voucher privatization waves in the Czech Republic. IPB was formed by a merger of the investment bank, Investiční, and the network of deposit-taking post office branches. Investiční had been created from the ČSTB in 1990 and separated into its Czech and Slovak components prior to its participation in the first wave of voucher privatization. In essence, the Czech Republic has one major commercial bank, one retail-oriented savings bank, a foreign trade merchant bank jointly-owned with Slovakia, and a merged investment/retail bank; three of these four participated in the first wave of voucher privatization.

Control of the big four banks is an important issue for the functioning of financial markets in the Czech Republic. These four banks had a combined credit market share of 63 percent in 1994, and they dominate the deposit market with a combined share equal about 75 percent. ČS with its more than 2,000 branches holds a monopoly position with respect to household deposits (about 95 percent of savings deposits in 1993 were collected by ČS).[30] According to its president, Jaroslav Klapal, roughly half of ČS's balance sheet is allocated to the interbank market. For prudent risk-management reasons, ČS lends to only 20 of the 59 banks in existence but the list is a closely held commercial secret. On the other side of the interbank market, ČSOB is a net borrower whose chairman, Pavel Kavanek, thinks is well-positioned to finance bilateral Czech-Slovak trade in hard currency now that the clearing arrangement between these two countries has ended.[31] ČSOB is aggressively developing new products to compete with the 'hungry' foreign banks that provide stronger competition than local institutions.

Recent reports indicate that ČS and ČSOB are discussing a merger which, if consummated, would result in the largest financial institution in the Czech Republic. Although official spokespersons from the Česka Narodni Banka (ČNB) and ČSOB discount the reports as speculative and premature, banking analysts supposedly welcomed the merger warmly as a complementary marriage that would lead to the creation of a bank big enough to compete with KB and with the foreign banks that are expanding rapidly in the Czech Republic.[32] The current market concentration of a 'big four' and the possible merger of ČS and ČSOB makes a duopoly or, at best, an oligopoly structure probable at least for the foreseeable future. Perhaps market discipline will be enforced in the Czech Republic by foreign competition, although foreign banks have traditionally been 'niche' players in host countries.

Like Czech companies, the Czech banks participated in the voucher mass privatization schemes. However, unlike the companies, banks were on both sides of the market. The major banks set up investment funds (IPFs) to acquire capital stakes in companies by participating in the two voucher privatization waves. Regulations restricting the holdings of any one IPF to no more than a 20 percent stake in any bank (or company) were enacted during the process. In the first privatization wave, IPFs collected 71.4 percent of the vouchers while individual citizens held the remaining amount. The ten largest IPFs acquired about half of all the voucher points distributed to individuals. Of these funds, six were set up by banks, namely ČS, KB, IPB, Creditanstalt, and the two largest banks in Slovakia. The three Czech banks' funds were among the largest five IPFs in the first privatization wave. The top five IPFs held 38.27 percent of the total voucher points disaggregated in the following manner: ČS 11.1 percent, IPB 8.45 percent, Harvard Fund 7.45 percent, Vseobečná Uverová Banka (Bratislava) Fund 5.84 percent, and KB Fund 5.43 percent.[33] The only non-bank fund in the top five was the Harvard Fund established by Viktor Koženy.

In the second wave of voucher privatization, somewhat fewer points were allocated (about 72 percent of the first-wave total). New IPFs appeared, the largest of which was established by Agrobanka. However, the percentage of vouchers placed with funds was lower (63.5 percent) and the concentration of points across funds was significantly lower in that the top five (ten) IPFs garnered only 21.1 percent (32.7 percent) of the total vouchers. The Harvard Group (two funds) was the only fund to appear in the top five in both waves. With the exception of ČSOB, the banks were privatized in the first wave. Although IPFs established directly by banks are forbidden to own shares of other banks, the law was circumvented by banks setting up investment companies owned by the parent bank and these companies in turn established IPFs that hold bank shares.[34] After the completion of bank privatization by vouchers, the five largest IPFs in the first wave obtained 41 percent of KB with the Harvard Fund alone acquiring 17.6 percent.[35] The IPB funds (twelve) obtained a 10.8 percent stake in KB, a 8.8 percent stake in ČS, and 17 percent of the shares of IPB. The KB fund acquired a 3.9 percent stake in ČS and 4.2 percent of the shares of VUB, the Slovakian commercial bank counterpart of KB. The KB fund also purchased 3.4 percent of the shares in KB. The ČCS fund is more diversified than the other four but it did acquire a 4.9 percent stake in KB. Hence, the banks and financial institutions in general established cross-ownership patterns among themselves through voucher privatization.

In addition to holding bank shares, the bank IPFs own up to the legal maximum of 20 percent in virtually all voucher-privatized companies. Of the approximately 280 IPFs in the Czech Republic, seven of the top ten funds by current market capitalization are bank funds.[36] The top three IPFs are the ČS fund with a capitalization of $296 million, the Harvard Dividend Fund with a capitalization of $159 million,[37] and the KB fund with a capitalization of $148 million. Through its fund, KB controls some 120 management and supervisory boards. Since KB has business ties with at least half of all Czech companies, the natural concern arises that banks may hold their client-companies hostage in non-market-based transactions by virtue of their ownership stakes.

A further situation affecting bank governance is the role of the state as owner by its NPF holdings. At the end of 1995, the National Property Fund (NPF) held 'core-investor' size direct stakes in the big four:[38] 48 percent in KB, 45 percent in ČS, 19.6 percent in ČSOB,[39] and 32.8 percent in IPB. Considering first KB, the state's total ownership stake is 50.5 percent con-sisting of the 48 percent held by the NPF and a 2.5 percent stake held by the Restitution Investment Fund (RIF). As of June 10, 1995 just prior to an offering of global depository receipts amounting to 3.2 percent of the out-standing ordinary shares, the other major shareholders in KB were the Harvard Group with 8.4 percent, the IPB funds with 5.3 percent, the VUB fund with 3.5 percent, KB's own fund with 3.3 percent and the ČS fund with 3.3 percent. No other shareholder, including any IPF, held a stake in excess of 2 percent at that time. The aggregate stake held by IPFs at the end of 1995 is 33 percent. Individual shareholders (DIKs) hold only 7.5 percent of the shares while foreign institutions have a 9 percent stake. Hence, the state has a majority ownership position in KB, IPFs in the aggregate have a core-investor stake, and the remaining shares are held widely by domestic individuals and by foreign portfolio investors.

In the case of ČS, municipalities hold 14.75 percent of the shares in addition to the 45 percent stake held by the NPF and a 3 percent stake held by RIF bringing total government ownership to 62.75 percent. Immediately after the voucher privatization of ČS, the Harvard Group held 12.9 percent of the shares and the major bank funds held the following stakes: IPB 8.8 percent, KB 3.9 percent, and VUB 1.6 percent. Viktor Kožený, the founder of the Harvard Group, attempted to influence governance at ČS but failed. By the end of 1995, IPFs as a group now hold 32.5 percent of the shares in ČS with the remaining 4.75 percent of the shares widely held by DIKs. As in KB, the government holds a clear majority ownership position and IPFs as a group hold a core-investor stake in ČS. The probability of a non-bank core investor emerging in either of the two large domestic banks in the Czech Republic is low given the current ownership configuration and the constraints on concen-tration of ownership by any single IPF. Insider governance seems to be firmly entrenched at KB under a strong CEO, Richard Salzmann. Hence, the gover-nance of the two largest banks in the Czech Republic remains in the hands of the state and insiders at this time.

The case of IPB is slightly different. The state holds a core investor stake of 39.6 percent consisting of the NPF's 32.8 percent and the RIF's 6.8 percent. The next largest individual stake at 14.7 percent is held by the IPB's own fund management company (První Investiční AS or PIAS). The Czech insurance company (Česká Pojištovna) holds 7.5 percent of the shares and the remaining 38.2 percent are held by IPFs and institutional investors. Again the state's ownership stake is dominant although not a majority holding. More interestingly, IPB's own investment fund group has a large stake and 45.7 percent of the shares are held by portfolio investors. The insider/state nexus retains a hold on governance in IPB as the major 'outside' investor is IPB's own IPF.

6. GOVERNMENT POLICY TOWARD BANKING: PRIVATIZATION AND FOREIGN ENTRY

In any economy in transition, the method chosen for privatization will influence bank governance and, as a result, bank performance. If shares are widely held and there is little or no concentration of non-state ownership, the state and/or insiders will have an opportunity to exert significant control over the bank. In the Czech Republic, the banks (with the exception of the foreign trade bank) were included in the first wave of voucher privatization. The result was significant cross-ownership patterns that strengthened the non-market relationships between banks and their company clients to the detriment of the governance of both. In the two largest banks, the state retains a majority ownership stake and IPFs as a group hold a core-investor stake. However, since no single IPF holds a stake in excess of 10 percent, insiders have successfully resisted non-state outside influence on governance. In the third large bank included in voucher privatization, the state retains a core-investor stake and the bank's own IPF is the only other investor with a stake in excess of 10 percent. Such a configuration provides ample opportunity for insider/state or solely state control in all three banks. Although voucher privatization is quick and politically expedient, it is likely to result in bifurcated ownership structures in which the state retains a core-investor-size stake while the preponderance of the rest of the shares are held widely. In the Czech Republic, voucher privatization requires a second round of ownership transfer to bring about independent non-state governance. In the interim, it entrenches informal non-market relations that will be difficult to break in the future. Hence, the Czech experience indicates that voucher privatization of banks with the state retaining a large ownership share is not likely to be market friendly.

In Poland, experiences with privatizations involving a SFFI indicate that a new private financial investor is likely to take an active role in bank governance and market strategy. The eclectic bank privatization method used initially in Poland left BSK in a situation whereby the MoF and ING participate in bank governance on somewhat equal terms. Since the IPO component of that privatization led to an extremely disperse distribution (consisting of three shares each to more than eight thousand individuals), these two owners wield significant control over the bank. Furthermore, ING is in the process of consolidating a substantial (about 15 percent) minority ownership position in BPH which was privatized solely by an IPO. Since BSK and BPH are both heavily branched in the southern (Silesian) region of Poland, ING appears to be taking an aggressive role in this regional market. ING is behaving the way a core investor would be likely to act with respect to internal governance and market position. Perhaps it is for this reason that the Polish government is actively seeking portfolio investors rather than foreign direct investment (that is, a SFFI) for its next IPO bank privatization.

The Polish experience with privatizing four SOCBs to date identifies three impediments to an effective transfer of governance to an independent core investor. First, pricing is problematic because of the political costs associated with the perception that banks are being sold at bargain prices in fire sales. Second, speed may prevent tailoring privatization plans to the conditions of the market and foreign demand. Both the absorption capacity of the domestic market and the option value of waiting must be taken into account. Third, a strong CEO can prevent the transfer of governance to non-state outsiders. With the state retaining a core-investor stake, the result of dispersed ownership is then continued insider/state bargaining over bank policy. A fourth lesson from Polish experience is the need to develop the transactional infrastructure before privatization occurs. The political costs incurred in the BSK privatization due to an overloading of the trading infrastructure could have been avoided if properly anticipated.

To date, Hungary has privatized three formerly state-owned banks of which two are controlled independently by outside non-state investors. The major lesson from this experience is that the search for a SFFI takes time but is likely to be worth the effort and patience. The transaction price is not as important as securing the governance of an independent foreign investor. Performance-based incentive contracts can attract SFFIs willing to put up their own reputational capital which is likely to be of more lasting value to the bank than any upfront financial capital. This is especially true when the financial capital from the privatization transaction goes to the state and not to the bank. As a corollary, a strong CEO can prevent the transfer of governance to an outsider as was evidenced in the case of OTP.

The Hungarian government's policy of permitting foreign entry to the banking sector influences the behavior of all banks as foreign competition imposes constraints on the activities of domestic banks. From the outset, the

Hungarian government pursued a more liberal licensing policy for foreign banks than any other country in the region. Even before the political change, foreign financial institutions exhibited a willingness to do business in Hungary. The Central-European International Bank Ltd (CIB) was founded as an off-shore type bank by six foreign banks[40] and the NBH in 1979. Unique in the region, CIB handled foreign exchange transactions for private clients. In 1988, CIB and its foreign shareholders founded a local bank (CIB-Hungary) to pursue forint transactions. Citibank Budapest Ltd[41] began operations on January 1, 1986. Hence, the combination of liberal licensing policies and the willingness of foreign banks to enter the Hungarian market early resulted in foreign banks having a more substantial market share in Hungary than they currently have in the Czech Republic or Poland.

A significant foreign presence in the banking sector may tilt the choice of the bank privatization strategy toward the search for a SFFI so that the resulting privatized bank will be competitive with the existing foreign banks. Experience in Hungary is consistent with this hypothesis. After granting a few initial licenses to foreign banks, the Polish government made a conscious decision to restrict foreign participation for three years. Rather than granting licenses for greenfield operations, the government allowed foreign participation only as a SFFI in a privatizing SOCB or by taking a stake in a failing smaller bank. Recently foreign bank licensing has been liberalized in Poland and the government has become interested in consolidating the domestic banks to create large enough banking groups to fend off the expected foreign competition.

The argument for consolidation of the SOCBs is based on a notion that the region is 'overbanked but underserviced.' Conceptually, the integration of a fragmented banking sector results in gains from both economies of scale and scope. Thus costs and, consequently spreads, should be lowered. Consolidation leads to asset pooling (risk diversification and lowered probability of excess withdrawals through netting) which, in turn, increases the stability of the banking system. Against these two significant benefits must be weighed the cost of creating large banks with significant political influence in the region. Such large conglomerates would be 'too big to fail' and prone to pursuing rent-seeking behavior through political channels rather than focusing on market-efficient, competitive strategies.

The issue of consolidation was first encountered in Bulgaria due to the way in which the two-tier banking system was created. Although the policy had been designed to foster competition by creating many independent banks, the extremely small size of most of the 59 newly born SOCBs combined with their highly concentrated (regionally and sectorally) balance sheets made them financially non-viable from conception. Hence, consolidation was undertaken to cluster the smaller banks with one or more of the larger specialized banks. The outcome of this process was the establishment of seven new banking groups. In addition, three separate specialized banks (two of which are insolvent) continue to operate with no SOCBs attached. While more concentrated than before, the Bulgarian banking system has not yet embarked on a major program of bank privatization due mainly to the weak financial situation of the banking sector resulting from the poor condition of the real economy.

The current Polish government considers the consolidation of domestic banks necessary as a defense against foreign takeover of the domestic banking sector when the Association Agreement with the European Union opens up the banking sector to European banks in 1997. Polish bankers and economists argue that the real sector has developed faster than the financial sector leaving Polish SOCBs with too small a capital base to make the large loans necessary for continued growth and restructuring of large state-owned enterprises. As mentioned above, the major concern with a consolidated banking sector in the region is the lack of competition and the potential for the exercise of monopoly power by the cartel. Will a few large multi-branched banks feel the pressure to provide a wide variety of financial products to a captive clientele? Will the cartel maintain high spreads and earn monopoly profits in the absence of competition? Will the lower costs be passed on to the customers in the form of better service at lower prices? Will large consolidated banks be deemed 'too large to fail'?

To complicate the issue, the Polish government faces the crucial question of sequencing. Which comes first for state-owned banks, privatization or consolidation? A tension exists between two distinct approaches to bank consolidation. The MoF, as the agent of the state owner, proposes to orchestrate the combination of the banks in an attempt to achieve the desired outcomes in a short period of time. The conceptually opposite market-based approach would allow for (or even encourage through the tax code) mergers and acquisitions of independent banks once privatized. Although admittedly taking longer to conclude, the decentralized method relies on negotiations between consenting partners rather than on an arrangement imposed by the parent state. Although quicker, the orchestrated approach runs the risk of creating a politicized governance structure in the consolidated unit that requires ongoing state involvement carrying with it the expectation of continuing financial support. Hence, the sequencing of consolidation and bank privatization will determine both the degree to which, and the speed with which, the state can withdraw from the banking sector after state-owned bank 'privatization.'

State withdrawal is crucial to the creation of a market-oriented banking sector. That consolidation may be seen as a substitute for privatization of SOCBs is dangerous. Consolidation of the type speculated about in the Czech Republic is particularly troublesome. The merger of a state savings bank having a virtual monopoly position in retail banking with a state foreign trade bank having a strong presence in trade financing and forex operations but lacking a branch network, marginalizes the interbank market by internalizing a large percentage of these transactions within the large consolidated conglomerate. Any government that is not committed to the potential advantages of having new owners, foreign or private domestic strategic investors, in the SOCBs may take this opportunity to consolidate the domestic banking sector into a cartel beholden to its political parent. Such a policy would be the antithesis of 'state withdrawal' and would lead to the creation of a politically driven, rather than market-based, allocation of credit.

7. POST-PRIVATIZATION: DO THEY BEHAVE LIKE REAL BANKS?

The objective of privatizing state-owned banks is to create the proper incentives and internal governance structure to ensure that the newly privatized banks act like private banks. To the extent that private owners seek maximal return, bank performance is influenced significantly both by the existing regulatory framework and the market structure which itself depends on banking regulations. In the EITs, even in those countries with a solid legal regulatory framework, actual regulatory practice is still evolving. Hence, both market structure and regulation are in a state of flux. The observed behavior of a privatized bank and the market structure evolving from the choice of a privatization method are key ingredients to the design of regulatory policy in the three countries studied here in detail. How does privatization change the behavior of a state-owned bank? A complete answer to this question is not yet possible due to the short time period over which we can observe bank performance after privatization. The first two privatizations of SOCBs occurred in Poland in 1993. An examination of their respective financial performance in 1994 relative to 1993 provides some partial insights. For WBK, ranked twelve by 1994 net profits, gross profit grew by 61 percent and net profit by 94.3 percent. Total credits extended by WBK increased by 16 percent and irregular credits by 2.7 percent. Its CAR increased from 9.3 percent to 10.6 percent while ROE and ROA both increased from 43.7 percent to 77 percent and from 1.8 percent to 2.5 percent respectively. For the banking sector as a whole, gross profit from 1993 to 1994 increased by 31.5 percent and net profit by 111.5 percent. Total credits increased by 31.2 percent and irregular credits increased by 14.1 percent. The average ROE and ROA increased from 24.4 percent to 36.9 percent and from 1.5 percent to 2.3 percent respectively for the banking sector. WBK, about an average or perhaps slightly above average performer in 1993, improved significantly in 1994 with above-average growth in profits.

Using preliminary data for the entire year,[42] WBK moves up to seventh ranked by net profit (excluding the number for BGZ which seems to be an aberration). More impressively, net profit grew by 82.5 percent and gross profit by 100.2 percent; both rates are the highest recorded by any of the nine regional banks. Located in Western Poland, WBK's dominance of the prosperous and rapidly growing Poznan region provides it with the opportunity to service many Polish-German joint ventures. WBK has taken the lead among Polish banks in retail and private sector lending with estimates that by the end of 1996 two-thirds of its loan portfolio will be to private firms. WBK is the only Polish bank to have opened a branch in Berlin.

For BSK, ranked second among all Polish banks by net profit in 1994, gross profit increased by 7.3 percent and net profit by 19.7 percent. Total credits extended by BSK increased by 27.3 percent and irregular credits increased by 30.7 percent. Its CAR increased from 11.2 percent to 14.9 percent while both return of equity (ROE) and return on assets (ROA) fell from 114.4 to 104.3 percent and from 5.6 to 4.8 respectively. BSK, already a significantly above-average performer in 1993, reverts somewhat toward the mean in 1994 but remained one of the strongest Polish banks.

For the first half of 1995, profits at BSK were up by 51 percent[43] and the proportion of bad debts was almost halved from 48.8 percent to 27 percent.[44] The share price rebounded and outperformed the WIG during this time. Using the same preliminary data as above for the entire year, BSK ranked third in net profit with a growth of 22.3 percent in net profit and 23.9 percent in gross profit. The first of these is above the median performance of the nine regional banks while the second is below the median. As the largest capitalization of the WSE currently, BSK accounts for about 14 percent of the total market value. Recently BSK was rated as Ba2 by Moody's for long-term deposits although it received a D for financial strength and 'not prime' for short-term deposits (both of these ratings at the very low end of the Moody's rating scale).

At the end of October 1995, BSK ranked fifth in equity behind the four large state-owned specialty and ahead of the other regional banks. Another signal of BSK's financial strength can be found in its performance in the stock market. As of January 26, 1996, BSK's shares were selling at PLN 185 or about $73, a high for the previous 52 weeks and almost three times the issue price in US dollars ($25). On December 19, 1995, the US firm Templeton Worldwide purchased a 5 percent stake in BSK offering another independent validation of its financial strength.

Since its privatization in the beginning of 1995, BPH ranks fourth to BSK in net profits, which grew faster in 1995 at a rate of 24.5 percent than those of any of the regional nine with the exception of WBK. Gross profits grew at 27.1 percent. As the second largest capitalization on the WSE, BPH received the same ratings from Moody's as BSK. One Polish analyst claimed that this rating could help both banks by giving them a more positive look and protecting them from any falls.[45]

In the Czech Republic, the three banks included in the first wave of voucher privatization have been under their new ownership structures since the beginning of 1993. However, it is difficult to compare bank performance before and after voucher privatization due to changes in the accounting and regulatory conditions. For example, a significant change in loan classification based on borrowers' debt servicing histories occurred in early 1994 rendering the comparison of the quality of the loan portfolio over time difficult. Due to the relatively short time span following privatizations in Hungary, the financial data necessary to assess its impact are not available. For these reasons, we do not attempt an evaluation of the performance of Czech and Hungarian banks after privatization based on financial indicators.

A separate indicator of how privatization matters is the effect it has on the bank's governance structure. All Polish bank privatizations have been accompanied by some personnel changes in internal governance. When WBK was privatized, EBRD placed two members on the Bank Council, joining the seven members already appointed by the MoF. The current ownership composition of WBK affords the state a core-investor stake of 30 percent, with AIB recently acquiring 16.26 percent of the equity in a new offering, and EBRD maintaining a 23.9 percent stake. The employees of WBK hold 14.3 percent of the total share value with the remaining 15.54 percent held widely. Hence, cooperation between AIB and EBRD would basically be a counterbalance to a coalition of the state and the employees. Control of WBK seems up in the air at this point with the potential remaining for an insider/state coalition having significant influence over decisions.

However, the most dramatic change in governance occurred in BSK, the one bank in which a private SFFI took a core-investor stake. After the privatization of BSK and during the 'Bank Slaski Affair,' the president of the Management Board resigned and the vice-president was recalled. At the May 1994 AGM, the previous Management Board completed its term and the Bank Council appointed a three-person new Management Board consisting of only one person who had served on the previous board (he was appointed the President of the board in July 1994). At the same AGM, a new Bank Council was also chosen. Of the seven members, only one served on the previous council. The chair and deputy chair of the Bank Council were not members of the previous council and one of the new members is an ING representative. Hence, BSK has revamped entirely its governance personnel since its privatization.

Currently, ING holds a 25.9 percent stake, and the state retains a 33 percent stake in BSK, with the remainder of the shares held widely. The new chairman of the Bank Council, Andrzej Wroblewski, describes the situation as having two big shareholders. Himself an employee of the MoF, Wroblewski considers himself an agent of both ING and the MoF. However, the fact that BSK is traded on the WSE limits the influence of the MoF, according to the chairman. Nonetheless, the MoF has significant influence over important policies. Wroblewski described a confrontation over dividend policy: the Management Board had determined that, over the next couple of years, BSK should aim for a dividend of 20 percent. However, the MoF as the largest shareholder wanted a higher dividend. The target for this year was adjusted upward to 25 percent and the chairman of the Bank Council concluded that the MoF did not act as true shareholder of the bank.

On relationships with the other big shareholder, Wroblewski was positive. He described the cooperation as developing well with the Dutch supplying know-how but also being very open to the opinions of bank management. ING did not always think that what they supplied was best and they did not act provincially toward BSK. ING provided considerable technical support to modernize BSK's operations. The marketing department and credit analysis procedures were revamped according to ING's recommendations.[46] BSK has started marketing the life insurance policies of the ING group in the Polish market. The two banks plan to launch a new stock market fund in the near future. Although Wroblewski reports that there was a tendency at BSK just after privatization to wait for ING to think of something, medium-term strategy is evolving. BSK intends to expand its product lines in both the corporate and retail markets. Fierce competition is expected in the corporate market for high-quality customers, so BSK is considering new instruments. On the retail side, BSK does not wish to sacrifice efficiency to expand its network. Rather the recent acquisition by BSK and ING of almost 15 percent of the shares of BPH indicate that the partners intend to use mergers and acquisitions to expand their network rather than build new branches. BSK is committed to concentrate its main business in the Upper Silesian region where it has good access to cheap retail deposits and proximity to some of the largest wholesale borrowers in Poland.

After the privatization of BPH, the Bank Council dismissed the president of the Management Board. However, the ownership structure of BPH is not conducive yet to the emergence of a non-state core investor. The state still retains a 43 percent stake, with the next largest shareholder being the EBRD with a 15 percent holding. Employees own 3.5 percent of the shares and WBK has a 2.5 percent stake. Adding to the shares currently held by BSK and ING, the impending purchase of Daiwa's stake results in a combined holding of slightly less than 15 percent. Currently the best chance for a non-state coalition involves the BSK-ING partnership with the EBRD. For the present, the MoF is likely to have a strong influence over BPH policy as evidenced by the plan to include the state's stake in BPH in the bank consolidation program. Perhaps the discipline imposed by the WSE, of which Wroblewski spoke, will leaven the MoF's large stake. In Hungary, the new owners of MKB, BLB and EBRD each placed one senior member on a six-member Board of Directors, joining four continuing Hungarian members. The general director of the board resigned and his post was assumed by one of the Hungarian members. To date, no senior bank executives from Germany have been put in place at MKB. Current ownership stakes in MKB are BLB with 25 percent, EBRD holding 16.68 percent and the APV Rt (state) retaining 27 percent. Although BLB has a strong enough position to assume the role of an aggressive core investor, it has not done so to date. In Hungary, the new non-private owners of MKB did place members on the governance board but have yet to take an active-investor role in bank strategy.

The situation in OTP seems even more predisposed to insider/state control. The CEO still maintains his chair of chairmanship of the Board of Directors. The APV Rt retains 25 percent of the shares while the two social security funds hold another 20 percent. Employees own a 5 percent stake, and the remaining 50 percent is widely held. Hence, with the assistance of the employees and the social security funds, the CEO can maintain insider control. On the other hand, when the social security funds align with the state, the block is sufficient to rule the day. The battle between the MoF and the CEO of OTP over control of the bank is likely to continue for the near-term.

In the Czech Republic, the state through the holdings of the NPF holds a dominant stake in both large banks. In KB, the NPF share is 48.7 percent while that of the top five investment funds is 41 percent. Of these top five investment funds, three are subsidiaries of the 'big four' banks, namely ČS, KB, and IPB. The NPF holds a 45 percent stake in ČS and the top five investment funds have a combined 27.2 percent share. Municipal governments also hold an aggregate stake of 20 percent in ČS. The major independent investor is the Harvard investment fund group, but their early attempts to challenge bank policy and assert independent governance were rebuffed. Although the NPF's share in ČSOB is only 19.6 percent, the state's stake in this bank is significantly higher and consists of joint Czech-Slovak ownership. It is only IPB among the big four in which the state's direct share of 14.8 percent is low enough to afford the possibility of the near-term emergence of an independent core investor. Between the cross-ownership patterns and the state's high stake in three of the big four banks, control of the Czech banking sector rests currently with the state. Witness the rumored merger of ČS and ČSOB that, if effectuated, would be orchestrated by the government and not driven by the market.

8. CONCLUSIONS: LESSONS FROM AND FOR THE VISEGRAD COUNTRIES

Of equal importance to whether or not privatization changes bank behavior and internal governance is the way in which the choice of the privatization method influences the evolving market structure. Crucial to the efficiency and stability of any banking system is a regulatory structure that is designed properly in accordance with the characteristics of the market. On this issue, conclusions can be drawn from the experiences of the three Visegrad countries. Clearly the feasibility of a domestic IPO hinges crucially on the absorption capacity of the domestic stock market. In April 1995, the average daily volume on the WSE was about $80 million, and the market had been rising during this period. At that time, 51 stocks were listed and the total market capitalization was about $4 billion. Selling about a 50 percent stake in BPH at the minimum price set by the government generated approximately $154 million or almost twice the average daily volume on the WSE. Currently, bank stocks account for about 40 percent of the market capitalization in Poland, and only three of the nine SOCBs have been privatized. Hence, the Polish authorities are considering strategies that combine the IPO approach with a significant influx of foreign portfolio investment. However, this strategy will not attract a non-state core investor.

The other two privatization options are not without their own pitfalls. Searching for a SFFI can be a time-consuming and politically tenuous process. The privatization of BB in Hungary failed when CSFB pulled out in the final stages of negotiation. Although WBK did not succeed initially in attracting a SFFI, AIB later bought a new issue at a substantially lower price. The option value of waiting to let the market determine the appropriate price can be a significant deterrent to the participation of a SFFI in the initial tender. The Hungarian foreign trade bank, MKB, did attract a SFFI, but it is a German public bank, BLB, that has not taken an aggressive stance toward governance or long-term market planning. Like the EBRD, BLB seems to be a passive investor. The only aggressive core investor to date in the region is ING, the private SFFI of BSK. However, partly due to the backlash from the BSK privatization, the Polish MoF is currently pursuing bank consolidation as a prior step to privatization of the remaining SOCBs. Because privatizing with a SFFI is likely to be slow and may even be politically dangerous, this strategy has lost favor with the governments in the region.

At the opposite side of the spectrum, voucher privatization is quick and politically expedient. However, experience in the Czech Republic points out the potential for significant cross-ownership patterns to evolve and strengthen further the non-market relationships between banks and their company clients to the detriment of the governance of both. Furthermore, both voucher privatization and IPOs are likely to result in bifurcated ownership structures. The state will retain a core-investor-size stake while the preponderance of the rest of the shares will be held widely. Such a configuration provides ample opportunity for insider/state or solely state control. In this case, the government as owner may pursue an agenda that is detrimental to the overall competitiveness of the banking sector as evidenced by the consolidation movements in Poland and the Czech Republic. The alleged Czech consolidation program is particularly troublesome in that it involves a merger of the state savings bank having a virtual monopoly position in retail banking with the state foreign trade bank having a strong presence in trade financing and forex operations but lacking a branch network. If consummated, this marriage would marginalize the interbank market by internalizing a significant percentage of these transactions within the large consolidated conglomerate.

Bank regulatory policies must be designed with a focus on the market structure that is likely to arise from privatization of the SOCBs. As the dominant financial institutions in these countries, privatized state-owned banks will play a central role in financial markets for the medium-term at least. The need to tailor both the design and the implementation of banking regulation to the market structure resulting from privatization policies seems to be a compelling message from the experiences of the Visegrad countries. More attention must be paid to regulatory policy when a privatization strategy is chosen.

Take, for example, the Czech structure resulting from voucher privatization. Such concentration might work reasonably well in a small open economy eventually linked with the European Union. Foreign competition could then provide the necessary market discipline in corporate markets. However, foreign banks tend to be niche players in host countries, leaving large segments of banking, in particular retail banking, to domestic banks. This analysis suggests that regulatory policy consistent with voucher privatization of banks should encourage foreign banks to set up commercial business and allow domestic citizens to hold retail deposits in other countries.

Unfortunately, the polar opposite 'bunker mentality' seems to prevail in the region. With the exception of Hungary, governments have restricted significantly foreign participation in the banking sector by making unattractive the terms on which foreign banks can enter. If such thinking continues, the privatization of state-owned banks by IPO or the voucher method will not lead to a healthy, competitive banking sector. Rather the new owners, be they outsiders or insiders, will simply reap the monopoly rents of a highly concentrated financial market.

State withdrawal is crucial to the creation of a competitive market-oriented banking sector. In the face of a perceived foreign invasion, consolidation of the domestic banks orchestrated by the state may be seen as a substitute for their privatization so as to make them viable opponents. Any government that is not committed to the advantages of having new owners, foreign or private domestic strategic investors, for the SOCBs may use this excuse to consolidate the domestic banking sector into a cartel beholden to its political parent. Such a policy would be the antithesis to 'state withdrawal' and would thwart the creation of a market-based financial sector. No economy in transition will be well-served in the long run by such short-term politically expedient solutions. Rather, the focus of government policy should be on designing strong regulatory and oversight structures to ensure competition on a level playing field and to provide the stability necessary for safe and sound banking to develop.

NOTES

1. A similar structure has been proposed by the government in Bulgaria.
2. The twinning arrangement was implemented in seven of the nine regional SOCBs.
3. The first bank floated on the WSE was Bank Rozwoju Eksportu (BRE) which was established in 1986 as an export development bank. It was privatized through an IPO in June 1992 and has been traded on the WSE since September 1992. BRE shares are widely held although Commerzbank (Germany) obtained a 21 percent ownership stake when a new issue was floated in 1993.
4. We use PLZ to refer to old zloty and PLN to refer to new zloty.
5. Reuters, January 16, 1996.
6. Since BSK was a larger bank than WBK, the expectation was that employees would be able financially to purchase a somewhat smaller percent of its shares.
7. An article in *Gazeta Bankowa* dated October 8, 1995 argued that the price of BSK shares in the IPO should be set at a PE of 8 or 9 leading to an issue price of at least PLZ 1 million.
8. According to the prospectus, 1.4 million shares could be reallocated from the tender to the IPO. Adding this number to the original allocation yields a total of 2.789 million shares in the IPO. Between November 3 and December 1, 817,644 valid offers were received totaling PLZ 7,993.2 billion ($400 million). Hence, demand exceeded supply by 5.73 to one. The Ministry of Finance allocated 2,478,384 shares to this group so that each person received three shares only. This information and some of what follows is taken from the annual report of Bank Slaski SA, 1994.
9. Within the employee offer, 646,369 shares were purchased at PLZ 500,000 ($25) per share and an additional 279,169 shares were purchased on preferential terms within the twelve months beginning December 27, 1993. The shares purchased by employees numbering 925,528 is approximately 10 percent of the total number of shares outstanding.
10. Christopher Bobinski, 'Privatization Dream Turns Into a Nightmare,' *The Financial Times*, February 7, 1994.
11. Budget revenues from these transactions would have amounted to approximately PLZ 2.8 trillion (about $140 million). According to the Ministry of Finance, the total proceeds from privatizing BSK amounted to PLZ 4.5 trillion ($225 million).
12. In addition, the Mexican crisis had decreased significantly foreign portfolio investment interest in emerging-market economies. The WIG bottomed out at 5904.7 in 1995 and stood at 8486.5 in mid-July, 1995.

13. Depository receipts are issued by banks that purchase shares and hold them in trust. American depository receipts are US-dollar denominated while global depository receipts are denominated in a currency-basket.
14. Article 78 of the 1989 Banking Act requires that an investor obtain the consent of the NBP before acquiring a stake that will allocate more than 10 percent, 20 percent, 33 percent, 50 percent, 66 percent, or 75 percent of a bank's voting rights.
15. 'Wedlock or Gridlock', *Institutional Investor*, December 1994, p. 66.
16. These are BG, BIG, BPH, BRE, BSK, Kredyt Bank, Polski Bank Rozwoju (PBR), WBK, Petrobank, and Pierwszy Polsko-Amerykanski Bank w Krakowie (PPABank) in which the Polish-American Enterprise Fund holds a large stake.
17. For a discussion of the pros and cons of centrally orchestrated consolidation and an analysis of the Polish situation, see Bonin and Leven (1996).
18. This and some of the information in the remainder of this paragraph are taken from *Economic and Legal Information From Poland*, Vol. V, No. 5 (October–November 1995).
19. The SPA has since been merged with the State Holding Company (AV Rt) to form the State Privatization Agency (AVP Rt).
20. The Banking Act of 1991 legislates that direct state ownership of any bank cannot exceed 25 percent by the end of 1997 although it is widely held that extensions will be granted for several of the large SOCBs.
21. Using an end-1993 exchange rate of HUF 100 per US dollar.
22. Using a mid-1994 exchange rate of HUF 102 per US dollar.
23. This paragraph draws on Kormendi and Schatterly (1996).
24. The total value of securities issued to all participating banks in this tranche was HUF 114.4 bn.
25. Creditanstalt itself had explored a possible offer earlier in the year but disengaged from the negotiations.
26. This paragraph draws on Kormendi and Schatterly (1996).
27. The specifics of the put and call options are confidential.
28. Perhaps this incident illustrates the importance given by all countries to maintain domestic control of the banking sector.
29. For an elaboration of this discussion see Chapter 5.
30. Mejstřík (1995), p. 12.
31. 'Economists Emerge From Obscurity,' *Financial Times* Survey: Czech Republic, June 2, 1995, p. IV.
32. Vincent Boland, 'Czech Banks Play Down Speculation on Merger Talks,' *Financial Times*, October 11, 1995.
33. Mejstřík (1995), pp. 14 and 15.
34. The test case was Investiční Banka which founded an investment company in 1990 that established 12 funds.
35. These data are from Mejstřík (1995), Table 7.
36. The data to follow are taken from 'Can Anything Tame the Fund Monsters?', *Central European Economic Review*, June 1995, pp. 24–26.
37. Adding the second Harvard Growth fund which is the sixth largest fund with capitalization of $91m yields a combined capitalization $250m making it the second largest behind CS.
38. These data are taken from the survey section of the *Financial Times*, April 26, 1996, p. III.
39. The state's share in CSOB is actually significantly larger as shares are also held by the CNB (26.5 percent), The Czech MoF (20 percent), and the Slovak National Bank (24 percent). Indeed, nine of the eleven members of the supervisory board of CSOB represent state institutions and only 9.9 percent of the shares are held by owners other than these government entities.
40. These are Comit Holding International SpA, Banca Commerciale Italiana Group, Bayerische Vereinsbank AG, the Long-Term Credit Bank of Japan Ltd, the Sakura Bank Ltd, and Societe Generale; each have a 13.2 percent share in CIB.

41. The NBH holds a 20 percent share in Citibank-Budapest.
42. As reported in *Rzeczpospolita*, January 22, 1996.
43. Performance figures for the first half of 1995 are from Toby Beck, 'Bank Slaski SA: ING's Silesian Protege,' *Business News From Poland*, September 19, 1995, pp. 13–15. End-1994 figures are from Bank Slaski SA Annual Report, 1994.
44. This change must be interpreted carefully. Until the beginning of 1995, every loan with a state guarantee had to be rated as 'substandard' and hence counted as an irregular credit (or bad loan in this terminology). At the end of 1994, the percentage of gross loans covered by state guarantees amounted to 18 percent (Bank Slaski SA Annual Report, 1994).
45. 'Analysts Lukewarm on Moody's Polish Bank Rating', Reuters, September 9, 1995.
46. Beck, *Business News from Poland*, September 19, 1995, p. 13.

3. The Role of Foreign Banks in Economies in Transition

A major development in banking throughout the world was the dramatic growth in international banking from about 1960 to 1985. Foreign banking growth spread from Europe and the US to Japan, the Pacific Rim and South America.[1] In the 1990s, foreign banking expansion has spread to the formerly planned economies of central and eastern Europe. There are a number of reasons for the spread of foreign banking activity: the increase in trade and foreign direct investment, the globalization of financial markets, the diminishing distinctions between banking and capital markets, the liberalization of financial markets around the world, and the increasingly free convertibility of currencies. All of these developments have occurred at a very rapid pace, even as differences in regulatory structure and other barriers to financial integration persist.

There are two distinct aspects of foreign banking activity: the cross-border activities of banks, really international banking, and the activities of banks outside their country of origin. Much of the remarkable growth of international banking activity consists of the cross-border activities of large banks. Growth in such activities parallels the growth of foreign trade and the development of international capital markets. We are interested in the second aspect of the foreign banking phenomenon, however, namely the activities of banks in foreign countries.

The activities of banks outside their home countries has two aspects as well. First, much of the growth of banks outside their home countries takes place in order to facilitate their international or cross-border activities. For example, much of the increase in foreign bank branching is associated with patterns of trade, foreign direct investment and migration. Also, much of the increase in foreign banking is centered in the global financial centers where Euro-currency capital markets and foreign exchange transactions are concentrated. Second, foreign banking activity has increased as financial services becomes a global industry and growth strategies for banks include operations in more than one domestic market.

Our interest in this chapter is the activity of foreign banks in the Central and Eastern European economies in transition (EITs). Both aspects of foreign banking activity noted above are relevant in the EITs. First, the development of trade and international investment opportunities in the transition economies leads to increased cross-border banking activities. Thus, banks enter the transition economies in order to facilitate the provision of international financial services. This phenomenon explains the growth of foreign branches in the transition economies. Second, the global business strategies of many banks include an extension of activities to the transition economies. Thus, many Western European and some American banks[2] have begun to extend their banking business in the domestic markets in the EITs. Domestic banking services can be developed by acquisition of existing banks, strategic alliances with domestic banks and by starting new ventures.

International and foreign banking activity is particularly important in the economies in transition for two reasons. First, the activities of MNCs and international activities of existing large firms are likely to be the leading growth sectors in the EITs. These are just the market sectors where the foreign banks are able to provide services. Second, the banking industry in the EITs was until quite recently entirely state-owned and continues to suffer from technological inefficiencies. Thus, the industry is ripe for joint ventures, cross ownership and foreign bank entry as part of both the privatization process and the development of a modern banking sector. The entry of foreign banks is likely to have profound effects on the competitive environment and the provision of services in domestic markets. Even relatively small foreign ventures in the domestic markets can have spillover effects that will influence banking practices generally.

Throughout the world, entry into the banking industry is subject to regulatory review to insure the adequacy of capital and the ability and honesty of the bankers. Regulation of bank entry is justified by the special role of banks as issuers of money assets and the potential for system-wide consequences of bank failure or malfeasance. The overall design of restrictions on bank entry and the appropriate regulatory framework are beyond the scope of our topic. However, what is of interest here is that there are often additional arguments raised with respect to the entry of foreign banks. In fact, it is common around the world to raise additional barriers to the entry into the domestic banking business of foreign firms.

The liberalization and harmonization of bank regulation in the European community has resulted in the expansion of cross-border banking strategies in Western Europe. The changes that have occurred are instructive for developments in the EITs of central Europe. In fact, the banking sectors of the EITs in central Europe are in many ways similar to those of the smaller European countries. That is, the banking sectors tend to be highly concentrated, there tends to be a significant amount of public ownership and foreign bank penetration is limited. Moreover, bad debt problems and technological inefficiencies are common. Finally, resistance to foreign bank entry is very common.

The business strategies of larger European banks in some of the smaller European community countries are similar to developments in the EITs.

In the next section, we take a very brief look at the structure of banking in Europe in order to place the EITs in perspective. The commonalities are striking and the European experiences provide a guide to what may happen in the EITs.

In the section that follows, we examine the arguments against foreign bank entry. There is an underlying current in banking discussions, particularly in the EITs, that the entry of foreign banks should be restricted. We muster and analyze every possible argument in favor of restricting foreign bank entry. We then examine foreign banking from the opposite point of view, by discussing what foreign bank entry can accomplish in the EITs.

The second part of the chapter provides a description of foreign bank activity in each of the countries examined in the project.

1. PERSPECTIVES ON FOREIGN BANKING

Although foreign bank activity has grown enormously, banking is an international industry in only a limited sense. Although international capital markets are very large, most banking activity takes place on domestic markets and most banking services are provided within national borders. The banking industry continues to be much less international than many manufacturing industries, such as the automobile industry. Most production of banking services is done by domestic companies within national borders.

The growth of international banking is part of the development of international capital market activity and is therefore concentrated in the major financial sectors such as New York, London, Tokyo and Frankfurt. Thus, the increase in foreign bank branches and new foreign-owned banks tend to be concentrated in these international capital market centers. Additional clusters of foreign bank activity tend to follow economic activity such as particularly strong trade relations and patterns of migration. The inroads of foreign banks in retail banking and domestic lending is still rather small.

There are several reasons why banking generally resists internationalization. First, service industries are generally less integrated internationally than manufacturing. Second, banking in most countries (with the notable exception of the US) is highly concentrated and therefore provides significant entry barriers.[3] In addition to concentration, state ownership of all or part of the existing banks creates a non-competitive environment and discourages foreign or any other new entrants. A surprisingly large number of generally free economies have significant amounts of state ownership of the banking sector; some data for Western Europe are shown in Table 3.1.[4] Third, and perhaps most importantly, national authorities are often opposed to foreign ownership of banking. For example, Denmark, Norway and Sweden did not allow entry of foreign bank branches until the mid-1980's and Sweden only lifted a ban on foreign ownership of banks in 1990.

Table 3.1 Distribution of Ownership of Total Banking Sector Assets, 1988

	Public sector %	Foreign sector %
UK	1	53
Switzerland	20	11
West Germany	50	2
Sweden	19	3
Spain	2	11
Portugal	87	4
Norway	20	0
Italy	68	3
Greece	84	5
France	42	14
Netherlands	8	13
Finland	11	1
Belgium	17	35
Austria	44	0

Source: Gardner and Molyneux (1990).

Comparison with some of the smaller European countries is particularly instructive. A Bank of Finland report echoes the concerns about foreign banks that are heard presently in the EITs:

> The presence of foreign banks in Finland was restricted, inter alia, in order to prevent foreign capital from gaining too much influence. Problems associated with the supervision of banks under foreign control and the fear that the room for manoeuvre in monetary policy would be curtailed by the entry of foreign banks in the domestic market help to explain the negative attitude. The ability of Finnish banks to compete on equal terms was considered to be a matter of some concern. (Savela and Herrala, 1992. p. 8)

The article goes on to say that attitudes changed when the benefits of competition became better understood, monetary policy began to emphasize international coordination and international cooperation set high standards for bank supervision. However, Finland did not allow foreign bank representative offices (with very limited functions) until 1973, subsidiaries until 1979 and branches until 1991. There are only eight representative offices, two subsidiaries and three foreign bank branches in Finland, and half of all these are less than ten years old.

Western experience is also helpful in understanding bank privatization in Central Europe. State-owned banks in France and elsewhere have been or will be privatized. The situation in Austria is particularly interesting because fears of foreign ownership of the banks has impeded the privatization process for almost five years. After much discussion, Austria is seeking to privatize the state's 49 percent stake (which commands 70 percent of the voting rights) in the second largest bank – Creditanstalt. There are no foreign banks active in Austria and suspicions about foreign control persist even as Creditanstalt itself has become one of the most active foreign banks in Central Europe. In 1994, negotiations with Credit Suisse and with a German group broke down because of Austrian nationalist opposition. The former Austrian chancellor, Franz Vranitzky, was quoted by Reuters as saying 'that the potential investor is Austrian or has a relationship to Austria is an important consideration.' The Austrian economics minister, Johannes Dits, was quoted as saying:

> Austrian national interests must be taken into account. The selling price is not the only criterion. It is important that Austrian influence should be maintained in the nation's second largest bank. (Reuters *Euopean Business Report*, August 9, 1995).

The strong expressions of nationalism in Austria have been echoed in the neighboring EITs to the east. It is interesting to note that more progress towards liberalization of bank ownership has already been made in these countries than in Austria.

Major changes in Western European banking have taken place because of the European Union directives that essentially create a single European market in all financial services. In the last ten years there have been a large number of cross-national acquisitions or mergers, purchases of minority interests by foreign banks and business alliances formed among existing banks. Many financial service firms are developing strategies that will enable them to develop as multinational firms and give them the opportunity to exploit the economies of scale and scope that might exist. However, despite these developments, most banking activity continues to be conducted by domestic firms.

Foreign banking has had only a limited impact because the costs of entry to the banking industry are often high. Nevertheless, the existence of cost differentials and economies of scale and scope lead many banks to develop international strategies. The internationalization of the European banks provides a longer history than the foreign banking experiences in the EITs, and the lessons drawn from the European experience are relevant to the EITs. For example, the strategy pursued since the mid-1980s by Deutsche Bank

(Germany's largest bank) in Spain and Italy is hard to distinguish from the strategies pursued more recently by Austrian and Dutch banks in the Central European EITs.[5]

As elsewhere, the market share of foreign banks is likely to increase slowly, and there is no indication that large foreign banks will dominate the industry in the smaller countries of Western or Central Europe. The 1988 data shown earlier indicate that the inroads made by foreign banks are usually quite small.The exceptions are very small countries that are integrated economically with their neighbors (for example Belgium) and international capital markets centers (for example the UK).

This overview of foreign banking strongly suggests that the banking sectors of the economies in transition are in many respects not so unusual. The EITs of Central Europe should be compared to other small industrial countries. In all such countries the patterns of banking structure are quite similar. Banking tends to be quite highly concentrated, and state ownership of part of the industry is common. In both formerly planned economies and free market economies, the powerful combination of industry concentration and state ownership gives the banking industry considerable power to protect itself from competition, foreign or otherwise. In addition, regulators are often sympathetic because they fear that competition may weaken or even lead to the failure of some existing banking entities. As a result, the industry is often very successful in keeping competitive pressures at bay. And one source of competitive pressure that is often discouraged is the entry of foreign banks.

Despite the concern about foreign bank entry, there is a significant amount of foreign banking activity in the EITs already. First, international banking has grown as a consequence of increased foreign direct investment in and trade with the EITs. Second, foreign bank activity occurs in several different forms in the EITs:

   (i) Representative offices and bank branches
  (ii) Joint ventures with domestic banks or purchase of minority interest
 (iii) Wholly-owned subsidiary in foreign country
 (iv) Strategic investment in domestic bank

International banking activity – cross-border banking transactions – often requires a physical presence. Thus, many banks have opened branches or established representative offices in the EITs in order to service their home country customers. Such offices can establish a presence in the market without any commitment of the foreign bank's capital in the host country. Often banks will establish such a presence on the speculation that banking business may develop. There are foreign branches or representative offices in all of the EITs examined, many of which are very small operations. For example, in 1995 there were 21 representative offices of foreign banks and three foreign bank branches in Poland. At the opposite extreme, Estonia and Bulgaria have just recently begun to grant entry to foreign branches. In each case, a number of foreign banks have expressed interest in establishing a presence in the country, often in anticipation of future needs.

There are several possible reasons why foreign banks establish actual banking entities in the EITs (foreign owned banks). First, their home country customers' activities might develop to the point where additional transactions services and lending are demanded. Second, the foreign banks may establish banking relations with domestic enterprises that have international activities. Third, the foreign banks may be eager to enter profitable niches of the banking business, such as the provision of services to wealthy individuals and the foreign communities in the EITs. Fourth, there may be a purely speculative desire to establish a presence in the industry.

The type of banking business started will vary with the motive. Citibank has developed a strategy which concentrates on firms with international banking business and on services for wealthy domestic customers which are served by wholly owned Citibank subsidiaries in the EITs. For example, although Citibank in Hungary is not competing with the OTP – the large savings bank – it does offer retail banking services such as ATMs and credit cards and aims to have 10,000 retail customers. Other banks prefer to keep their capital commitment to a minimum and to avoid large investments in infrastructure. In such instances, joint ventures or minority share holding with domestic banks is common. It is difficult to generalize about the foreign bank ventures because they vary from corporate shells to significant competitors in the banking business.

In the first several years of the post-Communist era, some of the EITs, particularly Hungary and Poland, were very liberal in allowing foreign bank entry. However, the authorities quickly became disenchanted with banking sector developments. New banks (domestic and foreign-owned) were popping up before an adequate regulatory framework was in place. Many of these ventures were highly speculative and poorly capitalized. In Hungary some of the new foreign banks ran up big losses, and in Poland there were bank frauds involving some of the new banks. Hungary has tightened entry requirements, and Poland has essentially stopped issuing new licenses as it seeks to have foreign entrants purchase existing institutions.

The market shares of foreign banks differ significantly among the major Central European countries. Hungary has been most hospitable to foreign banks, and there are almost as many foreign banks as Hungarian-owned banks. At the end of 1994, the foreign banks held close to one-fifth of total bank assets and the share continued growing in 1995. In Poland, the foreign banking share was barely more than 2 percent when the foreign stakes in the privatized banks are ignored. In the Czech Republic, where the banking sector is highly concentrated, the foreign banks are active in a few niches. In 1993, the majority foreign banks issued about 3 percent of total credits.[6] However, the foreign bank share was growing rapidly and by the end of 1994, Čapek (1995) indicates that it exceeded 6 percent and over one-third of new credits issued.

As an alternative to developing a bank or when the regulatory environment discourages it, the foreign bank may develop its advisory services and act as an investment banker. In the Czech Republic, where the privatization program preceded any efforts at banking reform, many Western financial firms entered the financial sector with non-banking entities. There are many Western investment and merchant banks, investment managers and brokers and only a few foreign banking ventures.

Since the banking sectors in the EITs are relatively undeveloped, some Western banks have ambitious long-term plans for growth. Such a strategy can involve a commitment to make large investments in business development. For example, the Austrian bank Creditanstalt has the largest foreign banking network in central Europe with offices in all of the EITs and 1400 employees. In addition, the Creditanstalt Investment Bank is a major player on the Budapest Stock Exchange and an important investment banker for corporate finance in the Czech Republic. It has more privatization advisory contracts than any other firm and is the only foreign bank leading the consortia that are being considered for privatizations in Poland. The bank is planning to expand into retail banking in Hungary and perhaps elsewhere. Creditanstalt has concentrated all of its international banking activity on the region. The manager of Creditanstalt in Slovakia, Thomas Uher, summarizes their strategy: 'We are returning to our roots for these are effectively our home markets.'[7]

Banking authorities in the EITs are anxious to channel foreign interest in directions that help them attain their domestic goals: the privatization and modernization of the banking sector. Thus, policy makers would like to develop strategic alliances between foreign banks and existing banks. In some instances this involves alliances with Western banks in order to provide business advice and start the process of modernization. In Poland, the so-called 'twinning' arrangements provided technical assistance without obliging the Western partner to make any equity investment. In some instances the twin arrangements did evolve into partial ownership and, in at least one instance, an option to gain control of a domestic bank. Generally, there are a number of examples of minority equity investments by and joint ventures with foreign banks.

More recently, the authorities in all three of the large Central European countries – Poland, Hungary and the Czech Republic – have been trying to use strategic investments by foreign banks as the vehicle for privatization. However, it has not been easy to bring such deals to fruition. Efforts to enlist a foreign strategic investor in the privatization of large state-owned bank have proven difficult. In the Czech Republic, Komerční banka has resisted such efforts. In Hungary, the negotiations for the sale of Budapest Bank were long and difficult. More than one effort to negotiate a strategic investment by a foreign partner failed before the deal with GE Capital was reached in late 1995.

The potential investors are reluctant for several reasons: first, potential foreign participants are not convinced that the balance sheets of these banks have been completely cleaned up; second, they are not satisfied with the quality of the management in the domestic banks; and, third, these banks are so large that investors worry about future government interference with the activities of foreign managers or owners. Interestingly, more progress has been made in Poland, where bank privatizations with the strategic investments by foreign banks have been made.[8]

Before we go on to examine the situation in the EITs in detail, we provide an analytic discussion of why there is so much apparent resistance to foreign banking.

2. ARGUMENTS AGAINST FOREIGN BANK ENTRY

The arguments presented to oppose foreign bank entry fall into two general topics. First, there is a general fear of foreign control and competition from abroad. Second, there is the possibility that the objectives and behavior of foreign banks will be different from domestic banks.

The first argument stems from the fact that banks are uniquely important institutions that often have enormous influence in the economy and also have very close relationships with the government. The fear that foreign control of the banks will lead to foreign control of the economy often motivates opposition to foreign bank entry. A corollary to this argument is that domestic banks, particularly if they are weak, should be protected from foreign competition. In addition, if the government assists the banking industry, such assistance should go to domestic institutions only.

The second argument is that foreign banks may have a different objective function than domestic banks. Their global profit maximization may lead to business decisions in the domestic economy which are undesirable.

In this section, we will list and evaluate the specific arguments for restricting foreign bank entry.

(i) Fear of foreign control

The entry of foreign banks will lead to foreign control of the economy. The argument here seems to be that foreign banks can be the leading forces in some kind of undesirable financial colonialism. In broad terms, the fear of foreign control implies that foreign participation in economic development should be discouraged.

Foreign participation in economic development, through foreign direct investment, financial investment or through banking, will lead to some foreign influence or control over the domestic economy. The feelings of nationalism that mitigate against foreign participation must be weighed against the foreign contribution to the growth process.

Actually, foreign direct or financial investment is more likely to be accompanied by foreign control than foreign banking activity. However, it would be silly to restrict foreign direct investment unless the domestic economy has sufficient domestic savings to finance growth. There have been restrictions on FDI in some of the East Asian tigers where large pools of domestic savings were tapped or created by repressing consumption and used to finance growth spurts while the domestic capital markets were essentially closed to foreigners. The approach has the advantages of creating pools of private domestic savings that are often needed to sustain the growth process. The situation in the European EITs may be fundamentally different. These countries are increasingly consumption-oriented, and it is not at all clear that the any policy could harness sufficient domestic savings to replace and modernize an aging capital stock. This is widely realized, and foreign direct investment is mostly encouraged rather than discouraged.

Direct investment, the purchase of productive assets, is relatively fixed and often illiquid. Thus, it represents a long-term commitment to the host nation by the investor. Even though the productive assets are subject to foreign control, the investors' interest and the national interests are likely to coincide.

Foreign financial or portfolio investment is more problematic than foreign direct investment because the assets are not fixed. It is not a coincidence that the terms 'hot money' and 'flight capital' have been applied to international portfolio investments. Portfolio preferences can change quickly, with profound consequences for macroeconomic stability in the host country.

Concern about the power over the domestic economy wielded by foreign portfolio investors has recently come to the fore as a consequence of the 1994 economic crisis in Mexico, which involved an exchange rate depreciation, a collapse in production and a massive accumulation of non-performing bank loans. However, the investors that were criticized for having precipitated the crisis were the holders (Mexican as much as foreign) of financial (portfolio) investments and not the owners of direct investments or the foreign banks.[9]

FDI in Mexico is generally viewed as being an important source of economic growth. The foreign banking sector does not wield any undue power. Thus, foreign financial investment can lead to macroeconomic stabilization problems which are difficult to surmount.[10]

Foreign banking and foreign portfolio investment are not the same thing. Foreign bank entry is a form of FDI in the financial services industry. Moreover, foreign bank investments are hardly flight capital, especially if the banking activity is funded by domestic deposits. Foreign banking and foreign portfolio investment are sometimes equated because foreign banks often provide portfolio services for foreign investors. The fact that foreign banks might facilitate portfolio investments should not be used to argue for foreign bank restrictions.

We have considered the reasons to be concerned with economic power wielded by foreigners through FDI and through foreign portfolio investment but we have not discussed foreign banking specifically. Banking activity – lending and deposit taking – by foreign banks is not likely to result in controlling interest over assets in the way that FDI can. However, banking activity by foreigners is often feared because the interests of the bankers can be pervasive. FDI is usually restricted to specific investments, but the successful foreign banker may have economic interests throughout the economy. However, the foreign banks are likely to have a commitment to the domestic economy, especially if their investment is fixed and their deposit base is from the domestic economy.

Since banks can exert influence over their loan customers, it is true that foreign banks will have influence over the economy. However, if their investment in the banking business is relatively fixed and their deposit base is raised domestically then their operations should not differ substantively from the activities of domestically owned banks. It would be silly for a country that can benefit from increased investment to restrict FDI, and foreign banks are simply a FDI in the financial services industry. Just as FDI in manufacturing is valued as a way of increasing the capital stock and productivity in industry, foreign banking should improve the efficiency of financial intermediation in the host country. However, there is one qualification that arises, because foreign banks and increased efficiency of intermediation generally will result in increased short-term portfolio flows. As noted above, such flows can be create difficulties for macroeconomic stabilization. Although foreign banks may introduce, facilitate and encourage portfolio investments, such developments would occur in their absence as the domestic financial markets develop. Interestingly, a reaction to the 1994 Mexican debt crisis has been increased discussion of the idea that the pace of financial market development can be too fast. Restrictions on foreign banks or on capital markets may be warranted until the domestic economy is strong enough to withstand potentially destabilizing movements of capital.

In conclusion, the fears of control by foreign banks are unfounded, particularly when they are weighed against the benefits of foreign investment. Moreover, foreign banking activity is best viewed as foreign investment in the financial services industry. The one general exception was the concern that foreign banking facilitates and encourages portfolio investments which can be destabilizing. Potentially destabilizing movements of portfolio investments might be a source for concern in the EITs once they move to full capital account mobility. For example, movements of financial capital out of the Czech investment funds could be a serious destabilizing force. However, the foreign banks in the EITs play only a small role in the portfolio investments in these countries.

There is one additional argument that may have specific application in the EITs. It is possible that the privatization of formerly state-owned industries will lead to an unusually large extent of foreign ownership of the economy. If such a situation were combined with an extensive foreign banking sector, then concern about pervasive foreign control of the economy might be well founded.

(ii) Protect infant industries

A corollary to the fear of foreign control is the desire to restrict foreign banks in order to protect the domestic banking industry. The infant industry argument is sometimes applied to banking in the same way that it can be applied to any other industry. However, the argument is usually made to support industries that will produce for import substitution. In the case of banking, foreign banks are producing financial services in the host country. The infant industry argument for banks would be applicable if the development of domestic banks would substitute for the importing of financial services. However, foreign banks are not importing services but producing them domestically.

Another aspect of the protectionist argument is based on the idea that the foreign banks are more efficient, their costs of production are lower, and therefore the domestic banks should be protected from unfair competition. This argument is made in the EITs to suggest that the foreign banks will 'steal' the best domestic customers and thus worsen the condition of the existing large domestic banks. This observation can be improperly used to justify protection of inefficient domestic banks. The argument is only valid if the cost structure of foreign banks can be shown to be always lower so that the domestic firms will not survive in the longrun.

In the short run there may be some additional arguments for protection due to the special nature of banks and the complex objectives of public policy towards banks. Banking in the EITs, as well as elsewhere, is highly concentrated. As a result the large banks have political influence, and policies that threaten their market share or profitability may be hard to enact. Moreover, there are reasons for concern about the viability of the large banks.

The disappearance or failure of existing banking institutions may entail large social costs. First, the payments system may rely on the branch network of existing banks. Even if these banks are inefficient banking businesses, their existence is important to maintain the payments system. Second, the large banks may be very large employers. Governments in the EITs may prefer to maintain existing institutions rather than increase unemployment.

Thus, the EITs may prefer to restrict foreign bank entry rather than bear the social costs of the failure of the large domestic banking organizations. The problem with this argument is that restrictive policies might remove any incentive that the large existing banks have to become more efficient.

If the domestic banks are 'too big to fail' and require some support, suppressing competition from new entrants can be a cheap form of off-budget support. Restricting bank entry (including new domestic banks) is a way of providing a hidden subsidy to the existing industry and temporarily avoiding the costs of restructuring the financial sector. By retaining their market share, the existing banks will have the time to undergo recapitalization and consolidations. Bank modernization does not occur instantaneously and restricting new entrants in the EITs will give the banks the opportunity to revamp their operations.

However, such delays also bear a social cost as the inefficient banks will continue to misallocate resources. Restricting entry enables the banks to continue their pattern of operation. If the banks continue to provide loans to state-owned enterprises and allow them to run up credits in order to maintain production, they will be inhibiting change in the economy.

In addition to the social cost arguments for protection, the special character of the banking industry leads to additional reasons to restrict foreign banking.

(iii) Banks are special

The special characteristics of banking institutions leads to both explicit and implicit government involvement in the banking sector in virtually every country. That is, it is common to find that the entire banking sector is implicitly or explicitly provided with government guarantees; the implicit view that all of the banks are too big to fail is quite common. Foreign banks may pay their share of explicit guarantees such as deposit insurance premiums, but wider implicit public sector guarantees are provided by the public sector. It is understandable that governments may not want to extend such guarantees to foreigners who will not be paying their fair share. In fact, such guarantees lead to a high frequency of bank nationalizations around the world.

Another aspect of the special role of banks is that even when they are privately owned, banks often function as an agent of the government. The centralized state planning agencies of the Soviet era have disappeared, but that does not mean that all government influence in credit allocation has disappeared as well.[11] In fact, it is common to have considerable government interference in credit allocation and the banks are often the vehicle for directing credit or providing subsidies. To some extent the banks profit from serving as intermediaries for the government, and there may be a desire to keep such profits away from foreigners.

Often the subsidies provided to the banking sector are quite explicit. For example, central bank credit is often extended to the banks at below-market interest rates. The banks often profit from special credit facilities for exports or for industrial development. Cheap central bank credit as a source of funds is a form of subsidy, and there may be well be a desire to avoid providing subsidies to foreigners.

(iv) Foreign banks have different objectives

The next argument is that foreign-controlled banks might pursue the domestic banking business in a fundamentally different (and less desirable) fashion than domestic banks. That is, the allocation of resources when the financial intermediaries are foreign would be different than the allocations made by domestic banks and will lead to different patterns of economic development.

The argument sounds like 18th century mercantilism. The mercantilist view is that the foreign bank will lend to industries whose exports are needed by the home country. However, the argument presupposes that the foreign bank will follow some specified set of home country interests rather than a profit-maximizing strategy that would be in the best interest of the host country. The mercantilist view that the foreign bank will be pursuing the national objectives of the home country to the detriment of the host country is not very convincing.

However, there are some alternative aspects of the argument that may be worth considering. Global profit maximization by a multinational banking institution may lead to different decisions than profit maximization by a domestic bank. Although this premise seems reasonable, it does not necessarily follow that foreign banks will be less satisfactory. One possible effect is that the foreign banks may be able to shift revenues and avoid taxation in the high tax rate host country. The loss of tax revenues on the banking sector are not very large but may still motivate regulators.

If foreign banks operate differently than domestic banks, their activities can have some distortionary effects. Foreign banks, because of their experiences at home and lack of host country experience, may emphasize lending for foreign trade and to large domestic companies with a foreign reputation. They are likely to have little interest or expertise in dealing with smaller domestic companies which may not satisfy international accounting standards. Thus, it is possible that foreign banking may distort the patterns of intermediation in ways that are not desirable.

(v) Regulatory differences

Differences in regulatory structure between the foreign bank's home country and the host country may lead to different objectives for domestic and foreign banks. If the host country regulations are more stringent, then foreign bank entry should be restricted. That is, the domestic authorities may simply not put great faith in the home country bank regulators.

This argument has merit with respect to the domestic activities of representative offices or branches. In these instances the exposure to risk in the home country carries over to their foreign activities, and the host regulators may not be willing to accept the same risk exposure. Such a situation is often handled by restricting the activities of foreign bank branches or representative offices.

The same argument cannot be made for foreign-owned or controlled banks in the domestic markets for the simple reason that such banks are subject to all of the banking regulations in the host country. The European Union banking directives, which are designed to create an integrated banking community, adopt this principle. They stipulate that foreign banks satisfy domestic regulations for all their domestic operations.

Differences in regulatory structure aside, it may simply be more difficult to apply regulations and bank supervision to foreign banks. The foreign bank may move activities between its domestic and home country operations, making it difficult for domestic regulators and examiners to monitor activities.[12]

Generally, small, start-up banking operations may be difficult to monitor and also may be prone to undertaking illegal activities. With relatively free banking, such institutions may spring up and result in embezzlement, fraud, money laundering and ultimately the looting of financial institutions. The threat of abuses is not restricted to foreign bank operations. Any new start-up operation could result in problems and therefore it might be advisable to make access to banking licenses difficult and to improve bank supervision. In the EITs, the costs of monitoring and auditing the many small and new banks may be very high and the government has no means via taxes or fees to recapture these costs.

Experiences in Hungary and Poland in the early post-Communist years suggest that this may be a significant issue. New bank entry (including many foreign banks) began before the authorities had developed an infrastructure for supervision and examination. It would have been reasonable to slow down the rate of entry if that would have avoided some of the problems that emerged.

It is possible that the foreign banks might be more easily used, or might even be set up with intent, for money laundering activities. With flaws in the regulatory and legal structure, a bank that is somewhat integrated with its foreign owners might enable domestic residents and businesses to evade capital controls. However, these observations mitigate in favor of high quality supervision rather than excluding banking sector investments by responsible foreign institutions. Again, it would be reasonable to exclude foreign banks that are likely to bring in banking undesirable banking practices (for example money laundering). As an example, the Estonian authorities are less than enthusiastic about the entry of Russian banks.

Difficulty in regulating foreign banks may weaken the monetary control ability of the domestic central bank. The ability of the foreign bank to move deposit balances across borders or offer very close substitute foreign deposits may make the task of monetary control more difficult. It is true that domestic monetary control would be easier if restricted entry and capital controls insulated the domestic economy from international financial markets. However, the consensus of modern thinking is that the benefits of financial liberalization and the integration of world financial markets are well worth the costs.

Capital account convertibility and the international financial markets limit the ability of small countries to conduct a completely independent monetary policy. Business cycle shocks are transmitted from country to country because trade and investment flows are large. Restricting financial market integration would only have a limited effect on this situation. Surely foreign bank entry increases the economic ties between countries that make them more vulnerable to shocks from abroad. However, the benefits of such ties are much greater than the costs of financial isolationism.

3. WHAT DO FOREIGN BANKS ACCOMPLISH?

In the previous section, we examined reasons why foreign bank entry is often opposed. In this section we will examine the contributions that foreign banks might make. There are three aspects of the question in the title that will be discussed in this section. First, what might foreign banks contribute to the economies and financial sectors of the EITs? We will begin with a list of potential contributions of foreign banks. This is simply the reasons why foreign banks might be advantageous and ought to be encouraged. The second aspect of the question is to ask when and why foreign banks will enter the markets in the EITs. The fact that a host country is receptive to foreign banking does not necessarily imply that foreign banks will want to enter. We will discuss here the conditions that will lead to entry. The third question is narrower in focus. That is, what do we expect foreign banks to be doing in the EITs? This question is rooted in the realities of recent developments and asks what the foreign banks have been doing and are likely to do in the near future.

Potential contributions of foreign banks

We begin with a discussion of the contributions that can be made by foreign banks in the EITs.

(i) Product and service innovation. The existing banking institutions in the EITs are often unlikely sources for innovation for several good reasons. First, they are often preoccupied with the problems of restructuring their loan portfolios. Second, they are unlikely to have personnel familiar with innovative banking services and may not have the profitability to invest in personnel and technology. Thus, foreign banks are likely to be major sources of product and service innovation. The entry of Citibank into retail banking for well-off customers in Hungary is a good example; the domestic banks would not have the expertise of ability to invest in ATM networks and transactions accounts.

(ii) Economies of scale and scope. The banking institutions of centrally planned economies were inefficient providers of the payments mechanism and the introduction of more efficient providers is desired. In the EITs, where banking is quite concentrated, many banks have sufficient scale for efficient operation. Foreign banks can bring in the banking technology that will enable the large banks from the planned economy era to exploit economies of scale. For example, institutions like Komerční banka in the Czech Republic and Budapest Bank in Hungary could benefit from cooperative agreements that would enable them to import banking technology.

Beside the handful of large banks in each of the EITs, there tend to be many small banks including many startups from the post-Communist era. Many of these banks are very small and efficiency argues in favor of consolidation. Foreign bank entry is a way of encouraging the consolidation by merger and acquisition of small institutions.

Also, foreign banks can introduce other financial sector activities insurance, portfolio management, brokerage activity which allows banks to exploit economies of scope. The existing banks in the EITs usually have little experience with these other activities and could learn from the foreign banks.

Of course, competition from new and/or foreign banks may have negative effects on the existing banks which we discussed before.

(iii) Environment of competition. The banking systems in the EITs were only recently carved out of the mono-banking systems of the Soviet era.[13] As a result, the management of these institutions have little experience with competition and market settings. Foreign banks would introduce competitive pressures that would benefit both savers and lenders.

(iv) Develop financial markets. The entry of foreign banks will assist in the development of financial markets. For example, foreign banks that lack a branch network to generate deposit financing of their activities are likely to turn to the interbank market. Thus, foreign bank entry will help increase interbank lending, develop the market and result in market determined interest rates. Another example is that the foreign banks may be able attract banking business that might otherwise go abroad.

(v) Spillover effects of good banking practice. Foreign banks are likely to introduce modern banking practices that were largely unknown in the planned economies. Their presence in the markets will hasten the spread of good banking practices. Examples include modern techniques for loan evaluation and efficient clearing operations.

(vi) Attract foreign direct investment. The presence of foreign banks in the EITs that can offer high quality banking services of all kinds will attract foreign investors. Foreign bank entry often follows FDI because the foreign banks serve their home country customers in the foreign market. However, it is also the case that the existence of foreign banks in the market reduce the costs of entry to firms from abroad. Thus, the existence of foreign banks is likely to increase the volume of FDI.

Reasons for foreign banks entry

Assuming that there are no barriers to the entry of foreign banks, what will motivate foreign banks to enter the EITs? This question is important because entry barriers aside, we do not observe enormous foreign bank penetration in many countries. Thus, it is important to examine the market characteristics that will or will not lead to foreign bank expansion into a domestic economy.[14]

Foreign bank entry can be considered in the same way economists examine the entry of multinational firms generally. MNCs will establish activities in a foreign country when they have a differentiated profit to offer to the host country market. Similarly, they will enter the foreign market when they have a cost advantage over home market producers. Cost advantages, often due to technology, and product differentiation are closely related. Either one will lead a multinational to establish operations in a foreign country rather than simply exporting to the foreign market.

In the absence of a differentiated product and/or cost structure, the multinational firm is more likely to export to the foreign market from its home country. In such instances, the foreign firm will utilize partnerships, dealers or representatives to compete in the foreign market rather than invest in an actual presence in the foreign country.

A foreign bank can conduct its business activities abroad without establishing a foreign bank subsidiary. This can be accomplished most simply by establishing a corresponding bank relationship with a domestic bank. A more distinct presence can be offered to home country customers with business in the foreign country through a representative office or a branch. However, all of these just extend home country banking in some limited ways to the foreign country, primarily to serve home country customers. Establishing a foreign bank, a FDI in the financial services industry, is quite a different step. A bank might enter the banking business in the foreign country if it can provide a differentiated product or utilize a cost advantage.

The increase in business international business activity in central Europe – for example FDI, exporting – implies that foreign banks will have activities in these countries. Thus, the rapid rise in correspondent relationships and representative offices is to be expected. However, do the conditions for foreign bank entry also exist?

The ability of foreign banks to provide high quality services and a full range of portfolio management, deposit and loan products indicates a product and cost structure that is clearly differentiated from that of the domestic banks. The serious management and restructuring problems of the domestic banks throughout the region suggests that the ability to offer a differentiated product will persist for some time. Thus, foreign bank interest in entry in the regions should come as no surprise.

Likely foreign bank activities

Foreign banks that have entered the EITs usually restrict their activities to those areas where they can offer a differentiated product and/or exploit cost advantages. In this section we summarize the likely activities of foreign banks in the EITs.

(i) Financial services to MNCs. This is probably the major activity of foreign banks and the major reason why they enter the markets. However, it is not at all clear that the domestic banks could provide such services and the presence of foreign banks is probably an important factor in the growth of activity by the MNCs.

(ii) Lending to the best domestic customers. Foreign bank lending activity starts with the best domestic customers, often those that already have international financial dealings. These are companies with accounting and reporting

systems that meet international standards. In some countries lending to high quality local customers is likely to grow because foreign banks may have a lower cost of funds (and perhaps lower loan rates), better services and services (for example for international payments) that the domestic banks cannot provide. In addition, domestic companies may be attracted by the imprimatur provided by an internationally know foreign bank.

This aspect of the foreign bank's activities is controversial because the local banks are often viewed as 'stealing' the best customers. Such competition can make it very difficult for the domestic banks to restructure their activities and they will therefore argue for protection from foreign banks.

(iii) Investment banking activity. There are a wide range of investment and merchant banking activities that were virtually unheard of in the centrally planned economies that the local banks know very little about. These can include advisory services for mergers and acquisitions and raising capital, underwriting of capital market instruments and making markets for securities. It can be expected that foreign banks and also non-bank financial institutions will enter such activities.

(iv) Retail banking is a less likely area of interest for foreign banks. Developing a branch network is expensive and buying existing branches can be risky. However, if the domestic banks fail to develop the products, services and information technology to provide retail banking, new entrants may well develop an interest. The example noted above of Citibank's expansion in Hungary is relevant. Citibank is developing a retail banking presence (through automated bank technology ATMs, credit cards, etc.) without developing a network of branches. This may well be a precedent to watch as other foreign banks may consider that entry into retail banking is attractive if expensive branch networks are unnecessary.

4. FOREIGN BANK ACTIVITIES IN CENTRAL AND EASTERN EUROPE

Each of the Visegrad countries have taken a different approach to bank restructuring: in the Czech Republic the banks were part of the voucher privatization process, in Hungary foreign entry was encouraged prior to any privatizations, and in Poland the emphasis has been on privatizations by public offerings, usually with the participation of a strategic investor taking control. As a consequence, the role of foreign banks has been different in each country. In this section, we describe the role of the foreign banks in the banking sectors of the Visegrad countries (in addition, there is a short discussion of foreign banking in some other European EITs).[15]

Poland

The key to understanding banking sector developments in Poland is that the government is very heavily involved in planning the evolution of the banking system. To some extent this is inevitable because reform of the banking system is tied to reform of the economy. Thus, the problem of the insolvency of the large agricultural cooperative sector will not be solved until the agricultural sector itself is restructured. Furthermore, there are still large banking institutions that are still government institutions, for example the savings banks and some of the commercial banks. Thus, the evolution of the financial system is still underway.

Nevertheless significant progress has been made towards the development of a modern banking system since the monobank system began to change in the late 1980s. A summary of the banking system structure in 1995 is shown in Table 3.2. The number of banks in each group does not provide an accurate measure of bank activity. Bank assets are concentrated in a few state banks (including the savings bank), the nine commercial banks that were separated from the central bank (NBP) in 1989 and perhaps 20 to 25 of the private banks and some of the foreign banks.

Table 3.2 Number of Banks By Type, Poland, 1995

Various state banks	15
Agricultural cooperatives	162
Commercial banks	9
Private banks	72
Foreign banks	9
Branches of foreign banks	3
Representative offices of foreign banks	21

The most important commercial banks are the nine commercial banks that were created from the central bank (NBP) in 1989. Four of the nine had been privatized by mid-1996. It is important to note that one of the privatizations – Bank Slaski (BSK) – includes a significant minority position by a strategic foreign investor: a 25.9 percent share owned by the large Dutch multinational bank, ING. ING has made a substantial commitment to BSK and the banking business in Poland. Stan Sczurek, the president of ING Bank Warsaw summarizes the strategy:

> We have committed so much to this country that we do not intend to stop investing, and if there were anything that would fit well with our operation here and world activities, we would consider it. We have signaled our intention to

increase our equity in Slaski and now it is up to the finance ministry to decide. (Reuters *European Business Report,* May 22, 1995).

The ING–BSK venture is planning to expand into investment banking with an investment fund and bond underwriting. ING has already managed commercial paper programs for the Polish subsidiaries of some MNCs and is planning to underwrite municipal and corporate bond issues by the end of 1995. Finally, ING is expected to increase its stake in BSK to majority ownership in 1996.

The first privatization in Poland, WBK in 1993, was done without any foreign participation, but AIB obtained a minority interest in a second offering in 1995. AIB has an option to obtain the EBRD's share in WBK and could ultimately gain a controlling interest.

There was a proliferation of banking licenses in the years 1990–1992. The number of private banks mushroomed, and many of them have had problems due to poor banking practice, bad debts and occasional fraud. In 1994, the NBP suspended four banks and about 15 small banks were taken over or merged. Only about one-third of the private banks are active banking entities, although a few have made it into the list of the largest banks in Poland.

In the same years, licenses were issued to a number of foreign banks and representative offices. Some of the foreign banks have expanded quite rapidly and have been very profitable. In 1994 the foreign banks had about 3 percent of commercial bank assets and 23 percent of the profits. Foreign banking capital (including strategic investments in Polish banks) was 8.5 percent of total banking capital, with the greatest share, about one-fourth coming from Holland. About 19 percent of the foreign bank capital comes from the US and between 10 and 15 percent from each of the following: Germany, France, Austria and the EBRD. Changes in exchange rates make it difficult to value the total foreign investment in Polish banking, but it probably is in the range of $100 million.

There is only one foreign bank – Citibank – on the list of the twenty largest banks in Poland, ranked by equity at the end of 1994. It is nineteenth with $42 million in equity and $411 million in assets. The list also includes several banks with foreign participation: the Polish Development Bank ($80 million), BSK ($152 million) and WBK ($51 million).

Foreign bank activity in Poland includes a handful of foreign banks, some joint ventures and the strategic investments in Polish banks. Table 3.3 lists the foreign banks in Poland; in addition there are a number of foreign bank branches and representative offices. The first fully licensed foreign bank was Raiffeisen Centralbank which started operating in 1990 and has about $7 million in equity. Besides its core banking activities, the bank does advisory

Table 3.3. Major Foreign Banking Activities in Poland

Ownership	Assets billion Zl. (end 1993)
American Bank in Poland	
57.4% owned by 3 US investors	
(Morrison-Knudsen, Bankers Trust, Time Warner)	2771
International Bank in Poland (IBP)	
joint venture of ABN Amro/BCI and Credit Lyonnais	
with shares held by IFC and some Polish banks	2237
PBR–Polish Development Bank	
6.2% owned by foreign banks	6582
Polish-American Mortgage Bank	
50% owned by Polish-American Enterprise Fund	303
Raiffeisen Centralbank	
100% owned by Austrian banks	3703
Wielkopolski Bank (WBK)	
privatized in 1993 with 23.5% ownership by EBRD;	
16.3% stake taken by Allied Irish via a $20 mn. capital	
infusion in Jan. 1995. Allied Irish's option	
on EBRD stake would give it controlling interest	20038
Bank Slaski (BSK)	
privatized in 1994 with 29.5% ownership by ING	40223
Citibank	
Fully owned by parent company	5011
BNP-Dresdner	
Joint venture received banking license in 1994	
Inter Bank-ABN Amro	
purchase in Dec. 1994 via a $20 mn. capital infusion	
BRE (Export Development Bank)	
Privatized in 1992; Commerzbank 21% stake	
via a $35 mn. capital infusion (new issue) in 1993	9135
Bank Rolno-Prezemyslowy	
20% owned by Polish American Enterprise Fund; investment	
by large Dutch bank (Rabobank) under discussion	202
Pierwszy Polsko-Amerykanski Bank w Krakowie	
47.1% owned by Polish American Enterprise Fund	752
Bank Creditanstalt	
100% owned by parent	1653
Solidarnosc Chase Bank-GE Capital Bank	
Founded in 1991 by D.T. Chase. Purchase	
by GE Capital of 90% pending	441
Westdeutsche Landesbank	
Banking license 1995	

Source: The Financial System in Poland: 1993-94

work, underwriting and leasing. Some of the foreign banks are small ventures that typically include investments from the Polish communities in the US or elsewhere. However, some of them represent efforts at market entry by major Western banks. Recent investments by large Western banks, through privatization and through investments in existing banks, indicate renewed and strong interest in entry into the Polish banking industry.

Foreign interest in the Polish financial sector is beginning to extend beyond banking as well. Citibank, Creditanstalt Securities and Credit Suisse First Boston are active as brokers. ING has introduced some capital market instruments, a private placement of dollar-indexed bonds and a commercial paper instrument. Finally, several investment banks have offices in Poland.

Government policy towards foreign banks has changed since the early 1990s. Originally, banking licenses were freely issued to both foreign and domestic applicants. Foreign banks were given a tax holiday and were even able to keep part of their capital in hard currency. Only a few foreign banks entered because of the economic uncertainties in Poland. Moreover, the proliferation of small, poorly capitalized banks with little banking expertise is viewed as a mistake. The minimum capital requirements for foreign banks has been raised and the tax holiday eliminated. Since 1992, the authorities have been very reluctant to issue bank licenses, particularly to foreigners.[16] Instead they are trying to channel foreign interest towards existing Polish banks as a means of promoting bank consolidation and the infusion of new capital. An interesting deal made in September 1996 illustrates this policy approach. A banking license was issued to Ford Credit Europe to establish Ford Bank Polska for financing auto dealers, leasing and sales. In turn for the license, Ford agreed to maintain a substantial deposit at WBK, which in turn takes over the deposits of a failed regional bank, Budgoski Bank. The entry of a new foreign bank is accompanied by progress towards the authorities' goals for the banking sector: consolidation and the infusion of new capital (a permanent deposit).

There has been some difficulty in finding strategic investors. One reason is that the 1991 legislation on bank privatization stipulated that a foreign investor would be limited to a 30 percent share of the bank. A strategic investor requires a larger stake in order to take an active management role. The MOF can negotiate higher shares. In fact, AIB is slated to take over the EBRD stake in WBK, which would give it majority ownership. Another reason is that the whole privatization process slowed down because the Warsaw Stock Exchange was not able to absorb all of the equity issues. The MOF has to balance the requirements of potential foreign investors against the resistance from the banks to strategic investors and the political reluctance to allow foreign control of banks.

In 1994–95, foreign bank interest in Poland was renewed, largely due to London Club negotiations on Poland's external debts to banks. There have been three instances of foreign banks obtaining a significant minority interest through a capital infusion, including ING's investment in BSK in 1994. This resulted in foreign bank capital infusions into Polish banks of almost $100 million; further negotiations with some of the German banks are underway. With the prospects of the Polish economy improving, additional foreign banks will be interested in purchasing Polish banks even if their balance sheets are not in perfect order. There is no other way at present to enter the Polish market and the prices of the banks are not high.

The Polish banking authorities have successfully attracted foreign participation in the privatization process. This is surprising given that the commercial banks continue to lend to their traditional customers. However, loan customers are supposed to have a documented business plan, and banks are maintaining adequate reserves for bad debts because they want to be privatized. Moreover, the banks tend to hold government securities rather than develop their lending capabilities.

The foreign banks have been influential in introducing lending operations but they tend to deal mostly with clients from abroad. The foreign banks have been profitable due to their high quality portfolios and foreign clients. The foreign banks have kept their bad debts to less than 10 percent of assets, while the Polish banks still have bad debts of up to 30 percent of total assets.

IBP is a good example of a profitable foreign banking operation. The corporate customers tend to be the subsidiaries or joint ventures of international firms that are known to the bank from abroad. The bank intends to enlarge its activities to include the largest and best known Polish domestic customers. Its interest is inhibited by concern about the reliability of information on Polish companies. However this still represents a very small part of total lending. In addition to lending, the bank is active in corporate financing for customers in Poland and provides advisory services on privatization issues.

Hungary

Entry of foreign banks dates back to the original banking reform in 1987. At that time Citibank was established in Hungary, originally as a joint venture with the NBH, but now solely owned by Citibank. Foreign banks were actively encouraged and there are now 19 jointly-owned commercial banks (full banking institutions with at least 50 percent foreign ownership). Table 3.4 shows that the foreign banking sector is an important component of banking in Hungary.

Table 3.4 Structure of Banking in Hungary, 1994

	Number	Assets (bn. HUF)
Large Hungarian commercial banks		
(assets over HUF 100 bn.)	6	2167
Other Hungarian-owned commercial banks	10	259
Jointly-owned	19	496
(foreign ownership share at least 50%)		
Specialized institutions	7	620
Investment banks	1	27
Savings cooperatives	255	184

There are two interrelated aspects of foreign banking involvement in Hungary. First, there are the jointly-owned banks which are essentially foreign banks operating in Hungary. Entry of such institutions is regulated by the banking law that requires minimum capital, approval of the principles, and so on but administration of the law encouraged new entrants. At times it has been suggested that foreign banking licenses be restricted so that foreign interests are channeled into participation in the privatizations of Hungarian banks, but there is no indication that this became policy. The second aspect of foreign banking is the foreign participation in the privatization of Hungary's large state-owned commercial banks. Government policy is to actively solicit foreign participation in the privatizations, and the government has set an (albeit unrealistic) end of 1997 deadline for privatization of the large banks.

The first aspect of foreign banking – the jointly-owned banks – has been very successful. The nineteen banks listed in the table account for 14 percent of bank capital in 1994 and 16 percent of bank assets. The second aspect – foreign participation in the privatization process – has been somewhat less successful.

The participation of a foreign strategic partner has been a major element in privatization plans.[17] A strategic investor that will bring managerial experience and a significant infusion of capital has been sought. The one successfully completed privatization, MKB, the Hungarian Foreign Trade Bank, included the participation of the EBRD and BLB, a large German bank. In 1994, the foreign investors paid $54 million for a combination of a share purchase and an infusion of new capital for new shares. That was the largest foreign direct investment in banking in the region prior to the Budapest Bank privatization in December 1995.

Late in 1994, the government attempted to privatize Budapest Bank in a similar fashion, with the participation of a strategic foreign investor. Four

Western banks expressed an interest and negotiations began on a plan for Credit Suisse to take a majority interest. In March 1995, CS discontinued its negotiations for reasons that were unclear, and the privatization process was placed on hold. Although the bank had been recapitalized through two government programs to clean up its balance sheet, there may have been questions about the quality of its portfolio and the ability of its management to introduce change. Nevertheless, several new foreign bidders for Budapest Bank emerged by the end of the summer. *The Wall Street Journal* (September 21, 1995) reported that ING and GE Capital Corporation were the front runners and that a deal was expected soon. GE Capital has already purchased a small foreign bank in Poland (Solidarnosc Chase Bank) and is developing an aggressive strategy to expand on the EITs (see *Business Week*, October 16, 1995).

In December 1995, GE Capital paid $87 million for a 27.5 percent ownership stake of Budapest Bank in a complex deal with some important features. GE has full managerial control of the bank, an option to purchase the EBRD and remaining government stakes, an option to put the bank in the hands of the state and an option to turn over certain bad loans.

The privatization of the largest Hungarian bank, OTP, the national savings bank, is underway and is supposed to be complete by the end of 1996. This case is a little different because the savings bank, which has diversified its activities into commercial banking as well, is in sound shape (see Chapter 5). So far, ownership stakes have been given to various state entities and sold to portfolio investors (including foreign investors through GDRs). However, the government is not seeking a strategic foreign investor and the privatization plan will limit any single foreign investor to 5 percent. In fact, an offer by George Soros to become a strategic investor in OTP was rejected by the government.

The comparison between Budapest Bank and OTP suggests that despite the active foreign bank role in Hungary, suspicions about foreign control persist. Foreign strategic investors are actively sought as a source of capital infusion but are otherwise discouraged. The policy is contradictory because if the role allowed to foreign investors is limited there may not be any foreign interest. Unless foreign banks have enough of a role to control or at least determine bank strategy, they are likely to eschew any interest in the privatization process. In addition, there have been two bank recapitalizations by the bank since 1993, and it is not completely clear that existing provisions for bad loans are adequate. This adds a great deal of uncertainty to a foreign buyer, especially if there is some concern that future recapitalizations may not be extended to foreign-owned banks.

The foreign banking presence in Hungary is, by any measure, substantial. As shown in Table 3.5, their asset share has doubled between 1990 and 1994. Their share of total capital declined because of the significant recapitalization of both large and smaller banks in 1993. The shares of total deposits and credits is somewhat smaller than the asset share. However, the share of entre-preneurial (business) deposits and loans are 29 and over 25 percent respec-tively. These shares grew substantially from 1993 to 1994. Thus, the foreign banks have made substantial inroads into business sector banking in Hungary.

Developments in 1996 indicate that the foreign bank presence in Hungary will continue to expand. *Business Central Europe* (September 1996) reports the following developments: ING acquired Duna Bank, Creditanstalt is expanding its branch network and that several European banks are interested in purchasing the state-owned Magyar Hittel Bank and Takarebank, a cooperative saving bank. The foreign banks (for example Citibank, Creditanstalt) and the domestic banks (for example OTP) are competing for retail banking credit cards, consumer finance, deposits, and so on.

Lending by the foreign banks is mostly new business with their multi-national clients with activities in Hungary rather than taking the most desirable loan business from the domestic banks. The jointly-owned banks can exploit their relationships with their home country owners to finance and provide services to foreign investors and to companies privatized with foreign participation. Between 1990–94, there were about 400 foreign investments in Hungarian privatizations. The largest number come from neighboring Austria (over 100) and Germany, and the largest investments are from Germany, the US and Austria.

Foreign banking in Hungary started with foreign trade financing but since 1994, the activities of the foreign banks have been extended. The large share of business financing is concentrated in short-term credits. NBH data indicate that the foreign banks in 1994 had a 35 percent share of short-term credits to the business sector and a 10 percent share of long-term credits. The reasons for this are that the foreign banks are more risk averse than the domestic banks and also have few long-term sources of funds. The other major activities of the foreign banks are capital markets (bond trading is dominated by the foreign banks), investment banking and advisory services. Despite their large market shares, the presence of foreign banks in Hungary has not had a large effect on the industry. According to Imre Tarafas, head of the bank superviso-ry office, the foreign banks have not yet influenced the development of banking standards and practice in Hungary; spillover effects have been minimal. Moreover, the foreign banking presence may inhibit the develop-ment of the Hungarian banks by making their staffing more difficult. The foreign banks attract the best professional staff from the domestic banks. Tarafas views the human resource problems to be more significant than the 'creaming' of the loan business.

Table 3.5 Large Banks and Foreign Shares of Banking Activity in Hungary

	Large Banks	Jointly-owned Banks
Assets		
1990	81.6%	8.0%
1992	76.4	9.6
1994	69.3	15.9
Subscribed Capital		
1992	58.9	23.3
1994	64.3	13.7
Total Deposits		
1993	76.0	10.8
1994	73.0	13.7
Entrepreneurial Deposits		
1993	67.6	23.6
1994	60.7	29.1
Total Credits		
1993	71.6	14.8
1994	70.2	14.4
Entrepreneurial Credits		
1993	66.6	18.6
1994	60.1	25.5

Source: National Bank of Hungary, (1994 data are preliminary).

We interviewed two foreign bankers with very ambitious business plans in the Hungarian market: Andras Simor, managing director of Creditanstalt Securities, and Tony Fekete, Citibank. Both acknowledge that the Hungarian banking market is overcrowded and that a period of mergers or even failures is likely. However, they argue that the Hungarian market is underbanked in terms of the provision of top quality banking services. Thus, they foresee a period of bank consolidation (of both small foreign and new domestic banks). In addition, many of the foreign banks will simply serve as a Central European outpost of major foreign banks whose value will only be realized if Budapest actually develops as the financial capital of Central Europe. However, some of the foreign banks will develop as major players in the domestic markets. Their ability to compete with better services and techno-logy will enable them to take a significant part of the market share of the existing big commercial banks. The management of the both Creditanstalt and Citibank foresee major roles for their institutions.

The foreign banking interest in Hungary is based on the view that the country is politically stable. In addition, its location and existing financial sector development lead many to believe that Budapest will be the major financial center to the east of Frankfurt. Simor of Creditanstalt adds that the most difficult problem faced in the Hungarian market is the development of human capital, the personnel needed for business development and expansion.

Table 3.6 Foreign Banking Activities in Hungary

Name	% Foreign Ownership	Assets, mn. HUF (end 1992)
Joint-owned Banks (at least 50% foreign ownership)		
ABN - AMRO	100	Founded 1993
Banque Indosuez	94	3,695
BNP-KH-Dresdner	74	12,254
CIB Group	66	USD 1039 mn.
(off-shore bank, founded in 1979 with special arrangements with NBH)		
Citibank	100	28,640
Commerzbank	100	Founded 1993
Creditanstalt	100	22,269
Credit Lyonnais	100	1,783
Europai Kereskedelmi	67	7,780
General Banking and Trust	50	21,121
Hungarian Volksbank	100	
HYPO-Bank	100	Founded 1993
Inter-Europa Bank	32	33,796
ING	100	14,660
Leumi Credit Bank	50	14,731
MHB-Daewoo	50	11,480
Nomura Investment Bank	61	1,252
Unicbank	72	27,638
WestDeutsche Landesbank	58	10,068
Foreign stakes in Hungarian banks		
Budapest Bank	60	145,490
MKB Hungarian		
Foreign Trade Bank	51	173,860
Mezobank	7	29,984
Postbank and Savings bank	15	123,019

There are, however, other risks as well. There is a regulatory burden that can be onerous. For example, the failure of the Agro Bank may result in a liability to the deposit insurance fund of all banks. Also, Fekete of Citibank added that liquidity risks are high in Hungary because the inter-bank market is not fully developed.

Creditanstalt views Hungary and the neighboring countries to be part of its home territory. The bank has been paring down other international interests in order to develop its activities in Hungary, the Czech and Slovak Republics, Slovenia and Poland. In Hungary, it plans to develop national coverage which includes retail, wholesale and investment banking. The retail part is just beginning with some small business lending planned and the opening of some branches. At the wholesale level, the bank provides financial services to large domestic and international clients. The investment bank is already active in the securities markets and creates and places non-traded instruments such as commercial paper.

Citibank's business plan for the Hungarian market (and elsewhere in Central Europe as well) is somewhat less ambitious. It is likely to restrict itself to consumer banking for high income and international customers, international banking and boutique financing. That is, Citibank will emphasize its ability to supply banking and financial services that would not otherwise be available in Hungary. A summary of foreign banking activity in Hungary as of 1993 is shown in Table 3.6

Czech Republic

The status of banking in the Czech Republic (CR) is very different from that in either Poland or Hungary for two important reasons. First, changes in the institutional structure of banking in the CR did not get underway until 1990. Second, economic changes in the CR have been shaped by the extensive voucher privatization scheme which influences all financial sector developments.

Table 3.7 Structure of Banking in the Czech Republic, 1994

State-owned banks	2
(Consolidation Bank, Export bank)	
Czech Commercial banks	15
Banks with foreign participation:	
minority foreign ownership	12
majority ownership	3
wholly foreign owned	10
Foreign bank branches	10
Construction savings banks:	
minority foreign ownership	3
majority foreign ownership	1

Foreign banks have been active in the CR but not as prominent as in Hungary and have not been actively brought into the privatization process as in Poland and Hungary. However, the foreign banks that have been established are likely to expand their market shares. Also, the remaining government ownership of the big four commercial banks is likely to be privatized without the use of the voucher system. It is very possible that the participation of foreign strategic investors will be sought.

The structure of banking in the CR (see Table 3.7) is highly concentrated in the hands of the largest banks. The four big commercial banks which were separated from the state mono-bank in 1990 and privatized in 1991–92 hold about 70 percent of all bank assets. If we add the next two largest banks – the state owned Consolidation Bank and the Agrobank, the market share of the six largest banks is over 80 percent.

The next largest bank – Živnostenská Banka (ŽB) – has a market share of almost 2 percent. It is also the largest bank with a significant foreign ownership.[18] The German bank Bank Frankfurt (BHF) holds 40 percent of ŽB and the International Finance Corporation (IFC) holds a 12 percent share. While the IFC is a passive investor, BHF is actively involved in management and in developing relationships with the German parent. The remaining banks in the top ten have market shares of around 1 percent and include the largest wholly foreign owned bank, Citibank. The other large foreign banks in the CR, for example HYPO Bank, Bank Austria, are about one-third the size of Citibank.

The number of banks grew rapidly from 1990 to 1993. Banking licenses were issued to both domestic and foreign applicants. As in Hungary, many of the new banks were poorly capitalized and soon began to have liquidity problems. The ČNB tightened its supervision, increased the minimum capital required and finally stopped issuing new banking licenses. The construction savings banks, a new type of institution, were an exception to this and several of them have been founded with foreign participation. However, these savings banks are as yet extremely small.

Further development of the foreign banking system could come about from the purchase of small Czech banks. The government is in favor of consolidation of the small banking sector and encourages foreign banks to purchase shares of smaller Czech banks. There have been several such purchases. In addition, foreign banks may be able to expand if the authorities decide to sell the large minority stakes that the National Property Fund holds in the big four commercial banks.[19] There was a moratorium on issuing new banking licenses to foreign banks but a few exceptions have been made (Westdeutsches Landesbank, Midland Bank). A summary of foreign banking activity in the CR is found in Table 3.8.

Table 3.8 Foreign Banking Activities in the Czech Republic

	Basic Capital Million CZK	% Foreign
Banks with 100% foreign ownership:		
BNP-Dresden Bank	500	
Citibank	350	100
Creditanstalt	882	100
Credit Lyonnais Bank	500	100
Girocredit Bank	300	100
Hypo-bank CZ	680	100
IC Banka	500 (427 paid in)	100
Interbanka	500	100
Raiffeisenbank	500	
Societe Generale	774	100
Banks with majority foreign ownership:		
Bank Austria	750	87
67% Bank Austria; 20% Cariplo		
(Milano); 13% Česká Spořitelna		
Bankovní Dům Skala	500	74
Živnostenská Banka	1360	52
40% Berliner Handels and		
Frankfurten Bank; 12% IFC		
Banks with minority foreign ownership:		
Agrobanka	3175 (3175 paid in)	4.8
Banka Haná	750 (749 paid in)	34
COOP-Banka	500	13
Česká Banka	2400 (1246 paid in)	49
Česká Spořitelna	3349	12
Komerční Banka	9502	8.8
Kreditní Banka	1121 (1123 paid in)	0.13
Moravia Banka	500	26
Plzenská Banka	600	1.7
První Mestská Banka	612	0.2
Foreign bank branches:		
ABN AMRO Bank		
Bayerische Verinsbank AG		
Deutsche Bank AG		
International Nederlanden Bank		
Osterreichsche Volsbanken AG		
Raiffeisenbank im Stifland		
Sparkasse Muhlviertel-West		
Všeobečna Uverová Banka		
Waldviertler		

Further plans for privatization of the Czech economy are developing slowly even though the government policy is to finish the process. The government is willing to allow foreign banks as partners in bank privatization. The directors of the huge Czech savings bank, Česká Spořitelna, favor a foreign alliance. However, Richard Salzmann, chairman of Komerčni Banka said that:

> We are not interested in having a massive partner. Three years ago that might have been a good idea, but now if we need advice, we can buy it. (*Wall Street Journal*, September 18, 1995, p. A13E)

There have been an increasing number of bank closures or banks under administration by the bank supervisors. In 1994 and 1995 there were two, but by mid-1996 there were eight. Most of these were due to large loan losses. In September 1996, Agrobanka, the fifth largest bank (though much smaller than any of the top four that dominate the entire industry), faced a liquidity crisis and the central bank organized a support package. In the spring of 1995, a Czech central bank official reported that four Western banks had expressed an interest in Agrobanka, which had just recently emerged from a negative net worth position. At that time, it was suggested that foreign bank interest in the privatization of the big four was possible and would be positively received by the authorities. The bank failures of 1996 may dampen foreign bank interest, and there has been little progress towards completing the privatization process of the big four. Nevertheless, the big four have good international credit rating and may be able to tap international capital markets on their own. However, the government rejected a plan to privatize the savings bank (Česká Spořitelna) and raise capital through the sale of global depository receipts (GDRs).

Despite the concentration of bank assets in the big four commercial banks, there has been substantial market penetration by the foreign banks. In 1990–91, the foreign banks limited their activity to foreign exchange transactions and services provided to their home country customers. However, by 1993–94, their activities had expanded. The German and Austrian banks in particular followed their clients and the foreign banks increased their market share and their scope of activities.

In 1994, the big four accounted for about 60 percent of total bank lending, down from 80 percent in 1991. The banks with majority foreign ownership accounted for 6.3 percent of total credits as of November 1994. The foreign banks held a greater share of short-term credits (9.4 percent) than of medium and long-term credits (6.7 percent and just 1.4 percent respectively).[20] The foreign banks deal mostly with a foreign or foreign-controlled customer base.

Table 3.9 shows the allocation of credits by type of client for the entire banking system and for the banks with majority foreign ownership. The growth of the foreign banking sector has been dramatic. Data for November 1994, indicated that the majority foreign-owned banks accounted for one-third of all credits granted in the month. It is entirely possible that the foreign banking presence in the CR will catch up with that in Hungary. The barriers to foreign bank expansion are no steeper in the CR than in Hungary. In both countries, the large banks, whether privatized as in the CR or largely state-owned as in Hungary, have a long way to go before they emerge as competitive modern banking institutions. Thus, there are ample opportunities for efficient foreign banks to grab market share.

Table 3.9 Distribution of Bank Lending in the Czech Republic

	All Banks	Majority Foreign Banks
Lending to:		
State-owned enterprises	26.8%	8.3%
Private and coop enterprises	59.1	31.7
Foreign controlled firms	4.8	54.8
Individuals	5.8	3.3
Other (incl. nonresidents)	3.4	1.9

In addition to the foreign commercial banks in the CR, there are a number of foreign non-bank financial firms active in the CR, for example, brokerage firms and investment banks. These non-bank firms are more active in the CR than in neighboring countries because of the important role of the investment funds. There is considerable foreign interest and ownership of the voucher investment funds. The foreign capital markets presence may lead to rapid development of non-bank financing in the CR. However, we do not have any data to substantiate the conjecture as yet.

Developments in the Czech banking sector depend on several questions that are not yet resolved. First, will the large banks that dominate the financial sector be able to clean up the balance sheets of the big Czech banks or will moral hazard problems result in more bad loans? Second, will the relationship between the investment funds and the banks lead to capital market synergies or problems in corporate governance? The resolution of these questions will determine the health of the domestic banking sector and the extent to which the foreign banks will grow.

The chief executive of Citibank in the CR, Karl Swoboda, provided some insights into the bank's strategy. Citibank targets large corporations in the

Czech market that meet its risk standards and attempts to develop a banking relationship with them. The business is relationship-driven rather than product-driven although the bank feels that it can offer a larger variety and quality of product than the big Czech banks. For example, Citibank can syndicate loans to Komerční banka, which has sufficient liquidity but lacks the sophisticated loan products. The targeted market consists now of about 300 firms including multinationals active in the CR.

In Swoboda's view, the large Czech banks have become more discerning in their loan practices and are setting aside adequate provisions for bad loans. Thus, they are competitive except in terms of the products that they offer.

Citibank is also active in the developing Czech capital markets. It underwrites bond issues, often in the international markets and commercial paper issuance is likely to start soon. However, Citibank will not follow a German banking model and enter corporate governance directly. The interlocking ownership of banks and corporations through the bank-controlled voucher investment funds is likely to lead to considerable involvement in corporate governance by the large Czech banks. Some of the foreign banks, for example the Austrian banks, have their own investment funds and will be involved with the corporate sector.

A somewhat different strategy is being followed by Živnostenská Banka, the largest Czech bank with a substantial foreign ownership. ŽB was privatized in 1992 with foreign participation; 40 percent of the shares are held by the German bank, BHF, and its French ally, and another 12 percent are held by the IFC. BHF has provided both capital and personnel to develop ŽB as wholesale merchant bank that specializes in medium size firms and private banking services. The bank follows a German model and participates in the governance of its customers.

Other Countries

Information on foreign bank activities in some other EITs with very different experiences was also collected for the project. In particular, we will briefly look at the role of foreign banks in Bulgaria and Estonia.

Changes in the mono-banking system in Bulgaria began in 1987 when seven specialized banks for industrial development were formed. A two-tiered banking system was established in 1989 when the branches of the Bulgarian National Bank were spun off to form 59 state commercial banks. After 1990, 10 private banks started operation and by the end of 1991 there were 78 commercial banks in Bulgaria. More than two-thirds of the banks had less than $1 million in capital and a Bank Consolidation Company was established in 1992. By 1995, a total of 11 state banks emerged from the consolidation process and the total number of commercial banks was reduced to 42.

The expansion of banking activity included the introduction of foreign banks. There are also some small privately-owned banks in Bulgaria, some of which have some partial foreign ownership. The Greek banks interest in Bulgaria stems from the fact that Greece is the largest investor in Bulgaria at present. The small presence of foreign banks in Bulgaria is not due to government resistance at the present time. Instead, the generally poor state of the banking industry and the country's foreign debt problems make Bulgaria less than attractive to investors.

Foreign banks in Bulgaria [21]
Raiffeisenbank (Austria)
> Started October 1994 with an investment of $7.7 million
> when the parent sold an earlier stake in the Bulgarian Bank for
> Agricultural Credit; Strategy is directed to export financing and project
> financing for foreign companies.

ING (Netherlands)
> Started October 1994.

BNP-Dresdner-EBRD
> Joint venture started in 1995 with $8 million capital.

Xiosbank (Greece)
> Started February 1994.

Union Bank (Greece)

ING, the Dutch bank with operations in most of the EITs, has a long-term strategy for business development in Bulgaria. The strategy focuses initially on multi-national corporations and then on Bulgarian exporters and trading companies. The bank does not envision that its activities will be very profitable in the short run. The ING presence in Bulgaria is nevertheless important in the long run because the bank wants to position itself for a prominent role in the privatization process, particularly as an advisor to foreign investors, as a market maker and investment banker. Thus, the bank does not want to compete with existing Bulgarian banks but, instead wants to serve new market segments as they emerge. Nevertheless, the Bulgarian banks opposed foreign bank entry.

The foreign banks did not play any role in the consolidation of the state owned banks. Several bank privatization proposals have been discussed in the last two years. They have led to little progress due to opposition from the government and the banks themselves. A few small banks have been partially privatized, again without any foreign participation. However, there have been a few small investments by the EBRD in banking ventures.

The overall picture of the banking system is not good; in 1996 there were several bankruptcies and in September 1996 nine banks were placed under special supervision by the central bank. The banking and foreign debt crisis that began in mid-1996 will lead to the closure of some banks and surely deter any foreign investors from extending their activities or interests in the Bulgarian banking industry.

In 1990 non-performing loans were one-half of all loans outstanding and one-third of GDP. The situation has not improved although the government has made several attempts to consolidate loan portfolios and recapitalize the banks. BNB statistics for the end of 1994 indicate that uncollectible loans are 15 percent and doubtful loans 60 percent of total loans outstanding. These statistics were considerably worse in 1996.

There are at least three reasons for the absence of foreign equity participation in the development of the Bulgarian banking industry. First, the government and regulatory authorities have never articulated a policy to encourage foreign equity investments in banking. Second, even if they had, foreign bank interest would be very limited because of the enormous bad debt situation in Bulgarian banks. Third, the country risks for investments in Bulgaria are very large because of the uncertain economic environment and the inability of Bulgaria to service its company risks. Hopes for improvement in this situation after an agreement was reached with the London Club of international creditors in June 1994 were dashed two years later by a banking crisis.

Estonian banking was part of the Soviet mono-banking system until the late 1980s. Estonia participated in the bank reforms of the last years of the Soviet Union which included the establishment of specialized state banks and some new commercial banks, including some private ones. In 1992, the Estonian banking system became independent of the former Soviet system and the Estonian currency was established in June 1992. A number of new banks were established and by the end of 1992 there were 42 commercial banks.[22]

Many banks soon found themselves in financial difficulty. The Tartu Commercial Bank, the first commercial bank established in the Soviet Union after 1989 the banking reforms, was the first Estonian bank to go bankrupt at the end of 1992. There were a number of reasons for the banking crisis in 1992 the weak capitalization of banks, poor banking practice inherited from the Soviet era, the freezing of assets in failed Russian banks, the overall difficulty of conducting banking business during a tumultuous transition from the Ruble zone to a national currency. The number of banks, due to consolidations, bankruptcies and de-licensing, was reduced to 22 by the end of 1993 and some further reductions have taken place.

It is not surprising that in this difficult environment, there has been little foreign banking activity. Foreign bank entry was allowed in 1992 and the American Baltic Bank started operations in 1993. At the end of the year it was the smallest commercial bank in the country with 0.4 percent of all bank assets. In 1993, the EBRD became a minority share holder in the Estonian

Investment Bank. The central bank is the majority owner of the investment bank that arranges currency loans for Estonian firms. Three Finnish banks have established representative offices in Estonia and two planned to change them into branches in 1994.

Several Russian and Ukrainian banks have expressed interest in entering the Estonian market but no banking licenses have been issued so far. There is substantial resistance to their entry for several reasons. First, there is political resistance to Russian influence over the Estonian economy. Second, there is concern that these banks would be substantially involved in money laundering and fraudulent activity.

The Estonian central bank favors foreign investment in banking as a means of increasing competition among Estonian banks and raising the level of banking practices. It is not clear whether or not this will lead to changes in the banking sector.

Foreign bank interest in the Estonian market may be limited for several reasons. First, the banking crisis in 1992 led to an overall lack of confidence in the banking system which persists. Second, the interbank market which is often used as a source of funds by foreign banks was practically non-existent until 1994. Third, the Estonian market is relatively small and there has been relatively little entry by multi-national corporations which require local banking services. (The economy is still tied in many ways to Russia, for example distribution networks, which discourages the entry of foreign firms.) Fourth, the capital markets are still in their infancy, the only traded securities are central bank short-term bills. On the other hand, the Estonian currency board arrangement seems to have successfully stabilized the currency and since mid-1994 there has been virtual full currency convertibility. However, the success of the currency board system limits the need for foreign banks to operate in Estonia. Currency convertibility and exchange stability enable both foreign investors and Estonian enterprises to fund activities abroad. Finally, legislation defining property rights was passed in late 1993. The planned voucher privatization of state owned firms will deepen the capital markets activity. These developments help create a favorable environment for foreign bank interest.

5. CONCLUSIONS

It is interesting to note that with all of the suspicions of foreign banks and the extent to which they might control the economy, every one of the EITs examined is basically in favor of foreign banking entry. It is viewed like any other foreign direct investments, as a means of both obtaining capital that contributes to economic growth and quickly improving the level of techno-logy. The only qualification in this regard is that the EITs would like to channel the foreign investment in ways that reduce the costs of reforming the existing banking system. Governments that are practically unable to reduce excess employment and improve the management of traditional banking entities would like to see foreign partners do the dirty work for them. Potential foreign strategic investors are often understandably reluctant to take on this role. As a result, it has often been difficult to find investors interested in participating in the privatization process. However, as the overall condition of the banking system in the EITs improve, foreign interest is quickly evident.

Foreign banks seem to find a way of entering markets where the underlying conditions are favorable. There seem to be three necessary factors for foreign bank interest. First, the economic environment must be fairly stable. Aspects of stability include the existence of commercial laws and a macroeconomic policy that avoids hyper-inflation and maintains the viability of the monetary system. The economic environment can be attractive even without full currency convertibility or a rapidly expanding level of output. Second, there has to be a payments system and an interbank market that allows for business dealings with the local banks. Third, there needs to be a presence of international firms, often from the home country, to provide a customer base that generates fee income for financial services.

Throughout the European economies in transition we see a dichotomy between governments which would like to channel foreign banking investments in a particular direction and foreign banks that are interested in unencumbered investments. This tension is healthy and has probably assisted in the reform of the banking structures. If a government values foreign investment and sees that foreign banks will only invest in thoroughly cleaned up banks, then it will have an incentive to make the necessary changes to the domestic banking structure. Alternatively, the success of new foreign bank entrants places competitive pressures on existing banks which should hasten the pace of reform.

The foreign banking presence is strongest in Hungary. Hungary encouraged the entry of foreign banks and joint ventures, and they currently account for a significant share of the banking market. The challenge in Hungary is whether additional foreign investments in banking can be harnessed to assist in the reform of the state owned banks. The ups and downs of the negotiations with various foreign potential partners for Budapest Bank leave this question still open. Budapest Bank was privatized in late 1995 but it is too early to evaluate the success of the deal (the details were discussed in Chapter 2).

In the Czech Republic, there would probably be considerable interest in expansion by foreign banks if a means for developing strategic alliances could be worked out. The partial voucher privatization of the banks and the high degree of concentration in banking makes this more complicated. A foreign strategic investor in any of the large Czech banks does not appear imminent. The new foreign banking ventures in the Czech Republic have become very aggressive and are growing rapidly. Thus, it is possible that the large banks will be threatened by new competitors before they can attract strategic investments. This combination of events could be destabilizing for the Czech banking system.

Poland is at a crossroads between the Czech and Hungarian examples. On one hand, the relatively new foreign banking operations are growing rapidly, and on the other hand the government has to devise a way of getting foreign investment to assist in the privatization and reform of the state-owned banks. The government has actively discouraged new foreign bank ventures and has succeeded in directing investment interest towards the privatization of Polish banks. Since the banking system is much less concentrated than in the Czech Republic, it has been possible to generate investment interest. It is reasonable to anticipate that future privatizations will continue to involve foreign bank participation.

There is barely any foreign bank entry in Bulgaria and Estonia. The reasons for this have more to do with the demand for entry by the foreign banks than policies that restrict their entry. In both of these countries the base of international customers is probably too small and, also, the existing domestic banking infrastructure is probably still too weak. Furthermore, the success of the Estonian currency board enables firms to raise capital outside of the country and to some extent holds back the banking sector. However, in both Bulgaria and Estonia, foreign banks will follow the path set earlier in the 1990s in the other central European EITs. That is, foreign bank interest will develop as the banks follow their customers into these markets.

Public policy toward foreign banks has differed across the EITs studied here. Poland does not currently issue licenses to foreign banks while Bulgaria treats foreign bank and domestic bank applications in the same way. These differences reflect the different stages of these countries in the transition process.

At the earlier stages of the transition, foreign bank entry is simply an indication that economic relations with the rest of the world are likely to grow. It would be silly to discourage entry of firms that will assist and encourage the development of trade, financing and investment. However, there is a risk of unbridled growth of the banking system that occurs before the infrastructure for bank supervision and examination have been put in place. In the early 1990s, both Poland and Hungary suffered the consequences of what used to be termed 'wild cat' banking. Currently, banking authorities in Bulgaria and Estonia are well advised to distinguish between new foreign bank entrants that will provide financial services for international trade and finance and new entrants without a long-run commitment to the country.

At later stages in the transition, foreign banks provide an excellent market test of the adequacy of reforms. More so than any other industry, the banking sector should meet international standards for the quality of management. The banking sector reforms should result with a banking sector with clean portfolios and adequate capitalization. Foreign bank interest in the privatization of a reformed banking sector provides a test for the success of reform.

Thus, the privatization of banks in Hungary and Poland has been slow to start because it was unclear that the reform process had been completed. But, the participation of ING in the BSK privatization and the forecasts that Budapest Bank will be privatized shortly with the participation of a foreign strategic investor, indicate that the banking systems in Poland and Hungary may be passing the market test. Both examples are instructive. ING was anxious to enter the Polish market and was blocked from starting up its own operation. Its willingness to participate in the privatization of an existing bank was reluctant and only developed slowly. However, the conclusion indicates that the Polish policy of restricting further foreign bank entry may be a success. In comparison, the Hungarian authorities were surprised at the difficulty in finding a strategic foreign investor. The reluctance of foreign banks indicated that the reform process in Hungary was not complete. However, the recent renewed interest in Budapest Bank indicates that progress has been made.

The situation in the Czech Republic bears comparison. Of course, it is more difficult to find strategic investors for the large banks in the very concentrated Czech industry. However, the absence of foreign interest is also a negative signal that the reform of the Czech banking system is not yet complete.

In all of the countries examined, there are examples of new foreign banks that are growing rapidly and making inroads in the local markets. The examples discussed earlier were Citibank and Creditanstalt. Despite the nationalist concern about foreign control, public policy has made no effort so far to block the growth of these companies. This is a very fortunate development. Comparison with foreign bank growth in Western Europe and elsewhere indicates that fears of such institutions is unwarranted. They are likely to have positive impact on the local industry through the introduction of new technology, new product innovation and competition in pricing. The best example of a positive externality from new foreign banks is that they encourage the development of the inter-bank market in funds. The reason for this is that the foreign banks will attract loan demand (from the local subsidiaries or customers of their home country clients) more quickly than they will be able to develop a deposit base. They are likely then to turn to the inter-bank market for funding.

In fact, the absence, until very recently, of significant foreign bank activity in the Czech Republic has probably slowed down the difficult process of reform of the big banks.

To conclude, public policy towards foreign banks has three components:

(i) in the initial transition stages, the benefits of a more open financial system must be weighed against the ability to monitor and supervise new entrants in an often unstable environment.

(ii) in the later stages, strategic foreign investments in the banking industry should be part of the privatization program because it provides a market test for the success of banking sector reforms.

(iii) new foreign banking firms should be allowed to develop because the benefits of competitive environment that they introduce outweigh any costs to the existing industry.

NOTES

1. See Brealey and Kaplanis (1994).
2. The large Japanese banks are conspicuous by their absence. There are two reasons for this: unlike their European counterparts, the Japanese have no tradition of business relationships in the Central European EITs. Also, financial sector development in the EITs in the 1990s coincided with the weakening of the Japanese financial sector.
3. For example, in 1989, the five largest banking institutions had a market share of 55 percent in France, 26 percent in Germany, 39 percent in Spain and 29 percent in the UK (*The Banker*, July 1990).
4. Often the state ownership consists of specialized lending institutions (for example, for agriculture or mortgages) and savings banks (for example, postal savings), but the larger percentages reflect state ownership of general commercial banking as well. On the structure of banking in Europe see Bisignano (1992). The pattern is not restricted to Europe; in Brazil, for example, virtually every state owns at least one financial institution and the largest bank is owned by the Federal government.
5. An analysis and case studies of bank strategies for internationalization is found in Hoschka (1993).
6. The share data here are taken from Bonin and Leven (1995).
7. 'A Long Haul: Foreign Banks in Eastern Europe,' *Eurobusiness,* April 1995.
8. The privatizations in Poland have not always been smooth; there has been much criticism of stock price manipulations – see Chapter 2.
9. See International Monetary Fund (1995).
10. For the past 20 years, there has been a rapid and almost universal movement towards financial liberalization. However, the idea of limiting portfolio investments with controls over capital flows is likely to be reconsidered.
11. Even in the US, a large fraction of credit raised is subject to some government influence through the provision of loan guarantees, insurance or the creation of loan pools.
12. The experiences of the Federal Reserve Bank of New York with Daiwa Bank, a foreign bank in New York, show that such concerns can be warranted. It is reasonable to suggest that the fraud by a Daiwa trader, the lack of controls and the efforts of management in Tokyo to cover up the losses could not have occurred at a domestic bank. It is simply more difficult to monitor an operation that is managed from abroad.
13. The earliest restructuring of the banking system was in Hungary and dates only back to 1987. In all of the other countries the restructuring did not occur until the 1990s.

14. See Barnea and Goldberg (1995). Israel provides an interesting example of a country where there are no barriers to foreign bank entry but, at the same time, little or no interest from foreign banks.
15. A comparative discussion of banking sector developments in the Visegrad countries is found in Bonin and Wachtel (1996).
16. There are some exceptions: BNP-Dresdner was given a license in 1994, reportedly as a reward for its efforts in behalf of Poland are with the London Club of bankers, Westdeutsche Landesbank in 1995 and Ford Credit Europe in 1996.
17. See also the discussion in Chapter 2.
18. There is some foreign ownership of the privatized commercial bank as a result of the voucher privatization and share trading. With the exception of shares owned by Slovak residents, the foreign share ownership is small. For example, 1.2 percent of the shares of the largest bank, KB, are held by foreigners and an additional 6.2 percent are held by Slovaks. There is no significant foreign participation in management.
19. As of early 1995, the NPF held 48.7 percent of KB and 40 percent of the savings bank, Česká Spořitelna.
20. Data are from Čapek (1995).
21. See Petkova (1995).
22. See Hirvensalo (1994).

4. Regulation of Bank Failures

1. INTRODUCTION

The attempt to target critical areas of the banking business in which excessive state interference has proven to be harmful to efficiency and market competition has directed us in this chapter to an examination of bank failures and how they are regulated towards a concentration on bank failures. Our reasoning lies within the historical tendency and the enormous capacity of bank crises, especially large ones, to induce processes that promote trends toward real and quasi-'nationalization' (or renationalization) of banking. This can occur in several ways:

- *outright renationalization of financially troubled private sector banks;*

- *overregulation as a reaction to troubles with the intention (and hope) of avoiding future failures;[1]*

- *informal interdependency between banks and government authorities as a consequence of 'soft' treatment of bank crises.*

In less-developed economies, it is in the field of bank failure where 'contractualism' is perhaps the most difficult to introduce. In the absence of contractualism, however, much broader market regulation is undermined than just that which addresses the banking sphere, though this in itself is a serious problem. The lack of clear, transparent government policies towards bank failures serves only to limit the efficiency gains other market reforms, especially deregulation and privatization, would otherwise bring about in EITs. Moreover, a lack of clear and credible rules and policies also limits the gains of banking industry privatization as the need for extended discretionary government interference in banking generates quasi- or dejure nationalization of affected segments.

In other words, bank failure is a crucial part of the general problem of state withdrawal from the banking sector, since misguided policies may generate mechanisms which in fact reverse, rather than promote reforms. 'Nationalization' in this broader, institutional perception is more comprehensive than its strict legal meaning: it means outright nationalization, as well as 'tantamount nationalization' (that is, development of strong informalism in the relationship between the government and the large banks' managements). This informalism, which can also occur in the interaction between the government and government-owned banks, is even more harmful than government ownership *per se* [2]. Implementing transparent rules in this area, however, is easier said than done because of the fear, justified in many cases, of contagion (that is, system-wide panic as a consequence of individual bank failure). Such panics are more likely to emerge in developing and transitional economies as a result of the credibility gap caused by historically unstable macroeconomic environments, frequent high inflation, and a high degree of bad loan creation in both the infant banking industries of economies in transition and the distorted banking competition of most third world countries. Also, major political disturbances, shaking the financial system, have been much more frequent in these countries than in the developed ones. And as a result, external shocks impact banks in these countries much more severely than in well-developed market economies.

Each of the sample countries in this project – Poland, Hungary, the Czech Republic, Estonia, and Bulgaria – has experienced something similar to the stabilization programs known in traditional development economics. In some countries macroeconomic reforms have addressed high (or near hyper-) inflation in conjunction with administrative price and import regimes in a manner that has treated these issues as interconnected. In other countries, and particularly in the Czech Republic where inflation has never really been 'high,' the core task of economic transition has focused upon the second task of price and import liberalization as a means of stabilizing inflation. Something close to a classical stabilization policy has been the centerpiece of macroeconomic reform in the early transition stages in the EITs.

Nevertheless, the monetary and often, albeit less often than needed, fiscal austerity associated with developing country stabilization episodes has posed a more serious challenge to the financial systems of the CEEs countries than is normally the case. In third world countries it is usually 'only' the jump in interest rates, other monetary tools of liquidity squeeze, and the subsequent sharp deterioration of the enterprises' financial position that worsen banks' portfolios in the early stages of economic stabilization. In EITs, however, these initial effects are often more drastic. When compounded by the fact that the banking sector is hit by these stabilization effects in a very early and extremely inexperienced stage of its development, its ability to adapt to the changing environment is understandably meager. Consequently, the propensity to accumulate bad assets at a fast rate is very high and renders the likelihood of bank failures in this period particularly large. In addition, banks in EITs have inherited bad loans extended in a different period, when the rules of the game were entirely different, for which they did not bear responsibility. As a matter of course, those bad loans were then rolled over, adhering the banks to bad clients. With the exception of Estonia, the banking sectors of our sample countries have received varied sector-wide assistance in their respective bailout or recapitalization programs. The intensity and scope of the assistance, however, was in the first year of transition relatively smaller in Czechoslovakia while significantly larger in Hungary. This disparity, though, has a broader and more complex relationship with the adopted macro- and microeconomic reform programs.[3]

The immense challenges confronting the privatization of traditionally large state banks have been discussed in Chapter 2. On the one hand there are strategic investors who are reluctant to risk their name and goodwill for acquiring, however cheaply, banks overloaded with bad assets in EITs. Conversely, there stands the monumental task of shaking up the corporate culture of nascent, even privatized, banks – a process which will undoubtedly prove to be incremental in nature and exhaustive at best. Moreover, Chapter 3 on foreign banking reveals the hesitancy of Central European governments with the notable exception of Hungary to build their banking strategies on attracting prestigious foreign banks to establish themselves as core financial institutions. This approach prevails despite the potential of foreign banks to rapidly improve the efficiency of credit allocation and the credibility of the countries' banking sectors in the eyes of the countries' depositors as well as that of potential international lenders.

For those two reasons (that is, the reluctance to involve core strategic partners in their most important banks and the reluctance of the most desired foreign banks to take over highly 'contaminated' local financial institutions) one cannot expect the impact of privatization to produce miraculous improvement in the operating efficiency of banks – particularly with respect to asset performance. The ratio of qualified to total assets in the EITs has historically been extremely high in international comparison, including comparison with other underdeveloped countries.

In Bulgaria, for instance, 37 percent of the loans of the United Bulgarian Bank (UBB), the fourth biggest Bulgarian bank as measured by 1994 assets, are qualified. The bank ended 1994 with a loss of nearly BGL 1 billion, largely due to the poor performance of loans extended in 1992 and 1993. This performance was reportedly the primary reason for the EBRD forsaking partial ownership stake in UBB. The seventh largest Bulgarian bank, Hebrosbank, declared BGL 8.5 billion, constituting 73 percent of total loans, as non-performing and substandard loans in 1994. A majority of the bad loans were extended in the 1991–93 period with 70 percent of total recipients being state companies. In Poland, 46 percent of the total credit of Bank Gospodarki Zywnosciowej, the traditional agriculture bank and the largest bank according to equity capital, was irregular in 1994. In the case of BSK, 27 percent of the total credit was irregular,[4] while WBK carries only 25.1 percent irregular loans. In Hungary the three initial large spin-off banks needed three consecutive rescue operations.

Even in the Czech Republic, which is usually mentioned in regional comparisons as a country standing out in terms of its banking system stability, the ratio of qualified to total loans at Komerční Banka was 43.8 percent in September 30, 1994. During 1994 the overall level of non-standard, doubtful and loss loans stabilized, but the quality of already existing non-standard and doubtful loans worsened, resulting in an increase in the level of non-performing loans. This situation compares unfavorably with the data in the international overview of the World Bank (1989), which found the situation extreme if 20 percent of loans in a given country are nonperforming. While it most certainly is partly a question of definition as to what ratio of a bank's or financial sector's assets are nonperforming, one has good reason to assume that, because of practically non-existing bankruptcy procedures, only a portion of the full problem surfaces in most EITs.[5]

Since experience suggests that banks' vulnerability is very frequent in transitional economies, turning to the body of international experience can provide good insight into how critical mistakes might be avoided. An effective system for handling bank failures should avoid the errors inherent in the extremes of the policy spectrum. On the one end of this spectrum lie policy choices pursuing unconditional bank, or even whole sector, bailouts. This seems to be a very extreme situation since almost every bank bailout program contains some kind of condition. Yet, evaluation of the short history of bank bailout campaigns in EITs reveals that most have been accompanied, thus far, by very weak conditionality criteria. Most typically, even firing managers responsible for substandard past performance is not yet a commonplace. In these cases the moral hazard problem of the bank managers is very acute: they interpret government action as calling for risky, and in many instances fraudulent, behavior and expect to be aided in cases of emergency. At the other end of the spectrum lie the absolute 'hands-off' solutions to bank or systemic crises. While there are no such examples of government passivity in cases of systemic banking crises, there do exist circumstances under which largely (of course in real life never entirely) hands-off attitudes concerning individual, even large, bank crises is evident. In this chapter we will discuss two famous episodes of *laissez-faire* approaches: the Estonian banking crisis in 1992 and the case of Baltija bank in Latvia in 1995.

Although the riskiness of banking has increased since the end of World War II in most of the market economies for a variety of reasons, one reason of particular interest to us is that of deposit insurance. While aimed at actually decreasing the systemic threat of individual bank failures, deposit insurance has gradually substituted for equity as a means to protect depositors and, in turn, has served to increase the moral hazard in banking (Benston, 1986). Nevertheless, some authors actually question or relativize the wisdom of focusing on the moral hazard problem as a major policy issue within the context of deposit insurance. De Juan (1995a) points out that in countries where bank failure bears the consequence of firing the responsible managers, the moral hazard problem may exist on the side of the depositors but not, or in a very weak state, on the level of managers. This may be a legitimate point concerning well established, mature market economies, but it is doubtful that many developing countries could demonstrate a strong systematic negative consequence for bank managers of financial failure. In any case, our task lies more in the identification of policy approaches that ultimately lead, in the transition from centrally-managed to capitalist economies, to fewer government rescue actions on behalf of banking institutions.

The chapter is organized as follows: section 2 highlights some of the experiences mature market economies have had with bank crises and with the problem of contagion; section 3 deals with the experiences in developing countries, recognizing that in many ways their lessons may be more relevant than those of market economies, as certain structural weaknesses in their banking industries reflect more the problems faced by banking industries in EITs; section 4 concentrates on the available experiences with bank crises in EITs, paying particular attention to the analysis of the 5 countries concerned, the Latvian Baltija Bank debacle and its consequences, as well as the Russian interbank-market crisis. Finally, section 5 asks whether or not EITs can realistically strive for more market-conforming solutions in handling bank failures. Particular attention is given to the issue of deposit insurance as a key instrument aimed at preventing an individual bank's problems from becoming a system-wide phenomena, although this method is very controversial within the professional community, especially in the US.

2. WHAT LESSONS CAN WE LEARN FROM THE EXPERIENCE OF MATURE MARKET ECONOMIES?

When evaluating international experience, we will primarily draw from the experiences of post-World War II US and Europe and the recently unfolding banking crisis of Japan. The importance of examining experiences in the developed countries is two-fold: first, the analytical literature currently available about public policy towards banking failures, particularly for the US is, quite simply, very rich. Nevertheless, such enthusiasm must be tempered with the recognition that the Western experience is only of limited relevance to

CEE. The fundamental difference in the two experiences lies in the lack of confidence in CEE, as in most developing countries, in the domestic financial sector. This gap renders their respective concrete policy task – achieving a radical increase in confidence – significantly different from that faced by policy makers in the US and other Western nations in general.

Second, studying the Western, and again, particularly the American, literature exposes the existence, more than elsewhere, of a vibrant, radical pro-market body of analysis. A comprehensive understanding by EIT policy planners of this body of work is vital, although the straightforward applicability of some of the radical policy proposals in CEE is clearly out of the question. Moreover, in seeking admission to the European Union, these countries will be subject to directives that constrain the policy choices of their policy makers because policy thinking on banking regulation in western Europe is much less radical than in the US.

The United States and the EITs

The cataclysmic experience of the Great Depression, even more than World War II, influenced institutional developments in finance and widened the divergence between patterns in financial sector development in the US and Western Europe. In both regions the trauma led to increased government authority in the financial sector. The US saw the expansion of the power of the Federal Reserve, a decrease in the reach of private banks due to the Glass-Steagall Act, which limited the powers of commercial banks relative to other financial firms, the establishment of the Federal Deposit Insurance Corporation (FDIC) in 1933 and geographical limitations in the banking business (Salsman, 1993; Pierce, 1991).

In most of continental Europe, while the Great Depression also led to increased government power over the financial sector, this transition occurred under the auspices of political regimes different from that in the US. In Europe, more informal ties developed between governments and large banks with the intended purpose of utilizing these banks for development purposes. The common denominator in both regions has been the trend towards gradual softening of the 'budget constraint' of the banking system. This observation alone illustrates the difficulty facing CEE policy makers, whose task is to gradually harden the budget constraint.

That banking has become riskier in the US in recent years is evidenced not only by the famous savings and loan crisis, but also by the acceleration of failure rates in the 1980s among the commercial banks (White, 1993). This riskier environment can be attributed most immediately to the wave of deregulation during the Reagan Administration, which pressed for stronger competition. A second look, however, suggests that since the introduction of deposit insurance and the imposition of severe limitations on bank portfolios during the Depression, banking has gradually become a less prudent and more risky venture in the US. Thus, we can view the banking crises of the late 1980s as either the short-term consequence of the deregulation that preceded it or the longer-term reaction to the regulatory protections of the Depression era. In the former case deregulation can be criticized, while under the latter interpretation, further deregulation appears to be the way to improve the security of banking.

Finally, in the US, part of the professional literature also challenges the wisdom of public investment in expensive banking supervision, which currently serves as a partial substitute for market control against excessive risk-taking. Much of the criticism is based on the inability of such supervision to offer guarantees of effectiveness (Benston et al., 1986). This, too, exemplifies the strong differences between the US and the EITs (as will be discussed in the concluding section of this chapter·

The key aspect of the American system that differs from the current Central European situation lies in US confidence in the financial system. This confidence is so strong that even a mild bank run would not cause a serious depletion in the deposit base of the banking system. Such a run would simply result in the reallocation of deposits from one bank (or financial institution) to another. In EITs, because of the system's fundamental vulnerability, which will remain a factor for the near future, much less than a full guarantee of household deposits would undermine the credibility of the whole banking system (even in case of a minor initial crisis) and result in deposit flight. The solutions to individual crises clearly need to take into account their impact on public trust more than do those applied in the US.

Deregulation has undoubtedly been one of the primary immediate reasons behind the American S&L crisis and the subsequent acceleration of bank failures. This should be of particular interest to the EITs, where early banking reforms should be viewed as a gigantic bank deregulation (from, of course, an incomparably high level of overregulation). Putting the blame on deregulation *per se* for the S&L crisis would be a false argument additionally because there are tools to mitigate the short-term risks of deregulation: primarily, the strengthening of capital adequacy ratios.

However, the point is made not to counter advocates for deregulation, but to insert a note of caution: when EIT governments pursue bank deregulation, they need to acknowledge that increased competition will inevitably result in some banks failing to adjust quickly enough to a more demanding environment. Yet since the EITs' experiences with early bank failures, most governments have become very cautious – almost lethargic – rather than bullish when implementing further reform. This is particularly the case with respect to market entry regulation. While at the beginning of reforms these regulations were typically very liberal, particularly as regards domestic investors, later reforms evolved on a much more cautious path. Minimum capital requirements were increased and central banks, or governments, became more meticulous in approving banking licenses.

The initial approach to domestic banks, however, was contrasted by a more restrictive policy towards issuing licenses to foreign banks. This has been the case even in some of the most reform-minded countries such as the Czech Republic, where a practical moratorium was in place for approximately two years, or Poland, where foreigners can get a license only by rescuing a failing domestic bank. With the benefit of hindsight, we can say that a better sequencing of measures to launch a two-tier banking system in the EITs would have seen regulators starting more cautiously, focusing more on higher minimum capital requirements for the issuing of new licenses, and then gradually easing the restrictions.

Japan's banking crisis

The Japanese banking crisis coming to light recently has strong similarities with the American S&L debacle. As in the US, the Japanese crisis was preceded by a major banking deregulation, which made competition fiercer and opened opportunities for thrift institutions to invest in previously restricted assets.[6]

The exhaustion of the Japanese Deposit Insurance Corporation's (DIC) funds by the bailout of Hyogo Bank and the two credit unions, Cosmo and Kizu, has triggered an urgent debate over strengthening the DIC. With the recognized level of problem loans in the Japanese system mounting to nearly $500 billion (approximately the size of capitalization of the financial sector), there exists the danger that the recent problems may affect a larger segment of the industry. The collapse of the real estate and stock exchange bubble that developed in the 1980s left some specialized banks with extraordinarily high levels of bad assets. This, in part, was also due to segmentation, a consequence of earlier excessive regulation of the market, which made large classes of banks dependent on interbank borrowing.[7] Central European bank regulators would do well to study this situation, as the problem within the region exists on a much larger scale, with savings banks usually controlling very large proportions of household savings.

Another problem, not unknown to EIT policy makers, is the imperfect real estate market. Heavy regulation, particularly of the land market,[8] makes valuation and selling of the collateral behind bad assets (or the assets themselves) particularly difficult. This is exacerbated by the attitude of Japanese regulators who, unlike the US regulators in the S&L crisis, do not encourage lowering of the book value of property to market value or below. The expectation among regulators and banks alike is that the market will ultimately pick up from recent 'unrealistic' levels and take care of the problem.[9]

The Japanese government must also contain the moral hazard (and the amount of taxpayers' money) involved in the seemingly inevitable bail-out of many financial institutions in the months to come.[10] In Japan, as in other countries, a large banking industry crisis represents a threat to the viability of the financial system because politicians are hesitant to bail out banking institutions with taxpayers' money when the magnitude of the problem reaches systemic crisis proportions. The problem is, of course, how to determine when the crisis has reached levels that justify pouring in large sums of public funds, and whether the crisis has become a systemic problem. A recent IMF report, in fact, explicitly criticizes the hesitancy of the Japanese government in managing the ongoing crisis. One of the sources of this hesitancy is a secretive corporate tradition (itself not an unknown phenomenon in CEE) that resulted in an unduly long period during which banks and the Ministry of Finance attempted to hide the magnitude of bad assets, in the hope that things would improve over time.

The other obstacle the government (mainly the Ministry of Finance) is facing is the attitude towards further deregulation of the heavily parceled Japanese financial markets. Segmentation was assumed to be a tool of maintaining stability by limiting cross-competition, and it seemed to work for the entire post-war period. Only since the recent crisis has the policy appeared in a different light, raising questions about the wisdom of strong specialization. From another angle it pushed the authorities to be lenient towards industry consolidation through cross-mergers between some large city banks and other financial institutions such as trust banks, credit unions or brokerage houses. This development is likely to accelerate and may well force the pace of changing the general policies towards segmentation.

Western Europe

In spite of wide-ranging professional criticism, the safety net under the American banking industry is still much more 'market-like' than the Japanese or the European models. In continental European countries, central banks are usually more eager to help troubled banks than in the US.[11] Furthermore the greater concentration in European banking makes the relationship between the banks and the central banks closer. US Department of Treasury report concluded that in most European countries the bank safety net is fashioned by the central bank, in coalition with the private financial sector. It is much more informal than the arrangement found in the US (US Treasury, 1991). However, in Europe, particularly Germany, the expansion of protective schemes from the 1960s through the 1980s went almost hand-in-hand with deregulation in such important areas as pricing (interest rates), the abolition of needs testing for branch network expansion, and so on The starting point, however, was one of much tighter regulation after World War II than in the US.

'Too Big To Fail' (TBTF) has become the de facto official banking doctrine of the newly integrated Europe since the European Commission's approval of the Credit Lyonnais (CL) rescue package. With their approval European authorities sent a dual message: while sanctioning the rescue, the Commission also forced CL to shrink its foreign activities. The sale includes 50 percent of the bank's European banking activities and 35 percent of its total activities outside France.[12] Thus the plan, endorsed by the EU competition commissioner, punishes the bank for trying to become Europe's biggest bank. This part of the package is important for addressing the moral hazard problem because the bailout would otherwise punish competitors who, unlike Credit Lyonnais, took heed of the costs and risks of a frenzied expansion. Still, the rescue package has outraged CL's main French private sector competitors. By asking only for the sale of assets abroad, the plan does not lower CL's domestic market share at the rate it 'deserves' given the bank's poor performance even in France. The package requires the bank to transfer its bad assets to a government managed 'hospital bank'. What the French government and the EU have designed is a very peculiar response to the CL crisis. On one hand the bank is forced to shrink its foreign activities, but on the other hand there are no sanctions on its domestic activities. Moreover, the situation could become even more complicated if CL is unable to sell the enormous amount of its foreign assets, since no particular penalty clause is attached to the EU verdict. It is no surprise that in the first year since the approval of the reserve package, one has witnessed a continuous further softening of the terms.

What the application of the TBTF doctrine means for CEE is that as long as TBTF prevails in Europe in a non-transparent way (that is, we do not exactly know which banks it applies to and any particular application depends partly on political bargaining power), it will be very difficult to convince CEE policy makers 'to be holier than the pope' and pursue far-reaching market solutions in situations of bank failures. TBTF has a self-perpetuating element: when the public recognizes it, large banks – and not healthy ones – will be preferred by depositors. This centralizes the banking system beyond levels which market rationality dictates, increases systemic risk, and increases the likelihood that the regulatory authorities will intervene in cases of individual bank problems.

Incidentally, there has been only one recent example of a 'hard budget constraint'-type handling of a major banking crisis in Europe, the collapse of Barings in the UK. Although Barings was not a commercial bank, the Bank of England handled its distress in a very disciplined fashion. This response may contribute to the improvement of internal control systems in banks and thus may have a broad impact on commercial banking. The Barings episode is likely to stimulate much thought on how to regulate derivatives trading and how to manage the risks involved.

Overview of Lessons from Developed Economies

The banking industry in Japan, Western Europe and the US is heading towards more concentration and consolidation. In Europe, however, it remains an open question as to how much this process will be constrained by national interest representation. In the US the gradual and ongoing erosion of restrictions on bank activities and location will make the drive towards consolidation much less constrained, but this will not affect market competition negatively for a some time to come. In fact, easing geographical limitations will, in many markets, boost competition. Generally, bank consolidation occurs without significant reduction in competition because of free entry, competition from non-banks and the internationalizaiton of markets.

Deposit insurance is another area where government policies can be a mixed blessing. Government-administered deposit insurance in the developed world also has a life cycle: in the early period its positive features outweigh the negative (moral hazard and principal/agent) ones. However, as the above-described dynamics of proliferation of control prevail, and as public perception gradually shifts towards government responsibility for deposits, the adverse characteristics become more and more dominant (Kaufman, 1995). Furthermore, as the banking industry slowly becomes quasi-nationalized, banking is increasingly perceived as a public utility. This 20th century historical trend now seems at odds with a more recent trend defining traditional banking as a less and less important industry, and financial products as more and more similar to 'normal' commodities that one can buy via telephone or, increasingly, electronic networks. Disintermediation is putting the whole problem in a new light in developed economies, and particularly in the United States.

An important aspect of the introduction of deposit insurance and financial safety nets in general is the need to combine them with intensified regulation. This puts banks at a competitive disadvantage to non-bank providers of financial services, which lately have included providers of payment services (Shibayama, 1994). Thus, in developed market economies, it is not only the moral hazard issue that causes legitimate headaches to policy makers, but the adverse selection problem, which ensues when overregulation decreases banks' potential efficiency and contributes to the pace of disintermediation by which banks are increasingly left with worse clients than other, less regulated financial institutions. Bank regulation is at odds with the trend toward increasingly similar financial products in countries with the right incentives. One might think that in the CEEs, which are characterized by rather obsolete financial technology, the challenge from non-bank financial companies would not be a serious problem. But this underestimates the pace of technological progress in CEE banking on one hand and, even more importantly, the potential for further progress following a good dose of competition in the financial services market, on the other.

The existence of a system-wide financial safety net creates perverse incentives. While deposit insurance is only one component of this safety net, a central part of any banking reform should be the reform of deposit insurance. The banking systems in CEE requires the establishment of transparent instruments and institutional structure for handling bank failures in order to minimize the creation of perverse incentives from the safety net.

3. DEVELOPING COUNTRY EXPERIENCES

So far we have examined trends in economic policy towards bank failures in the developed market economies. The examples of developing countries should be at least as revealing and, in many ways, more important than those in the sophisticated market economies. Like cases in the developed markets, the distress of financial enterprises has become a major issue of policy concern in developing countries. As the 1989 World Development Report concludes, 'not since the 1930s have so many firms in developing countries been unable to service their debts. The inability of firms to service debt has caused distress for many financial institutions.' Indeed, just as in the mature market economies, the 1980s and 1990s saw a historically unprecedented number of banks becoming insolvent in an unprecedented number of countries, including many in the Third World.

As was pointed out in the introduction to this chapter, one of the main characteristics of most developing (or underdeveloped) countries' economic systems is the lack of confidence in the financial system. This means that when choosing between short-term security, with all its risks of moral hazard, and hard budget constraints, Third World countries, like their post-socialist counterparts, usually have a very narrow path to walk – more like a tightrope – to avoid the collapse of the financial system and acting responsibly for building a long-term, safer and competitive financial sector. Latin American experience with bank failure and contagion seems to be particularly relevant, since the situation in which banks operate resembles in many ways the climate in CEE. When predominantly short term liquid liabilities stand against short-term assets plus a large amount of government securities, the macroeconomic and market environment are very volatile (see

Rojas-Suarezand Weisbrod, 1995). Experience shows (Sundararajan and Balino, 1991) that in developing countries relatively small crises can very easily trigger full-blown systemic problems, which must be then managed with extraordinary measures. It is very rare that an established and formalized financial safety net, including a deposit insurance scheme, can withstand the pressures of such periods.

Interestingly enough, for the newly emerging market economies the crisis sometimes may start not in the financial sector, but with the payment difficulties of large companies in different sectors. The well-known Chilean financial crisis in 1981 started with the failure of a large sugar factory and spread to the financial sector later. Similarly, in the same year, the Philippine financial crisis started with the payment problems of an industrial company, as the dishonored bills left behind by textile magnate Dewey Dee triggered a chain of financial sector troubles (Sundararajan and Balino, 1991). Nor is it unknown in the most developed market economies that troubles of large non-financial companies trigger major disturbances in, or generate liquidity support of, the financial sector. Ambrus (1995) offers a number of interesting examples demonstrating that even in the United States, the Fed has occasionally felt obliged to intervene, explicitly or informally, in order to prevent the troubles of non-financial companies from spreading to the financial sector.

Concerning the degree to which developing countries rely on market solutions to bank distress and what institutions and mechanisms contain the spread of distress, the most important lesson according to the previously cited World Bank study is that although only a small minority of the countries have explicit deposit insurance schemes, in an overwhelming majority of bank failures the depositors have actually not been hurt at all. Implicit deposit insurance is still the name of the game in most cases, with predictably negative consequences for market discipline. Financial liberalization that is not closely harmonized with improving the quality of banking supervision has often resulted in crises which, given the fragility of the financial system, governments were usually unable to handle without generous bailout actions. Talley and Mas (1990) highlight many examples of this and quite rightly put Spain in the 'developing country' basket in terms of the bank safety net. In that country, deregulation started in 1969 in a way which left the once over-protected private sector and government-owned banks unprepared to face the oncoming competition. In the Spanish case as well, capital requirements were not strengthened in the time of deregulation. Here as in the mature market economy examples quoted in the previous section, subsequent systemic challenges to the stability of the national banking industries generated a process of increasingly explicit government responsibility for an ever growing part of depositors' funds.

Experiences in Venezuela, Mexico, Argentina, Brazil and elsewhere demonstrate the importance of policy which affects post-stabilization bank failures.[13]

Specifically, the establishment of contributory deposit insurance funds should be a policy priority. Although it would be too optimistic to believe that these funds will be able to contain a potential crisis in the short-term, the Argentine (and Hungarian, as will be seen in the next section) examples seem to suggest that, as a first step, one may want to establish the funds, even if the government still needs to intervene in the case of a crisis at any sizable bank. The next step could then be to fine-tune the process and the instrument. Where skillful management is available, setting up a contributory deposit insurance fund may still be a credibility gain in the eyes of an under-informed public, even if at this stage it is unrealistic to expect that the fund will be self-sustainable.

As Talley and Mas (1990) rightly point out, while an explicit deposit insurance system (DIS) may be a good thing in a developing economy environment, it can also very easily constrain the ability of the government to bail out a failing bank. Therefore, they argue that relying entirely on a DIS can be more costly than having an implicit depositor protection. Of course, as previously pointed out, there is hardly a country in the developing world where a major bank crisis could have been solved entirely on the basis of a formally established protective system. In that sense 'informalism' (that is, a deliberate government ambiguity) is always present even if a DIS itself is supposed to contain contagion. A well-managed ambiguous government 'poker game' with the banks may result in a better outcome than a formally established protective system. A possible trajectory is that in an early phase of shaping the new institutions and rules of the banking sector, informal solutions are and will be combined with developing a formal safety net as, over time, more responsibilities are shifted to the formal system. Also, successful consolidation of the economic system means that financial deepening and general credibility of the financial system progresses and allows a greater burden to be placed on the market when sorting out bank distress. However, the question remains as to what are the preconditions for playing the poker game well, without exposing the bank managers and depositors to more moral hazard than with other, more rigidly formalized, solutions.

Another policy measure that is even more relevant to our topic relates to bank privatization. In judging privatization, the quality of the purchaser institution rather than the cash generated by the sale should be the most important consideration. The value of this advice lies in the quality of privatization potentially serving as an important determinant of the frequency of future bank crises.

4. EXPERIENCE WITH BANK FAILURES IN CENTRAL AND EASTERN EUROPE

Bank bailouts – generic problem

As shown in the previous two sections, the gigantic 'deregulation' of banking which occurred at the end of 1980s and continued through to the beginning of the 1990s, caused major systemic disruptions in the financial sector. Banks needed wholesale bailout in most of the countries of CEE. However, within this general picture there was a great deal of variation in the approaches to bank distress.

It was found that most of the initial comprehensive bank bailouts of the state-owned commercial banks (SOCBs) in CEE had several common characteristics: (i) they were expensive; (ii) they paid attention mostly (sometimes almost exclusively) to solving the immediate systemic crisis; and (iii) they paid very little or no attention to the long term consequences of those campaigns. Therefore, most of these initial bailout episodes have been suboptimal from the long-term point of view, and have demonstrated the need for repeated rescue actions in a relatively short period of time and increased the explicit national debt to a large extent. Nonetheless, there have been significant differences within this picture, even among the five countries examined here.

Most of the sample countries have created legal conditions for bank bankruptcy; however, these legal provisions have remained for the most part without any practical use. Those problems which characterize enterprise bankruptcy in the post-communist economies are even more crucial in the cases of banks, where confidence in the health of the institution is an even more critical part of its value than in the case of, let us say, a steel mill.

Country experiences – Hungary

(i) Bad debt situation and the bank rehabilitation program. Both Hungary and Bulgaria stand out in this comparison as the two countries which started the economic transition with excessive national debt, making the debt burden of the enterprise sector also the largest in the region. These two countries have applied repeated and costly rescue programs (Dobrinsky, 1994). The major difference between the two countries, however, is that as a result of the combined effects of much stronger structural reforms in general, and deeper banking reforms enhancing competition in particular, the operative efficiency of the Hungarian banking industry presently is much better than that of Bulgaria.

In Hungary, a series of profound structural reforms caused stronger pressures on banks' asset portfolios much earlier than in any other country in our sample and, arguably, in the whole region. These reforms included draconian bankruptcy legislation enacted at the end of 1991, relatively quick progress in banking regulation (including accounting, prudential rules, and provisioning) also in 1991, and allowing intense foreign competition in the banking industry earlier than in the other countries. There are economic arguments for and against the rationale behind the radical Hungarian policies but, in their defense, it should be noted that these reforms fostered operational adjustment and reform on the microeconomic and banking levels much faster than in most of the other cases in the region. While the Hungarian experience yielded a relatively large number of bank failures (Agrobank serving as just one example), one cannot necessarily draw the conclusion that Hungary's problems with the banking sector are necessarily 'more serious' than in the other sample countries. Because of harsher microeconomic restructuring measures as well as a more stressed macroeconomic environment, the country's banking sector was exposed to great challenges from 1992 until well into the 1990s. This environment has created a more competitive environment in the banking sector than in any other transition economy. These circumstances are important to acknowledge because most of the literature usually points only to the negatives, that is, the generous enterprise and bank bailouts from 1992 which resulted from structural reforms. This stands in sharp contrast to the slowness of structural reforms in 'over-leveraged' Bulgaria, and in the region in general. And indeed, from 1995 the sector in general returned to healthy profits and balance sheet expansion. Within this general example there are outstanding examples and less spectacular ones. However since the collapse of Agrobank in early 1995 no sizeable bank has experienced any liquidity problems and all of them have reported some profits.

(ii) Bank insolvency legislation and treatment of large banks' crisis. Predictably it is Hungary, ahead of the rest of EITs in putting in place most of microeconomic restructuring mechanisms, where formal bankruptcy proceedings have already been applied. The National Bank of Hungary may consolidate a loss-making bank and supply an emergency loan to a financial institution if the institution's own capital is to decrease by 25 percent or in case of another emergency situation. Bank bankruptcy may be initiated by a financial institution or State Banking Supervision, which imposes a prohibition of a payments on financial institution until a court announces an adjunction order. Liquidation must be initiated if the financial institution is unable to effect its due payments within three working days. In the course of liquidating a financial institution, no compensation for depositors is allowed. The largest case of formal bankruptcy proceedings in Hungary is that of Ybl, which concluded in Budapest Bank taking over the bank and creating Polgari Bank

('Civic' Bank), an intended private banking operation, in its place. Polgari Bank has also assumed the job of recovering the bad assets of Ybl on a contractual basis with the liquidator of the failed bank.

Bulgaria

(i) Bad debt situation and the bank rehabilitation program. If there is a strong case for applying a Begg–Portes-type solution to the bad debt problem in any country, it is Bulgaria.[14] The stock of initial enterprise debt towards the banking sector at the beginning of the economic transition there had the least economic merit in the operational efficiency of the indebted enterprises. However, the Bulgarian government did not opt for creating a carte blanche for its economic agents which caused a further accumulation of confusion over who is indebted and for what reason. The result was the 1993 bailout program (Dobrinsky, 1994), which failed to solve the problem and constituted a textbook case for further expensive bailout needs. In fact, because of the lack of economic merit to the bailouts as well as their magnitude, the program shifted the responsibilities from the shoulders of the bank managers to those of the government. The unusually large size of the bad loan portfolio in the state banks has been attributed to the inherited hard currency denominated loans for which the banks bear only very limited responsibility. The 1993–94 program only partially cleaned the portfolio and in this way created the conditions for the reproduction of the problems. Because of the large share of these inherited hard currency denominated banking assets, the ratios of bank credit to GDP and M2 to GDP are unusually high in Bulgaria in comparison with countries of otherwise similar characteristics of inflation and monetary policy matters. The inherited debts, including those denominated in hard currency, were rolled over almost automatically in hopes of future government assistance. The result was the virtual collapse of the financial system in 1996.

(ii) Bank insolvency legislation and treatment of large banks' crisis. In Bulgaria there is no specific regulation of bank bankruptcy. Bulgarian law provides for voluntary liquidation, when the bank is solvent and possesses sufficient liquid assets to pay, without deferral, its commitments to depositors and other creditors. Legal procedures for declaring insolvency may be instituted upon the proposal of the Central Bank.

As noted earlier, the bad loans' conversion program of 1993–94 in Bulgaria provided only a partial solution to the financial problems of the major state-owned commercial banks. Of the five countries examined here, Bulgaria's economic system seems to have changed the least dramatically; that is, of the web of factors demanding reconstruction in such a manner as to achieve something of a comprehensive reform, Bulgaria has undergone the smallest transformation of the five countries. This is also true of credit practices: the chain of 'revolving' credits extended to indebted state enterprises has been broken less completely than in the other sampled countries. This contrasts sharply with the depth of market deterioration of Bulgarian enterprises. At least two factors suggest that the market environment has deteriorated the most in Bulgaria. First, Bulgaria had in the past relied the most on the Soviet market for its goods within the COMECON and, therefore, its collapse affected Bulgarian industrial enterprises the most dramatically. Second, the Yugoslav war has isolated the country as much if not more than any other non-warring economy in the region. If we add to this scenario the fact that Bulgaria has a very small and open economy we can understand the effect of East European changes on its traditional companies. To illustrate, the fall of industrial output in Bulgaria between 1989 and 1992 was 50 percent, while the decrease in the other CEE countries for the same period was: 34 percent in the Czech Republic, 30 percent in Hungary and Poland, and 51 percent in Romania. The structural reform policies of Bulgaria have not provided the needed economic impetus either. Large scale privatization as well as bankruptcy procedures were until very recently all but nonexistent, which caused a slowdown in the microeconomic adjustment process compared with those countries pursuing bolder structural reforms. For the above reasons, banks have encountered substantial difficulties searching for new clients, as the whole policy environment has not really required any particular soberness in lending to traditional clients.

Lack of clear government policies explicating realistic rules and expectations towards banks has led to an acute moral hazard problem in Bulgaria. The performance of Economic Bank in 1995 illustrates this point. The poor performance of the bank in 1994 would seem to dictate that it will be particularly sober in new lending. Estimates, however, suggest the contrary: interest received for the first six months of 1995 was only 57 percent of interest due.

The problems of Mineralbank and Economic Bank in particular reemerged soon after the debt conversion program. Because debt conversion bonds carry very low interest, the resulting high concentration of such bonds in these two banks has led to severe liquidity problems. The coupon rate over the dollar-denominated bonds was equal to 6 months LIBOR and on lev-denominated bonds to 1/3 of the base interest rate, or 72 percent in 1994. Partly as a result of the submarket interest over these assets (the conversion affected more than 50 percent of Mineralbank's total assets), Mineralbank ended 1994 with a loss of BGL 670 million and Economic Bank was in the red of a magnitude exceeding BGL 2 bilion, even though in September, 1994 BNB purchased bad debt bonds on face value (that is, well above the market rate) of BGL 8.8 billion. Also in September, 1994 Mineralbank's share capital was raised from BGL 292 million to BGL 730 million.

In 1995, the government tried to mitigate the problems by considering two methods of injecting extra liquidity into those banks. According to the Bulgarian National Bank (BNB), it would have bought back the conversion bonds on favorable prices, that is, on face value. The receipts would then have been cleared against the debt of these banks towards BNB. However, the government adopted the proposal of the Ministry of Finance instead. As a result, the 'bad loan bonds' have been replaced by new government bonds at the old market price (BGL 728 per BGL 1000 face value) with the provision that this money be used to clear the banks' debt towards the central bank and the State Savings Bank. A new and potentially progressive element of this scheme is that it tightens administrative control over the banks through the introduction of strong measures regarding salaries and obliging banks to sell certain branches. If executed, those measures can contribute to shrinking the two banks and thus to breaking the old, loss-making credit connections with traditional industrial structures. This may, in turn, give room for other, potentially efficient banks to expand in the subsequent vacuum.

In the years to come, the Bulgarian government will be facing some very difficult problems. The two aforementioned banks are not the only ones which will require operational and structural surgery. The United Bulgarian Bank (UBB) – the fourth largest Bulgarian bank in terms of 1994 assets – ended the year with a loss of nearly BGL 1 billion due, according to the bank's management, to the low return of bad debt bonds and unpaid state guarantees on preferential loans extended to the agriculture and the mining sector. It is estimated, however, that a substantial part of the loss is due to the poor performance of the loans extended in 1992 and 1993. Bank Biochim, which after a prolonged dispute with the Bank Consolidation Company was left out of the consolidation process, ended 1994 with BGL 300 million loss. The same reason was given: negative net interest income due to the below-market interest on the bad debt bonds.

Poland

(i) Bad debt situation and banks rehabilitation program. Although Poland was not able to avoid a major bailout program, that program stands out for the complexity of its design and the incentive structures built into it. The 1993 Law on Financial Restructuring of Enterprises and Banks provided for a decentralized approach, making commercial banks responsible for upgrading their asset portfolios, with the government playing an important but subsidiary role (Belka, 1995). The banks were required to create separate Difficult Loans Divisions (DLDs) to administer the whole program of cleaning up their asset portfolios. DLDs were assigned significant resources in terms of money and personnel from both the banks' own means and

external sources. To strengthen the positions of DLDs and provide an incentive mechanism, their directors became members of the banks' boards.

Banks could use several methods to improve their asset position. They could have the debtor repay the credit, initiate a bankruptcy of the indebted company, sign a court settlement with the debtor, or sell the existing loan on the secondary debt market at the going price. In 1993 seven of the nine commercial banks initially included in the program (two were dropped since they had managed to clean up their portfolios without the help of the state) received 11 trillion zloty in the form of fifteen-year low-interest (3 percent) treasury bonds, which were, however, not tradeable for three years. This made possible creating reserves for loans written off or exchanged for shares. (Belka, 1995).

Yet as discussed in Chapter 2, there were major bailout episodes outside the program, including two of the largest commercial banks (BGZ and PKO); their recapitalization amounted to a significant fiscal cost later. An important characteristic of the Polish program is that it started when the economy was already beyond its post-transition crisis and the companies' liquidity position had started to improve markedly. Thus, the main advantage of the Polish scheme may well have been indirect, that is it helped to avoid more centralized programs interfering more intrusively with the market mechanisms.

(ii) Bank insolvency legislation and treatment of large banks' crisis. Polish banks which are encountering difficulties and are faced with the threat of insolvency are required to notify the National Bank of Poland (NBP) of the situation and devise 'rehabilitation measures.' The NBP has the discretion of instituting such measures on its own if bank customers' deposits are threatened. If it is discovered that a bank's funds have decreased by 50 percent or more and the current managers decide not to pursue rehabilitation, the president of the NBP may decree that the bank should be liquidated or taken over by another bank.

Czech Republic

(i) Bad debt situation and the bank rehabilitation program. Czechoslovakia, and later the Czech and Slovak Republics, avoided in the early years of transition particularly costly bank bailout programs with the exception of an early operation in which a special type of evolving credit was taken out of the commercial banks' portfolios and was put into a special Consolidation Bank. Since Czech and Slovak public finances too, are in the best shape compared to other countries in the region (the Czech Republic has arguably also left behind the 'transitional recession'), both the Czech and Slovak Republics seem to have the most stable banking systems of all EITs. However, the relatively 'hands-off' approach of the Czech Republic in relation to bank bailouts

was rather an exception region-wide. Also, as discussed in Chapters 2 and 3, deregulation, particularly concerning competitive challenges from foreign banks, has been more cautious in the Czech Republic than in Hungary or even Poland. So far the Czech Republic has traded the innovation of its banking industry for its security. In 1996, however, the structural weakneses of the Czech economy came to the surface. The higher margins caused by the much more closed and oligapolictic banking system no longer satisfactorily offset the poor lending performance of the larger banks. The collapse of two mid-sized banks shook confidence in the whole system. The slow pace of microeconomic (enterprise-level) restructuring also contributed to the troubles of Czech banks in 1996.

(ii) Bank insolvency legislation and treatment of large banks' crisis. In the case of the Czech Republic, to preempt and offset the detrimental bank failures, the government has codified the following provisions: 1) remedial measures and penalties, 2) conservatorship, and 3) revocation of banking licenses. The Czech National Bank (CNB) has provided for the implementation of either monetary fines or restriction from certain activity. Conservatorship is enacted when the above measures have not remedied the situation. It can also take place if the bank's financial position declines precipitously or has continually been unstable. The revocation of a bank's license is undertaken when: a) the situation is so dire that a conservatorship will not effect a solution or b) if a period of conservatorship has failed to turn the institution around. Czech banking law also permits revocation of a bank's license when the business is in violation of relevant EU Directives such as a bank's 'inactivity in its major line of business.'

Estonia

(i) Bad debt situation and the bank rehabilitation program. Estonia has not orchestrated any general bailout program although the three banks affected by the November 1992 crisis represented 40 percent of the deposits in the entire banking sector.

(ii) Bank insolvency legislation and treatment of large banks' crisis. The Bank of Estonia is entitled to initiate bankruptcy proceedings immediately after it has enough evidence of a credit institution's insolvency. During bankruptcy proceedings, a credit institution can be reorganized through a merger or acquisition procedure. A credit institution has to be liquidated due to bankruptcy when it has become insolvent and also if there is at least one client whose justified claim cannot be settled and no moratorium has been enforced on the credit institutions. Thus, in Estonia, like in the Czech Republic, but unlike in Hungary, the Central Bank has strong statutory discretion over bank insolvency.

In November 1992 three of the largest Estonian banks, Tartu Commercial Bank (TCB), Union Baltic Bank (UBB), and North Estonian Bank (NEB), representing 40 percent of commercial credit at that time in Estonia, became insolvent. Eight smaller commercial banks were closed in 1993 for failing to meet new capital requirements. The handling of the three bank failures by the Estonian government is often cited in the international policy debates as an exemplary hands-off approach to bank failures which has paid off spectacularly.

Although, the Estonian government's approach to that crisis was praiseworthy, two important aspects of the crisis should be noted:

First, as the crisis of the three major banks hit the system (resulting in a combined total of as much as 40 percent of the country's deposit base) the whole economic system was in flux and, due to the previous Soviet galloping inflation and to the fact that exit from the Soviet economy had just been completed, banking did not yet play a major role in the economy. In fact, the 1992 credit to GDP ratio was 13 percent, while M2/GDP was 16.8 percent in the first quarter of 1993, and time and savings deposits/GDP was 4.6 percent. Therefore, a major shakeup of the industry did not greatly affect the economy to the extent that it would have in a country with a considerable savings base.

Second, some of the large commercial banks were inherited from the Soviet era as Estonian branches of the Soviet specialized banks. Some of these banks have become partly owned by private Russian structures as their parent banks went through an ownership transformation. For this reason, their severe treatment had a strong political dimension and a more *laissez faire* attitude was easier to implement. A good case in point is the merger of UBB and NEB after the freezing of their foreign exchange deposits by the Soviet Vneshekonombank in 1993, as well as the liquidation of the Social Bank (successor to the Estonian branch of Zhilsotsbank) in 1995.

Mismanagement was the main cause of difficulties at TCB, a problem inherited from the Soviet banking culture. The main reason for the problems of UBB and NEB was the freeze on assets deposited at the Vneshekonombank in Moscow, which made up 63 percent and 64 percent respectively of the total assets of the two banks. After deciding that rescuing TCB would be too expensive, the Bank of Estonia put it into compulsory liquidation. UBB and NEB were merged and recapitalized with government long-term securities (Hansson, 1994; Hirvensalo, 1994).

The resolute behavior of the Bank of Estonia gave a clear signal to other banks that financial strategy must be reoriented to the demands of the market economy. The 1993 Annual Report of the Bank of Estonia observed a turn in the behavior of banks from speculative to careful, with more attention being paid to risk analysis and diversification. These changes in tactics resulted in the growth of foreign assets and a very careful domestic credit policy. The bank crisis also provided a lesson for the bank customers, who began to select banks more carefully.

Summary of the country experiences with large bank crisis

As is clear from this overview, with the exception of Hungary, each country's bank insolvency regulations explicitly empower the country's central bank with discretionary powers in order to manage individual bank distress. Even in Hungary, where powers over failing banks are more evenly spread among different governmental agencies, small banks' distress is increasingly handled in a discreet way through the cooperation of the Ministry of Finance, Hungarian National Bank and the Banking Supervision Board.

One can not, of course, expect that governments in transition economies would soon be able to solve large banks' crises with legally well prescribed, transparent methods. The problems are simply too momentous even after the first phase of the generalized, campaign-like bank bailout programs which we described earlier. The recent period seems to be a time of individualized, case-by-case methods of assisting troubled banks, with the aim to prevent the spread of the disease. In Hungary, for example, the consecutive bailouts have recapitalized the large banks to a level corresponding to the Basel capital adequacy standards. The bailouts have been very costly, particularly as governmental ability to meet legitimate social needs has decreased.[15] In these circumstances there is especially strong public incentive to discontinue the routine of helping large state-owned banks.

It is critical to prevent an overambitious investment program, as well as to force these banks (with supervisory authority and on the basis of state ownership) to follow a prudent employment policy. Not only inherited portfolio and inherited clients (that is, the bad debt problem), but also frenzied investment into new activities and into the workforce has perpetuated the problems created by the large state-owned banks in EITs. Large banks in the last few years have been busy expanding into new territories, following the German role model of Allfinanz, without much regard to their own financial limitations (that is, implicitly assuming that the authorities will help them out in case of financial difficulties). At the depth of this strategy was an unspelled and many times unconscious consensus between the banks and the regulatory authorities that the country 'needs' a few large, diversified 'national' banks. This low cost sensitivity also exists in employment policies: the level of employment in large domestic banks is a significant multiple of the employment of foreign banks of comparable balance sheet. Domestic banks argue that they can not afford the high quality cadre and high level of computerization of IT foreign banks have. Moreover, they argue, the type of products in which they can be competitive need higher levels of employment. However, if a right balance is not found (and certainly it is not along recent employment levels) they descend into a vicious circle with their poorly trained, and on balance expensive, cadre. The wage push on the labor market affects banks as well and wage increase has been robust even though the banks' lack of profitability has not justified such a lavish approach to wages.

The solution to this dilemma is that the authorities in their capacity as regulators and, in most of the cases, as owners of the banks must provide for effective management by proper incentive systems and by direct interference to shrink loss making banks during periods of financial losses and improper provisioning against low quality assets. Probably the most natural tool is what the Hungarian government has applied in 1995 when it covered past losses (accumulated negative profits) by decreasing the capital of two of the largest, predominantly state-owned, banks' (MHB and K&H) to one-fifth and one-tenth, respectively. This operation then needs to be followed by a rigorous execution of adjusting the banks' balance sheets to the new capital bases.[16]

Private sector bank crisis

One of the typical crisis paths in banking in the transition economies finds an indigenous private sector bank attempting to syphon away deposits from the established players. In the beginning these banks are assumed to support an ambitious lending program or, in a worse case, to channel funds into non-banking businesses of the very same entrepreneur or circle of entepreneurs. A worsening liquidity crisis of such banks may then perpetuate an accelerated increase of the interest rates in order to meet earlier commitments. The most dramatic example for such pyramid schemes is Latvia's Baltija Bank debacle. This case illustrates the typical problem in the region's banking industry: only an extremely few indigenous domestic banks have succeeded so far in becoming major players in the market. Baltija tried, through its vigorous expansion, to do just that. To succeed, it needed to expand its branch network to enable it to syphon away deposits from the already ailing savings bank. It also needed to dramatically increase the interest rates in order to orchestrate the shift more quickly. The 'Ponzi scheme' pyramid the bank finally arrived at also contributed to major imbalances at the savings bank, and ultimately, after Baltija had become the largest domestic bank, to its demise.

The groundwork for Baltija Bank's rapid growth and subsequent collapse may have been laid by the 'asset hole' in the Latvian Savings Bank, caused by the transfer of deposits to the Moscow Sberbank at the time of Latvian independence. The Latvian Savings Bank was unable to either compete for new deposits or retain current ones because it could not offer the competitive rates of private banks. The latter captured three quarters of new loans by mid- 1994. The growth of banks like Baltija was also aided by the sell-off of Bank of

Latvia's (BoL) branch network and the attractive interest rates (as high as 50 percent) offered on deposits.

Latvia's financial system has become a safe haven for Russian flight capital and money laundering. Ethnically, it has been made possible by Riga's large Russian population, estimated at three-quarters of the city population. The financial sector grew up on the transfer of Russian exports in the initial years of independence. By common international perception the country is overbanked. That interpretation, however, depends on how one views the aspirations of the country's powerful bankers who would like to shape Riga as a financial off-shore base for Russia. This development has been facilitated by the radically liberal approach of Einars Repse, governor of the BoL. In the period 1991–92, minimum capital requirements were set at a very low level ($200,000) and 63 new banks were established in a very short period of time. After the Banka Baltija crisis in May, 1995, the minimum capital requirement was increased by the BoL to $2 million beginning January 1996. In the last couple of years the seemingly unstoppable growth of the sector came to a halt as fat trading and forex profits expired. As a result of the quasi-pyramid scheme, one fifth of the Latvian population had deposits in the Banka Baltija. The international press and Latvian officials primarily blamed Russian depositors for the crisis, though how much such a claim can be substantiated is debatable. Allegations suggest that InterTek, a Russian bank ranked 49th in a recent *Wall Street Journal* listing of Russian banks, may have made deliberate attempts to destroy Banka Baltija through the issue of phony securities. After the collapse, a major portion of the Baltija's loan portfolio and assets was ceded to InterTek, which caused a run on deposits. The crisis deepened by the authorities' laxity in the early signs of crisis. The bank was taken over by BoL on May 23, 1995 and on June 9, the Prime Minister announced that the government would fully pay out deposits up to 500 lati. Unsatisfied deposits are estimated at $360 million. The government asked the EU to make 45 million ECU of unused G-24 credit available to cover the losses of depositors. As a consequence of the crisis, money in circulation has contracted sharply, by an estimated 9 percent by June 27, 1995. In June alone, the country's gold and hard currency reserves fell by $10 million. Moreover, interest rates increased and, because of its autonomy, the BoL was able to refuse the extra credit line support for the government. Indeed, the politics of the crisis reveal a strong banking lobby which opposes stricter regulations.

The crisis of course spread to other banks. By mid-1995, 12 banking licenses had been suspended including those of some other sizeable banks such as Latvian Deposit Bank and Kredo Bank. The crisis also spread to some extent to Estonia and Lithuania. During June, in Lithuania a major bank, Aura Bankas, collapsed.

Another example of an ambitious indigenous private sector bank was the First Private Bank of Bulgaria. It experienced some problems with branching costs and bad assets; as of the end of 1994, 22 percent of the bank's loans were qualified. The bank managed to end 1994 with BGL 10.6 bilion profit before taxes. However, the bank's finances deteriorated in 1995 as economic conditions in Bulgaria worsened. Rapid credit expansion took its toll and in 1996 the bank' s license was suspended.

A rare successful case of indigenous bank development is Hansabank of Estonia. In fact Hansabank's success is quite remarkable within the 4 years old Estonian financial market. Not only has it become the largest domestic bank, but by acquiring 30 percent share of the Estonian Savings Bank it now dominates the market. Since Estonia's is the most open financial market of all EITs because of the currency board, external competition can still prevent a monopolistic situation.

In Estonia, the events in neighboring Latvia accelerated the construction of a new deposit insurance plan. Beginning July, 1996, deposits of up to $10,000 will be insured. Deposits of legal entities will start to be insured in the year 2000.

Failure of small banks

The large number of failures of small domestic banks in the whole region tells a tale different from that of the large banks. These failures, despite vast differences in intensity of occurrence, show quite a similar pattern region-wide and demonstrate two explicit categories of banks: those established by government organizations (branch ministries, communist youth organizations, other social, governmental organizations or powerful pressure groups) and those created by ambitious local entrepreneurs. The central motives of the founders of the former group were obtaining advantageous financing for some categories of enterprises, as well as establishing vehicles for tax avoidance, spontaneous privatization, and/or money laundering. In nearly each of these cases the purpose and mandate of the banks was, to a greater or lesser extent, in conflict with the dominant market principle according to which the goal of a business is profitability. Therefore, very few of these financial institutions have generated profitable businesses. The ones which did succeed, such as Tourist-Sport Bank in Bulgaria departed from their founders' intended profile quite early on; however, the sweeping systemic crisis in 1996 bankrupted even this relatively sober institution. Typical cases of banks established with a mission incompatible with market rules are the so called 'pocket banks' in the countries of the former Soviet Union. These were created for the purpose of obtaining cheap central bank finance for the companies or the ministries which established them.

Among banks founded by indigenous entrepreneurs the motives were also not especially compatible with the idea of proper business ventures. Many entrepreneurs established banking operations in order to get cheap credit for other parts of their rapidly growing business network or sometimes for money laundering purposes. Still another motive was the tendency for young, dynamic entrepreneurs in EITs to view banking as a lucrative, fancy business. Some of these bank founders were also intent on seeing that the state banks did not 'support' the new and ambitious entrepreneurial class with credit. Without much prudent assessment these financial entrepreneurs entered into an industry where prudent behavior is of the utmost importance. Most of these entrepreneurs were, instead, the biggest risk takers. Paradoxically, if it was not for their propensity toward risky business, they would not have grown as rapidly and would not have established banking operations.

Some elements of the Russian private sector banking exemplify a phenomenon appearing in every Central European country – a private sector bank founded on the basis of high risk, sometimes criminal, business ideas. Early laxity of entry rules – low minimum capital requirements and liberal government or central bank licensing – helped in the creation of this situation. It is no surprise that most of these banks proved to be failures. In these cases many bank owners fled with the depositors or partners' money, emptied the bank to benefit other parts of their business, or simply went bust because they collected, early on, expensive deposits and bad loans and did not fully appreciate the difficulty of this particular market. A few smaller banks went bankrupt because of disregard for cautionary rules on the concentration of positions toward single clients. In many cases these loans went to insiders. An understandable lack of the special corporate culture that banking requires has further diminished the chances of these 'early birds' to become successful financially.

Governments and central banks have handled small bank and large bank failures differently. Most small banks do not have a large retail depositor base, although a few, like the ones mentioned above, have made fast inroads to household deposits by offering high interest rates and sometimes also good services. The bankruptcy of banks without significant deposit bases is, therefore, not perceived particularly adversely by households and usually does not threaten systemic disturbances. Some of the ways of handling small bank failures include central bank acquisition followed by a merger into larger banks and a direct merger into a larger bank arranged by the regulatory authorities.

(i) Russian interbank crisis. In the category of small bank failures the collapse of the interbank market in Russia in August 1995 is an interesting case, and although Russia is not a part of this study, the interbank crisis has provided us with a number of important lessons. First, it is worth noting that Russia has taken a path different from the one followed by most of the other

post-communist countries in terms of the development of its new banking industry. Prolonged inflation has withered away most of the old specialized banks. Also, Russia did not follow the Central European path of creating large spin-off banks from the credit branches of the central banks. Instead, some emerging indigenous private sector banks have gained an ever increasing significance in the country's finances. Their rapid growth was fuelled in the early years of economic transition by cheap central bank credit, by easy speculative gains in the developing forex markets, by highly lucrative returns on Russian government debt instruments and by various fee and arbitrage services other than crediting the enterprise sector. However, the position of many small entrepreneurial banks has become more difficult with the stabilization efforts of the government and the central bank in 1995. Business sector credits increasingly have turned out to be non-performing and the central bank has not pumped as many subsidized loans into the banking sector as was earlier the case. Interestingly, after the appearance of early warning signs in Russia, it was not the depositors whose panic transformed isolated failures into a systemic problem but the collapse of the interbank market. This is not surprising given the extremely small depositor base of most of Russian banks, which has resulted in their heavy reliance on the interbank market.

The creditor banks reacted to the first signals of crisis (open positions of some smaller banks at the end of the trading session) by increasing their rates up to 500 percent overnight, and in many cases refusing to offer credits at all. This caused significant difficulty for the banks in vulnerable liquidity position. The money market practically shot up for two trading days as the government tried to inject liquidity into the system by heavy buying of government securities from the banks.[17] During these days of crisis at least 300 small banks were practically bankrupted.

This episode has also offered an opportunity to achieve a leap in consolidating the Russian banking sector. A large portion of bank failure does not necessarily create a problem if they do not, as was the case in Russia, represent significant depositor base or fulfill any traditional banking functions. The Central Bank of Russia's initial reaction, injecting liquidity into some healthier and larger banks through buying government bonds, has contributed to significant concentration of cash flow in the hands of the stronger, more professional banks.

Judging from the aftermath of the crisis, the consolidation and rehabilitation process may take more time than generally expected. As of October, 1995, Russian money markets were still lacking liquidity, with the volume of interbank credit operations dwindling for lack of trust and rumors that cash shortages may again hit the banking sector. Most banks, doubting the financial health of other banks, limited the number of their credit trading partners to 10–20 banks and assumed a 'wait-and-see' position.

In recent years, central banks have become very cautious about issuing banking licenses in EITs. They also have increased minimum capital requirements to equal or approaching EU levels. Though this is a welcome change, an overzealous closing of entry opportunities carries an inability among domestic entrepreneurs to create full-fledged financial institutions. In these situations, only a very limited number of financial companies, mostly traditional large domestic banks and large international players, can enter the market. This may have very negative implications for competition, particularly if regulation of non-bank financial services providers is too rigorous as well. Whereas the danger of the first couple of years of transition was lax entry rules (particularly in the CIS countries and the Baltic states) it is becoming increasingly clear that most EITs are entering a phase in which their banking policies should be most concerned about maintaining competitive situations in domestic markets. This is particularly true if one reflects upon the changing regional political climate: presently, each country has established sizeable banks which are interested in closing the market and are able to lobby for their case.

5. SHOULD REGULATION OF BANK FAILURES BE MORE MARKET-ORIENTED?

It must be clearly understood that whatever one thinks about the desirable direction and implementation of banking reform internationally, particularly in Western Europe and in the US, such policy prescriptions do not necessarily have full and direct relevance to CEE. There is a rapidly emerging international consensus among policy analysts that market discipline in the banking sector has seriously eroded in the developed economies over the past six decades, following the traumatic experience of the Great Depression. In Flannery's (1995) words, 'the broad (formal or informal) guarantee structures we presently observe in the US, Europe, much of Asia, and Japan have gone too far in absorbing private credit risks on behalf of sophisticated depositors.' The explicit and implicit safety net that has been stretched underneath almost the whole banking industry in the developed world has made banking safer (at least for some time), but has also increasingly shifted responsibility for safe and sound banking from those who actually run the businesses to the government.

This shift is already hurting the long-term safety and efficiency of the banking industry in mature economies, as best illustrated by the Japanese government's mishandling of the banking crisis of the 1990s. Since the end of World War II, the Japanese financial system has embodied stability, with no bank failures for decades. It seems, however, that this governmental overcommitment to extreme financial sector stability has also meant that the magnitude of the problems that were swept under the carpet was not realized until the recent cyclical, but unusually deep, recession of the Japanese economy. Lack of tougher market conditions for banks in the last decades may well be responsible for a larger government bill in the recent wave of bank failures.[18]

All developed countries have to consider the costs of bank bailouts. There is a trade-off between higher systemic risk in connection with potential bank bankruptcies and adding to the national debt through costly bailouts. If nothing else, the state of public finances in the developed world will keep the question of government bailouts of banks high on the agendas of governments and policy planners.

In the most advanced economies the basic direction of banking reforms seems to be to maintain the overall security of the system by decreasing the government's role and by intensifying competition in the industry, thereby creating the right incentives for better risk diversification and quicker improvements in efficiency. There are several alternative schools of thought about how to best reach this goal.

The main elements of a gradualist reform could include: decreasing the level of deposit insurance coverage (thus providing incentive to depositors to monitor bank institutions); introducing risk premium fees over banks' assets towards the deposit insurance scheme; differentiating between the treatment of transaction and other short-term deposits, as opposed to long-term time deposits; introducing an obligatory minimum subordinated capital (to assets) ratio (Kaufman, 1995); and making the role of the central bank, as lender of last resort, more transparent than is the case in most market economies.

The alternative to gradual reform is a more radical institutional reshuffling, the so-called functional approach. It divides a failing bank's transaction and savings accounts and requires transaction accounts to be backed with fully liquid and securely collateralized assets, so that the payment function of the banks is fully protected.[19] Government guarantees and rigorous supervision cover these accounts, and as a result, the bank's savings accounts do not receive undue subsidies in the form of government deposit insurance.[20] A variation of this proposal is what Talley (1993) summarized under the heading of 'fail-proof banking.' It requires a bank's transactions and short-term liabilities to be institutionally separated and matched by riskless or low-risk assets. The other functions of a bank should be divested or put in a holding affiliate. Under this solution, transfers other than tax payments and dividends between the transactions unit and the rest of the holding would be forbidden.

Interestingly, in CEE, the savings banks are relatively close to Talley's fail-proof bank ideal – a large part of their balance sheets consists of transaction instruments, while on the asset side they usually have a large proportion of low-risk instruments. What this and other ideas about narrow and fail-proof banking tell us is that one may well want to be more cautious about expanding national savings banks' licenses. On the other hand, the general practicability of Talley's plan is doubtful. Usually it is more depositors' savings and less their transaction accounts that are of concern to policy-makers. The narrow banking idea will hardly relieve the political pressure on governments to bail out depositors in cases where large deposit-taking institutions fail. Furthermore, 'narrow banking' is particularly vulnerable in a Third World or EIT environment, where it is not only short-term political concerns, but also macroeconomic issues, stemming from the general vulnerability of the country's financial system, and the consequent fear of major capital flight, that incline policy makers to protect depositors.

When discussing the reforms proposed for EITs, two considerations must be kept in mind. On one hand, we cannot assume that optimistic expectations about reforms in leading economies will necessarily come true. The trend in banking regulation in developed countries will have direct relevance to the relatively small CEE countries. If the need to build depositor confidence enjoys considerable priority and if the leading European countries keep supporting their banking sectors through bailouts and a variety of other implicit subsidies (of which government-sponsored deposit insurance is one), the trend will have certain relevance to the competitiveness of domestic banks in the EIT financial markets. Over the short and medium run, a more market-oriented, and therefore more 'risky,' environment may again mean that depositors will tend toward putting their money into safer West European banks within very easy reach.

Although it is intellectually tempting to contemplate the consequences of more free-market solutions to our problem in EITs than those prevailing in Western Europe, at this stage it is probably premature to advocate such radical reforms. While we have not yet arrived at a complete understanding or consensus on the full economic effects of the short-term monetary contraction that a hands-off government attitude to any major bank's distress would bring about, one should always be sensitive to the very volatile political environments with which we are dealing. The free market approach would have to be maintained for a long period of time in order to gain credibility in the domestic and international public and financial markets. Allowing any major bank to fail would undoubtedly invite vicious political attacks and make the longer-term results of such plans doubtful. To be sure, we would also readily admit that any middle-of-the-road approach is likewise vulnerable to political opportunism and informal interference.

Governments need to strike a balance between over-confidence in the system (that is, they need to avoid massive flight out of the domestic banking system in the short run) and the moral hazard problem caused by unconditional bailouts. When trying to assess the significance of the moral hazard problem, one should certainly not pursue a purist agenda. It is essential to realize that downward risk has already been softened, not only in the banking sector, but in the entire economy (even in countries with developed markets) through, just to mention the most fundamental and widespread instrument, the spread of limited liability over many decades. The realistic goal is, therefore, not to eliminate but to mitigate the moral hazard problem (de Juan, 1995b).

The problems associated with this balancing act in EITs can be differentiated from those in other countries primarily for the simple reason that the magnitude of bad loans is larger. This is the case for two reasons. First, in earlier reformers like Hungary, an inherited stock of bad loans caused the initial problems. Second, in other countries (the later reformers or, like Poland, where the old stock has been inflated away) operational inefficiencies, inherited clients rather than assets, the lack of both professional experience and a culture of prudent bank management, and underlying corporate governance/incentive problems have caused a higher share of bad assets than in other regions, and certainly higher than in OECD countries. For this reason, the initial phase of transition bailout of banks by monetary or fiscal tools was almost inevitable.

This approach, or, more precisely, industry-wide bailout campaigns, is, or definitely needs to be, largely concluded in all of CEE. Previous policies should be replaced by more sophisticated approaches that help to reconcile the needs of the day with longer-term policy goals. A case in point would be direct government (or central bank) assistance shifting to individual bank problems so that the authorities are able to decrease the moral hazard without compromising overall security of the financial system. Indeed, in some CIS countries, especially the Ukraine, it is recognized that more general bailout episodes may still have to occur. If the overwhelming importance of confidence building in the system is true for countries with low- or medium-level inflation, one needs to accommodate the fact that the governments in these countries will still have to step in many times. Agrobank in Hungary and the Czech approach of placing problem banks in the hands of the central bank are the most obvious examples to illustrate this second stage of bank bailouts. Agrobank also is an interesting case because the way in which it has been handled demonstrates similarity with other European countries' handling of problem banks. This approach includes full bailout of depositors, inability of the deposit insurance scheme to fulfill its functions, and the way the authorities have obliged the large banks to step in with a 'lifeboat.'

As was stated in Section 3, in underdeveloped markets macroeconomic shocks to the system have most frequently initiated large-scale problems in the banking sector, making intervention inherently difficult for the authorities to resist. In underdeveloped economies, as in EITs, these shocks are usually caused by government mismanagement and particularly high budget deficits. Governments which want to be responsible for their banking sectors must first act responsibly in macroeconomic purposes by putting their public finances in order and making their macroeconomic management predictable in the long run. Naturally, in the EITs, it is the Czech, and to a lesser extent, the Slovak example which comes to mind. Predictability of macroeconomic management and low inflation helps make their banks, though far from immune, much more resilient to sudden policy changes and unsustainable budget deficits. In such a situation, it is easier to gamble with the banks than in an environment where authorities' resolve is frequently tested in the marketplace.

Tax rules governing provisioning against bad or doubtful assets should not create perverse incentives. Provisioning should be part of the costs of the banks. Ministries of Finance, in their efforts to catch tax revenues, in some countries are ambiguous on this issue. This can only lead to more, cumulative bailout costs to the treasury at a later time.

When system-wide bailouts are no longer necessary, but, because of fear of deposit flight from the whole sector and/or significant shortening of the deposits' time-span, individual bank bailouts still are, the main emphasis needs to be on proper incentives so that recovery is efficient and banks receive the message of government resolution. Unless there is a compelling reason to maintain incumbent management, it should be replaced in banks where government bailout involves public funds. If it is a majority government-owned bank or has been nationalized in the bailout, the contract of the new management should be structured so that a strong financial incentive is put in place to re-establish solvency and liquidity of the bank, concluding in its privatization.

Bank bailout needs to be orchestrated in such a way that the bank's shareholders (unless, of course, it is fully state-owned) carry financial responsibility for the losses. A government bailout that does not hurt the shareholders establishes the wrong incentives. Part of the accumulated losses of two large Hungarian commercial banks, for example, were covered by a capital decrease in 1995. On the basis of that lowered capital, they can meet the required capital asset ratio only if they greatly reduce their balance sheet. In other words, they must effectively sell large portions of their assets. If government authorities are able to exercise the capital requirement, the result will be the loss of market share and significance of the poorly performing bank. Notice that in EITs problem banks are more likely to be within the state sector rather than the private one. Thus, the suggested tough treatment leaves room for market expansion of healthier banks and in this way advances the 'privatization' of the industry. This treatment is usually very painful and bank managers will always have plenty of examples as to how this hurts the public interest. The truth is, however, that in most cases it directly improves the industry's efficiency. Even more important is the disciplining message this kind of government treatment of ailing institutions carries to the rest of the market, as was case with the government management of the Estonian bank bankruptcy episode in November 1992.

Expansion of rescued state-owned banks should be contained by the owner and/or the supervisory authority. It is a common practice of many state-owned banks in the EITs to use government financial support to continue investing in the expansion or maintenance of their branch network, in expensive technology and new product lines, or in new additions to their business holdings. As long as these banks carry large amounts of bad assets on their books and their operational efficiency (credit, treasury, risk management, and so on) does not reach adequate levels, government control of that expansion is needed to avoid moral hazard on the part of managers who count on additional bailouts. Overemployment, typical of these banks, should also be targeted by various measures of the state in its role as owner supervisor.

The American literature also contains a good stock of arguments questioning the rationale for a supervisory authority. Those arguments are based on the notion that supervision may cost more than the benefits it can deliver, especially in a period of rapid technological and product changes in the banking industry. We would not go as far as to advocate unsupervised banking in EITs, although supervision there is generally in an infant state and has not performed particularly well in forewarning authorities about upcoming crises, let alone preventing them. However, since we do not advocate an elimination of the banks' safety net in CEE, it is compatible with this paper's intent to advocate the energetic strengthening of the supervisory functions of the state.

The question then becomes how to distribute different functions of the government towards the banking sector: as shareholder, as lender of last resort, as privatizer, and as supervisor. In addition, administrators of the deposit insurance scheme also have to fit into the universe of different authorities. Although it is usually desirable to have checks and balances in bank 'supervision' in a broad sense, and although de Juan's point (1995b) about the flaws of the central bank taking over supervisory authority is appreciated, it is nevertheless unsettling to have so many agencies around the banking sector as is the case in some CEE countries. Such supervision creates an environment characterized by a low capacity to coordinate and a generally low ability to manage on one hand and a high capacity to create public confusion through publicizing the disagreements of government agencies on the other. There is a vast number of differing solutions to this institution-shaping problem. What we advocate here is for governments to assign the authorities of the different agencies in the context of their cooperation in potential bank distress.

Role of deposit insurance

As logically follows from the above discussion, we support the establishment of explicit deposit insurance agencies in EITs, in spite of the fact that the record of such schemes in developing countries has been modest thus far. We treat official deposit insurance schemes as a potentially important step on the road to establishing credible, safe and sound financial markets. The alternative to this would be accepting, albeit perhaps temporarily, the fact that only informal deposit insurance is a realistic alternative for the immature market environment of the EITs. Certainly it is better not to introduce any explicit deposit insurance than to have a heavily compromised one. However, we also think that in the more advanced EITs the time is ripe to create such agencies, since on balance they can contribute to increasing clarification of government treatment of bank distress, provided the deposit insurance structure is carefully designed. We do not believe, though, that deposit insurance schemes themselves can handle even individual bank crises in the immediate future if those banks are sizeable – ability of that nature will come later. Additional government support will still be needed in the case of a large bank. There are an infinite number of ways to construct a deposit insurance scheme.

At first glance one may think that a voluntary arrangement, supervised by an industry association, would be a more desirable insurance arrangement. However, we are skeptical about this solution on two grounds. First, we believe that in most of the countries of the region industry associations are not yet, and for some time to come will not be, mature enough to supervise a true insurance scheme. They may represent interests of a particular banking group or may simply be immature professionally.

Also, in cases where they administer the scheme, they may simply use it for political pressure to extract public funds for the support of the industry. Second, more generally, a deposit insurance scheme is basically a public good to the extent that the safety of the banking system is a public good. Therefore, it should not be under the influence of the professional association of the banking industry, but under the representatives of the public, that is, the government. Involving industry associations on the basis of determining the rules and practices of the deposit insurance agency is another matter and should be welcomed. Similarly, any involvement which leads to more responsible banking practices should be welcome.

In all instances, the deposit insurance fund should be a government agency. The question emerges, which government body should be responsible for supervising the scheme and what should be the scheme's (fund's) prerogatives? Theoretically there can be four broad alternatives: it can be supervised by the Treasury (usually the Ministry of Finance in the EITs), by the central bank, by the parliament, or by the banking supervisor. Parliamentary supervision seems to be the worst solution, as it would leave the fund open to manipulation for short-term political purposes. Of the other three solutions, the preference seems to be for the ultimate responsibility to lie with the Finance Ministry, with an obligatory consultation mechanism with the central bank and the bank supervision. This is the best, although not a fool-proof, guarantee for a potentially cheap use of public funds and due consideration for the safety of the banking system in general. However, there can be many variations to this rule depending on the distribution of responsibilities for the banking sector between the three aforementioned institutions.

One particularly complex issue is the establishment of the supervisory and regulatory prerogatives of the deposit insurance agency, since it can collide with the responsibilities of the banking supervisor. The deposit insurance governance mechanism has to accommodate two principles: it must be transparent enough to serve the public interest, but it also needs to be broad enough to enable the fund (or the decision-making body above the fund) to use different rescue methods, depending on efficiency, in solving a particular problem; the governance mechanism also must enable the fund to make and execute decisions quickly in crisis situations. Financially, the government must develop a mechanism to enable the fund and/or the supervisory body to identify problems early on and to exercise control over banks in jeopardy before a full crisis has developed.

Deposit insurance schemes should balance the primary objective of protecting depositors for the sake of accumulating confidence in the domestic financial system with their role of educating the public to select carefully that bank which they trust with their savings. The best tool to achieve this is limited coverage, although the limits have to be realistic and maintainable for the government in case of a crisis. In Hungary, for example, the cut-off limit officially is HUF 1 million. However, when Agrobank failed the Hungarian authorities rescued all depositors. This seems to suggest that the limit which Hungary established was too optimistically high. A better policy would be to establish a higher coverage limit and even officially declare government support at that level, than to establish a low limit and then be forced to carry out a comprehensive bailout. In the current conditions of CEE, $10,000 (roughly the Hungarian case) seems too low; on the other hand, $100,000, a sort of rule of thumb in many countries, is too high at the presently low level of household wealth. The coverage limit should then be established somewhere in between. We do not advocate differentiation between different types of depositors – the level of protection should be unitary. The system should not protect deposits in foreign currencies, since the country should protect its own legal tender and savings in that tender as part of a general effort to attract demand for the domestic currency.

Even with the above-mentioned limit, coverage should only be 'almost full.' If the country's aim is, as it should be, to strive towards a competitive financial sector and a financially educated public, it should not give full protection even to small investors. Therefore, under the limit, we advocate a near-full (90 percent) coverage. An additional protection level significantly below the first rate could also be established. In a stylized CEE we imagine the following rule:

up to US$50,000	90% coverage
from US$50,000 to 150,000	50% coverage
from US$150,000	no coverage.

This type of arrangement seems to be politically dependable, while still enhancing at least some degree of competition and prudent savings behavior.

The level of coverage premium should be established based on international experience. Given the extreme risks associated with EIT banks in the present period, however, governments need to support, or 'capitalize' the system. It should be done by an up-front contribution with the understanding that, over time, the government will gradually disengage from the system. Regardless, tax payments and the obligatory reserves of a healthy banking system contribute enough to the budget to make this investment worth its price. The contribution can be a one-time investment or a matching contribution over a short period of time. We do not believe that for the next few years it would be technically feasible to think about introducing the principle of risk weighted assets (or liabilities); however, there may be a few easy examples where this principle could, to a limited extent, be adopted. For instance, if a bank pays a significant amount of interest above the market rate, 20 percent for example, that bank's deposits can not be protected by the system. This decision has to be publicized so the public can be informed about changes. As a general principle, the deposit insurance authority needs to publicize the circle of banks and deposits it protects on a regular basis, let us say quarterly. Premiums have to be established *ex ante*; we do not find justification for any *ex post* charges on the participating banks. Such changes would heavily penalize the most prudent banks. For any bailout costs expanding beyond the fund's resources, the government must take a guarantee.

Membership in the deposit insurance scheme needs to be obligatory for domestically owned banks, at least during a transition period. A more complex question is that concerning membership of majority foreign-owned banks or the branches of foreign banks. Here the European Union directives must be applied; they explicitly call for harmonization of the deposit guarantee provisions in the member states. Regarding participation of non-member states' banks in EIT deposit insurance schemes, it can be voluntary if the home country standards provide for better coverage, and obligatory if this is not the case.

As is clear from the above deliberately simplified list of issues in constructing a deposit insurance scheme, such a task is a highly complex enterprise. Of paramount importance in establishing such a scheme is that it should be constructed such that the government can maximize the likelihood of future credibility of the institution. In other words, the government needs to do everything possible to set up deposit insurance rules so that they can be observed in its operation.

The determination of the government to privatize the industry and to increase banks managers' interest can be a very strong incentive for better performance in the short run and for improving the quality of the market actors in the longer run. Thus, properly managed privatization of the banking sector, which also avoids the kind of mismanagement Chile experienced in the 1970s before its banking crisis, can be a powerful vehicle to make the industry more solvent in the delicate reform period. Within the region, the design of the Polish banking privatization is the best example; it provided the right incentives by privatizing the well performing banks in the consolidation program.

Entry rules have a great impact on the banking industry. Since the initial period of transition is over, we do not need to argue particularly for rigorous limits, as de Juan (1995b) does. On the contrary, we should emphasize that most of the EITs outside the CIS have entered a period of their economic transition in which the worry should be that authorities may close the market, rather than make it too open as discussed in Chapter 3. Of particular importance is the easing of extra difficulties facing foreign banking investors in some countries (Hungary and Estonia are the exceptions in our sample) for the sake of the future dynamism and long-term safety of the industry. Rigorous examination of the prudence of the new entrants is still, of course, an important objective.

A way of increasing market discipline on banks is to require them to issue some minimum amount of subordinated debt. Requiring a minimum ratio of subordinated debt to total or risk-weighted assets is another way of shifting risk to the private sector, since the risk preferences of subordinated debt holders would be similar to those of the deposit insurer. This is because the holders of such debt receive at most a fixed return on their investment, but, like the insurer, may suffer unlimited losses in case of a bank failure. Thus the market discipline exerted by subordinated debt holders would be similar to the discipline the deposit insurer imposes.

A major predicament in using subordinated debt as a disciplining tool in CEE is its potentially high cost to banks. With the high risk of bank failure, the subordinated notes must offer an attractive coupon rate, which will make them expensive for banks. Alternatively, if the coupon rate is low the market will be thin. Also, with equity banks can withhold dividends and provision earnings; with debentures they must pay interest. This may impose an additional burden.

A partial solution to the above problem may be the issue of zero-coupon subordinated notes as part of bank managers' compensation (or bonus). The notes should have medium-term maturity, offer attractive yield, and be redeemable only if certain standards of profitability are met. The bank managers could either hold the bonds or sell them in the secondary market but not below the issue price. This will give them an incentive to keep the bank healthy if they want to redeem their bonds at the date of maturity and realize the original yield. Alternatively, if they want to realize capital gains on the secondary market, they will have to improve the bank's profitability and make it attractive for investors. Subordinated debt of this type can also be issued to shareholders instead of dividends. In both cases, the instrument should lead the owners and managers of a bank to take a better care of it.

The status of the savings banks, both in terms of regulation and market strength, affects countries' options. In cases where the savings bank enjoys strong protection by a full deposit guarantee and/or a legally codified monopolistic situation, the crisis of other banks poses relatively less systemic risk. Of course another question, addressed in Chapter 5, is how to regulate and supervise the savings bank and what to do with its monopolistic position. In countries where the savings bank moves energetically into corporate lending, there is a supervisory and regulatory task to consider regarding the potential systemic risks arising from an inexperienced bank with a very strong initial cash-flow.

It also follows from the above presentation that regulation of the safety net protecting banks is not an issue where exact recipes or an international consensus would prevail. The issue is far too complex and views are too divergent to hope for that. However, if a broad agreement concerning the direction of reforms can be shaped (which critically depends on whether the mature market economies reach any convergence on the subject), the international financial institutions need to pay more attention to, and be more assertive regarding the reform performance in this area of the recipient EITs. The issue first needs serious dialogue between the developed countries on one hand, and between developed countries and the international financial institutions on the other. Given the importance of the safety of the financial sectors and the need to establish transparent and credible rules, regulation of the safety net around banks is worthy of serious international efforts.

NOTES

1. This political economy point is particularly well stated in 'Hooked on Financial Red Tape.' *The Economist*, July 22, 1995.
2. There are countries outside the EITs where contractualism is so strong that it mitigates the dangers inherent in unclear ownership and governance structures, with Germany serving as a prime example.
3. For an explanation of the implications of different policies and starting points for the intensity of the bailout programs see Mizsei (1994) and Mizsei and Székely (1995).
4. In 1994 this share was about 50 percent because any loan with a government guarantee had to be qualified as substandard. This nonsensical accounting rule was eliminated in 1995.
5. Bankruptcy laws by now are present in most EITs but only a handful of them (particularly Hungary and Estonia) actually use them.
6. 'Japan Catches Up in Bank Failures.' *New York Times*, September 10, 1995.
7. See 'Risky Removal of a Support System.' *Financial Times*, September 19, 1995.
8. See 'Japan's Quiet Bank Bailout.' *The Wall Street Journal*, October 17, 1995.
9. 'A Reflection on the State of Japan's Biggest Banks.' *The Economist*, October 14, 1995.
10. 'Clearing up the Mess.' *The Economist*, September 2, 1995.
11. For an extensive overview of handling bank failures in different countries see Goodhart (1995).
12. See *Financial Times*, July 27, 1995, and *The Economist*, July 29, 1995.
13. 'Latin American Bank Failures.' *Financial Times*, August 17, 1995.
14. The Begg–Portes proposal calls for a compete initial write-off of pre-transition debt in the enterprises' balance sheets. See Begg and Portes (1992).
15. In 1995 the service of government debt out of the bailout amounts to approximately 2 percent of GDP.
16. Since this chapter was written, events have demonstrated that the policy described was correct. MHB was sold at the end of 1996 to ABN AMRO, one of the strongest and most internationally minded European banks. The sales price and the pledge of immediate further capital investment was almost 200 million USD.
17. See 'Russian Banking Sector Faces Shake-Out.' *Financial Times*, August 26, 1995.
18. See 'Cosmo's Supporters' Club.' *The Economist*, August 5, 1995.
19. For an analysis of the functional approach, see Shibayama (1994).
20. This approach is also identified sometimes as the 'narrow bank' approach.

5.   Retail Banking in Central and Eastern Europe

1. INTRODUCTION

In this chapter, we examine three major issues concerning the role of savings banks in the economies in transition. First, what is the appropriate role for Savings Banks (SBs) in financial intermediation in the present and future phases of economic transformation. Second, what is the present role of SBs in CEE, in particular the countries examined here: Bulgaria, the Czech Republic, Estonia, Hungary, and Poland. Finally, what are the feasible transition paths for SBs which can be regarded as reasonably fast, while at the same time keep costs of transition and the risk attached to it reasonably low. Naturally, these three main questions raise a large number of subsidiary questions about several aspects of financial reforms in general in CEE, institutional development of SBs, market structures, and so on, which we shall take up in the subsequent sections.

Section 2 discusses the main characteristics of financial intermediation in CEE. Section 3 focuses on the relative importance of retail financial markets in the region. Section 4 discusses the main characteristics of the financial reforms typically pursued in the first phase of economic transformation. These characteristics explain in large part why SBs have not at all or only very slowly been evolving into modern retail banks in the region. Section 5 describes the presently prevailing market structures in retail banking in CEE. Though there was an explosive increase in the number of banks throughout the whole region resulting in an increase in the degree of competition, banking markets remained highly concentrated in CEE. As new banks mainly penetrated commercial banking markets, the dominant overall positions of SBs remained unchanged. That is, retail markets are still highly distorted. Section 6 investigates the possible roles SBs can play in the evolving banking systems of CEE. As we shall point out in the subsequent section on policy measures, it is very important for policy makers in CEE to have a vision of the future development of the banking (financial) system, and to design and pursue a policy package for SBs that fit into this vision. Section 7 summarizes the policy options to facilitate the future development of retail

141

banks (SBs). The major dilemma is between stability and efficiency (competitiveness).

The remaining sections discuss the specific characteristics of some of the countries that are covered by the project, giving specific examples to support the reasoning and suggestions we make in the preceding sections. The section on Hungary is the most detailed because the industry has changed more quickly than in some of the other countries examined, access to information was easier there and the authors were more familiar with developments in Hungary.

2. FINANCIAL INTERMEDIATION IN CENTRAL AND EASTERN EUROPE

The first phase of financial reforms in CEE was characterized by an emphasis on state-owned commercial banks (SOCBs) and their relationships with state-owned enterprises (SOEs).[1] SOCBs had a virtual monopoly in financing SOEs, particularly long-term financing for larger firms. These inherited loan portfolios and the bad loans emerging in them in the early phase of transition (Begg and Portes, 1992) made SOCBs natural candidates for the role of 'the agent of change' (Wijnbergen, 1994). Thus, major parts of available financial and human resources were devoted to the cleaning up of the loan portfolios of SOCBs (Mizsei and Székely, 1995) and to the reorganization and preparation of SOCBs for privatization (Ábel and Bonin; 1994, Bonin, 1995).

The other important common element of the reform strategy was the emphasis on increasing the number of (competing) banks (and financial institutions in general). To this end, entry barriers (capital requirements) were set at sometimes very low levels so that new private banks could be set up in relatively large numbers.[2] Moreover, in many CEE countries[3] there was a period at the beginning of economic transformation in which licensing standards were rather lax and the importance of making sure that 'fit and proper persons' own and manage banks was neglected. As a consequence, new ('zero') domestic banks very quickly started to create serious problems and the failures of such banks shook the trust in the banking systems througout the region. Increasing the degree of competitiveness is indeed a very important element of any financial reform program, but there seems to be a limit on the speed with which it can be achieved.

While there is a widely held view that financial deepening is a necessary condition for fast growth in CEE (catching up with developed countries), experiences since the beginning of economic transformation clearly show that there are several, very important preconditions to this process. Furthermore, if the pace of financial deepening is higher than what the prevailing conditions in the financial system allow, the negative consequences are sizeable. There are a large number of bank and lender consolidation schemes (Mizsei and Székely, 1995) with very high projected costs to the state. The burden on the governments of the bail-outs of state-owned and private commercial banks is enormous.

The reasons why the state is willing (or is forced) to undertake these obligations are wide ranging. The 'too big to fail' argument is much too familiar in this regard. With the exception of Estonia, authorities in CEE did not have the courage to try to test what happens if this argument is rejected. In fact, with very few exceptions, authorities were afraid of the failure of any bank or non-bank financial institution, big or small, because, perhaps, they thought that such failures can undermine the future development of the financial sector.

The essence of financial deepening is that primary savings are channelled to net borrowers to an increasing extent through independent (preferably privately owned) bank and non-bank financial institutions. In order to mobilize primary savings and keep costs of borrowing as low as possible there should be a sufficient competition among financial institutions. To this end, it was felt that the type and number of financial institutions should be increased by lowering entry barriers, introducing liberal licensing policies, liberalizing financial markets (allowing foreign competitors to enter the market or compete through cross-border business). Further, competition between different types of financial institutions (instruments) was promoted through financial liberalization – removing interest rate ceilings and thus increasing the mobility of primary savings and price competition.

To sum up, the strategies that policy makers in the region adopted[4] in this regard led to several undesirable outcomes. The major problems were related to (a) too rapid increases in the number of competing units; (b) trust in the capacity of SOCBs to restructure (privatized) SOEs; (c) a misunderstanding of the basic nature of economic (industrial) restructuring and, thus, a neglect of the 'de novo' segment of the emerging private sector, which turned out to grow much faster than anticipated (Ábel and Székely, 1995, Konings et al., 1995); and finally (d) a neglect of the retail segment of the banking market, in particular that of state-owned SBs (SOSBs). From the view point of the present chapter, the latter one is the most important issue, though the neglect of 'de novo' enterprises is also related to SBs.

3. THE RELATIVE IMPORTANCE
OF RETAIL MARKETS

The major factor determining the size of the retail banking industry is the net financial wealth of households and its composition, retail customers. This is in turn determined by the size and the composition of the net wealth of these groups and other retail customers.[5] In countries which experienced high (near-hyper or hyper) inflation, had non-liberalized (repressed) financial markets and lacked even partial convertibility (allowing for forex denominated deposits), previously accumulated financial wealth has been to a large extent eroded and real wages declined substantially. This was the case in Estonia to some extent and in Poland right before stabilization.

As Table 5.1 shows for Estonia, household financial savings and, thus, retail (deposit) markets may lose their importance in such countries. However, as the figures for Bulgaria and Poland suggest in the same table, this is not necessarily the case, as inflation can erode the assets of other sectors and forex cash is always a 'safe haven' for households.

We shall not discuss household non-financial (real) assets here, but concentrate on the portfolio structure of households.[6] In CEE portfolios consist of banking products, cash and non-bank securities. As Table 5.9 shows, even for Hungary, the country with perhaps the most advanced financial structure, cash holding is very high and the share of non-bank securities is limited, though rapidly increasing.[7] High cash holding is normally explained by an underdeveloped payment system and the high shares of black and grey economies. As the figures for Hungary suggest, product (for example, plastic cards and high yield liquid retail products) and technological (for example, ATM) innovation may reduce cash holding substantially, creating further extra potential for the retail industry.

The relative importance of retail markets is further influenced by the financial positions of other bank customers, mainly the corporate sector and the government. That is, in countries where the financial positions of enterprises are strong, as in the Czech Republic, the relative importance of retail markets tend to be smaller. The Czech example is an interesting one. As Table 5.4 suggests, the net financial position of households *vis-á-vis* the banking system (a fairly good approximation for net financial wealth) is rather strong in the Czech Republic. Comparing Tables 5.4 and 5.7 (using USD for this comparison),[8] we can see that net financial wealth of Czech households (held in banking products) is more than twice as much as that of Hungarian ones (the populations of the two countries are practically identical). Still, if we compare figures for the two countries in Table 5.1, we can see that the relative size of retail deposit markets is smaller in the Czech Republic and, unlike in Hungary, it is slowly decreasing.

Table 5.1 The Shares of Retail Deposits and Loans in Five CEE Countries

		Deposits		Credits
Bulgaria				
	BGL[a]	Forex[b]	Total[c]	Total[d]
1992	68.7	25.5	56.0	3.1
1993	72.6	33.9	63.8	2.6
1994	74.8	45.5	64.3	1.6
Czech Republic				
	CSK/CZK[a]	Forex[b]	Total[c]	Total[d]
1991	50.8	62.7	51.8	6.9
1992	46.3	67.8	48.3	7.6
1993	44.6	79.6	47.5	6.5
1994	44.4	69.6	46.3	5.6
Estonia				
	EEK[a]	Forex[b]	Total[c]	Total[d]
1994	24.8	14.5	23.0	7.7
Hungary				
	HUF[a]	Forex[b]	Total[c]	Total[d]
1991	42.4	66.3	47.5	11.0
1992	45.5	70.7	50.2	10.3
1993	46.4	62.1	50.2	10.0
1994	49.1	72.4	55.1	9.8
Poland				
	ZL[a]	Forex[b]	Total[c]	Total[d]
1993	54.5	95.9	69.0	6.8
1994	54.9	95.5	69.3	7.7

Notes:

a) Shares of household (private) domestic currency denominated deposits in total domestic currency denominated deposits.

b) Shares of household (private) forex denominated deposits in total forex denominated deposits.

c) Shares of total household (private) deposits in total deposits (domestic currency +forex denominated).

d) Shares of total household (private) credits in total credits (domestic currency +forex denominated).

Source: Authors' own calculations based on Monetary (Banking) Survey data published for
             Bulgaria in the Annual Reports of Bulgarian National Bank (various issues), for the
             Czech Republic in the annual report of the Czech National Bank, 1994, Tables III and
             V, pp. 77–82; for Estonia in Bank of Estonia Monthly Short Report, July 1995, Tables
             6, 10,15, 19, pp. 51–58; for Hungary in National Bank of Hungary Monthly Report,
             March 1995, Tables VII/1 pp. 140–143; for Poland in National Bank of Poland,
             Information Bulletin, Nov. 1994, Statistical annex in Table 5.

Table 5.2 The Shares of Forex Deposits and Loans in Five CEE Countries

	household deposits	total deposits	total credits
Bulgaria			
1992	13.3	29.2	37.2
1993	12.1	22.8	45.1
1994	25.4	35.9	48.2
Czech Republic			
1992	9.8	11.1	2.9
1993	13.2	9.2	4.1
1994	12.7	8.3	5.6
Estonia			
1994	10.6	16.9	7.8
Hungary			
1991	30.0	21.5	2.6
1992	26.2	18.6	3.0
1993	29.4	23.8	2.7
1994	33.7	25.6	3.3
Poland			
1993	48.7	35.0	
1994	49.0	35.6	

Notes: Shares of forex deposits and credits in total deposits and credits of the respective kind.

Source: Authors' own calculations based on Monetary (Banking) Survey data published for
              Bulgaria in the Annual Reports of Bulgarian National Bank (various issues); for the
              Czech Republic in Czech National Bank Annual Report, 1994, Tables III and V
              pp.77–82, for household – credits in Statistical Yearbook of the Czech Republic, 1994,
              Table 8-2, p. 163; for Estonia in Bank of Estonia Monthly Short Report, July 1995,
              Tables 6, 10, 15, 19 pp. 51–58; for Hungary from National Bank of Hungary Monthly
              Report, 3/1995, Tables VII/1 pp.140–143; and for Poland, National Bank of Poland
              Information Bulletin,11/1994, statistical annex, Table 5.

Table 5.1 summarizes the share of household (retail) deposits in total deposits for the countries considered here. As currency substitution is very strong in the region (Aarle and Budina, 1995), besides shares in total deposits, shares in domestic currency and forex denominated deposits are also given. Due to the usual path of relaxing regulations on forex deposit holding by corporate units followed in the region, households typically have a much higher share in forex deposits than in domestic currency denominated ones. Table 5.2 indicates the relative importance of forex denominated instruments (deposits and loans).

An important finding we can make based on figures in Table 5.1 is that there is a very strong asymmetry in the relative importance of retail markets. While, with the exception of Estonia, retail deposits are the largest segments in each country, retail loans are much less important. With the exception of Hungary, where the inherited amount of subsidized housing loans still carry a sizeable weight,[9] the shares of retail loans are below 8 percent of the total credit market, and no significant increase can be detected in these shares. The decline in the shares for Hungary reflects the repayments of and write-offs in the old housing loans. The major factor explaining these very low shares of retail loans is the virtually complete lack of new mortgage (collateralized) loans to retail costumers. The reasons for this are the lack of the necessary legal regulations and infrastructure and high inflation. We shall discuss this issue in more detail in the section on policy measures.

As mentioned earlier, currency substitution is very strong throughout the entire region. Table 5.2 gives the shares of forex deposits in retail deposits and total deposits, as well as that of forex loans in total credits.[10] Currency substitution is traditionally the strongest in Poland, but it shows very high and rapidly increasing level in Bulgaria, in particular in the credit market. Bulgaria and Estonia[11] are the countries where currency substitution is actually stronger in the corporate sector than in the household (retail) sector. As the description of the Hungarian retail sector in Section 10 demonstrates, currency substitution is so strong that parallel retail markets have emerged in forex and domestic currency denominated products. Though these markets emerge partly because of the lack of full convertibility, it is far from certain that forex based products (for example, debit cards) will disappear after full convertibility is established.

Another important characteristic of currency substitution in the region, again with the exception of Bulgaria, is that its degree is higher in deposits than in credits. Though, as we mentioned above, these figures do not cover direct forex borrowing from abroad, they certainly suggest that domestic banks, including SBs, are exposed to a considerable amount of exchange rate risk. Actually, while SBs may have a sizeable amount of available forex loanable funds, enterprises borrow in forex from abroad. This is obviously not an optimal situation.[12]

4. FINANCIAL INTERMEDIATION AND SAVING BANKS: THE FORGOTTEN BANKS?

In the monobank system, the savings bank was typically one of the specialized banks, basically an arm of the central bank (monobank) with the function to collect household savings and channel them to the central bank (basically to the budget).[13] It lacked any kind of autonomy over risk management or credit allocation. It offered very basic products and services (time and saving deposits and a very basic form of money transfer) and enjoyed a wide branch network and a full monopoly in retail banking. Even though in many countries, there existed savings cooperatives, there was no competition of any kind between the savings bank and savings cooperatives.

While this was generally true for the five countries under discussion here, each of them had some special characteristics that are of some importance to our discussion. In Poland, the major difference was that there emerged two separate savings banks, PKO BP and PEKAO SA. PKO BP dealt with domestic currency denominated savings and transactions, while PEKAO SA collected forex savings. The latter transferred the collected forex savings to the Foreign Trade Bank (Bank Handlowy). As currency substitution was perhaps the strongest and the regulation on forex the most liberal in Poland during central planning in CEE, PEKAO SA collected a significant proportion of household savings. In Hungary, OTP (the Hungarian Savings Bank) dealt with both domestic currency and forex savings, though the restrictions on holding forex deposits were relaxed much later and in a much more gradual manner than in Poland. On the other hand, Hungary started to reform its financial system somewhat earlier than other CEE countries, and it introduced measures to integrate retail and corporate markets in an early phase. In Estonia, the national savings bank emerged only after secession from the USSR. The assets of the separated (from the USSR Sberbank) bank were never actually recovered from the legal successor of the Sberbank in Moscow. Moreover, the hyperinflation while still within the ruble zone practically fully eroded previously accumulated savings, at least those that were kept in ruble denominated deposits. That is, the Estonian Savings Bank practically inherited only the branch network, the staff and the institutional culture of the former Sberbank.

The role and relative importance of SBs are closely related to the net financial position of households (individuals) or the share of the net financial wealth of households in the total net financial wealth of a country. Some of the CEE countries (Bulgaria, Estonia, and Poland) went through a phase of very high, sometimes hyperinflation while still controlling the interest rate to a large extent. This eroded the real value of households' net financial wealth kept in domestic currency denominated financial instruments to a large extent.[14] In these countries, the relative importance of household primary saving, though depending on the extent of currency substitution before the beginning of the inflationary period (Aarle and Budina, 1995), was much less than in countries where macroeconomic stability was largely preserved throughout the entire period (the Czech Republic and Hungary in our sample). As our analysis in the section on Hungary below shows, while real GDP declined rapidly, real (gross) household financial savings increased significantly. Actually, in Hungary the household sector has been the major source of primary savings. The other extreme in our sample of countries is Estonia, where household savings were largely eroded and a substantial part of what was left was kept in cash. Not surprisingly, as we shall discuss in more detail below, household deposits (the dominant form of financial instrument kept by households) are still a small part of total deposits (some 25 percent).

As we pointed out in the previous section, the first phase of financial reforms in CEE focused on SOCBs and their role in restructuring SOEs in financial distress. Thus, at least in the first years of economic transformation, SBs were very much neglected by authorities. They were regarded as 'too big to fail', but 'too costly to restructure.' Old management was kept in place, and the typical strategy was to let newly created SOCBs and the new banks to gradually take over retail markets. As a result, the market positions of SBs eroded. The extent of erosion depended on the duration of this period of neglect and the erosion of the real value of household savings. New forms of deposit insurance were established only very recently, if at all, thus an implicit (or explicit) state guarantee applied to the SBs. This, to some extent, preserved their market positions, depending on the extent of financial repression (real interest rates on household deposits).

It was only with a considerable delay that authorities realized that SOCBs and new banks have very limited capacities to enter retail markets and that allowing price competition by liberalizing the banking system (allowing and inducing the migration of household deposits) without introducing proper (prudential and other) regulation and banking supervision can be a very costly and/or dangerous option. The fraudulent behavior and collapse of some of the new 'zero' banks shook the confidence in banks (in the financial system in general) and called the attention to the strengthening of 'ownership control' over SBs.

The (partial) liberalization caused another difficult problem, at least in Hungary and Poland where SBs were active in financing housing investments. Liberalization removed interest rate control over the liabilities of the SBs in these countries, but did not do so on the asset side, that is, the interest rates on the housing loans[15] granted in the past did not change. This asymmetric liberalization did of course create enormous cash flow and structural problems for SBs in these countries. The two countries applied rather different solutions to this problem. The Hungarian solution, though it was only partial, did clean up the loan portfolio of OTP, allowing it to turn itself into a market-oriented institution. Though the profitability of OTP did to a large extent depend on the yield of the bonds it received in return for the old housing loans, apparently a sufficiently large amount of resources was freed for investments in information technology and human and physical assets in order to improve products and services offered to retail costumers.

Changing old management and starting to exercise 'ownership control' were also important elements of the apparently successful turnaround of SBs in the Czech Republic, Hungary, Estonia, and to some extent in Poland. This was an important change in governments' attitude towards SBs in the region, with Bulgaria being the only notable exception among the countries under consideration here.

5. MARKET STRUCTURES AND COMPETITION IN RETAIL BANKING

Even though the number of (commercial) banks increased rapidly in every CEE country, banking markets in CEE are still characterized by high degrees of concentration. The large SOCBs (some of them already privatized) that were created after the break-up of the monobank system still dominate banking markets. The only genuine exception among the countries under investigation is Hansabank in Estonia, which is by now the largest commercial bank in the country and which started to operate as a de novo (or 'zero') bank.

Retail banking markets are even more concentrated, in certain cases basically serviced by a single bank. Even in Hungary, OTP, though it has lost a sizeable proportion of its initial market share, still dominates the retail markets.

The overall market shares of SBs depend on three major factors: first, the net financial position of households; second, the portfolio structure of households (that is, on what part of net financial wealth is kept in banking products); third, the degree of concentration in retail markets. In Section 3, we analyzed the relative importance of retail markets, that is, the shares of household deposits in total deposits and household loans in total loans (see Table 5.1). We also pointed out the asymmetry between the relative importance of household deposits and credits and also the differences in this regard among the countries under investigation.

Table 5.3 Market Position of SBs in CEE (in percent)

Country Bank Year	Bulgaria SSB Dec 1993	Czech R. CS Dec 1994	Estonia ESB May 1995	Hungary OTP Dec 1994	Poland PKO BP Dec 1993
Market share in household deposits					
total	58.5	61.9	43.2	66	25.4
domestic currency				70[c]	40.8
forex				55[c]	9.1
Market share in total deposits	37.3	36.4	19.1	48.7	20.7
Share of household deposits in total deposits		82.5	52.8	80.8	84.9
Share of household deposits in total liabilities	87.3	66.6	44.7	66.3	62.0
Memo item: the share of household deposits in total deposits in the country	63.8	46.3	23.0[b]	55.1	69
Market share based on balance sheet					
total	11.0		16.1	31.6[c]	14.1
Market share in households loans					
total housing loans		92.2	34.7	70.0 90.0	98.0
Market share in total loans	8.7	14.6	14.4	12.1	
Share of household loans in total loans		35.9	26.	057.1	76.0
Share of housing loans in total loans				49.7	71.0
Share of household loans in total assets	15.1[a]	12.0	10.5	20.5	41.0
Memo item: the share of household loans in total loans in the country	2.6	5.6	7.7[b]	9.8	6.8

Notes: a) Total loans
b) December 1994
c) December 1993

Source: Authors' own calculations based on Monetary Survey data published in Czech National Bank Annual Report, 1994, National Bank of Hungary, Monthly Report, 11/1995, Bank of Estonia Monthly Short Report, 7/1995, National Bank of Poland, Information Bulletin 11/1994, and the balance sheets of the respective banks and years.

Household credits are only a small part of total credits (less than 10 percent) in each country, the smallest being in Bulgaria (1.6 percent in 1994), while, with the exception of Estonia, household deposits form one half to two thirds of total deposits. The Czech Republic is also a notable case in this regard, not only because the share of household deposits is somewhat less than 50 percent (46.3 in 1994), but also because the share of household deposits has been continuously declining since the beginning of economic transformation (see Table 5.1). The relative importance of household deposits has a strong impact on the overall market positions of SBs (as measured by, for example, their balance sheet totals).

Table 5.3 gives an overall view of the market positions of the Savings banks considered here. They fall into two groups – OTP and ČS with large shares, and all of the rest. Naturally, besides the relative importance of household savings, the structure of retail markets also has a strong influence on the overall market shares of SBs. The low overall market share of ESB (Estonian Savings Bank) is largely explained by the low share of household savings.[16] In the case of PKO BP, the low overall market share is mainly explained by the market structure. PKO BP is only one of the two major SBs with a very low market share in forex deposits. Given the fact that currency substitution in Poland was traditionally very strong, perhaps the strongest in the region (see Table 5.2), this meant a low overall market share for household (retail) deposits. The low overall market share of SSB (State Savings Bank in Bulgaria) in Table 5.3 is somewhat misleading because of the special position of the Foreign Trade Bank which is also included among the CBs.[17]

Regarding the other group, the relative importance of household savings was significantly higher in Hungary than in the Czech Republic (see Table 5.1). Though the market share of OTP in this market was also slightly higher than that of ČS, the difference between the overall market shares of these two banks was mainly attributable to the differences in household saving.

Not only are SBs the dominant (largest) retail banks, but they also heavily depend on retail deposits. With the exception of ESB, the share of household deposits in total deposits are above 80 percent for these banks and in total liabilities above 60 percent. Regarding their loan portfolios, the importance of retail loans, again with the exception of ESB, is similarly high. That is, these banks are truly retail banks, at least as far as their deposit collecting and lending activities are concerned.

The relative size of their household loan portfolios are, however, very small (around or below 15 percent of total assets). The somewhat higher share for Hungary and the considerably higher share for PKO BP are due to housing loans. In these two countries, even during central planning, a considerable proportion of new dwellings was financed by concessional bank loans provided by OTP and PKO BP, respectively. Unlike in Poland, in Hungary, a considerable part of these loans has already been removed from the balance sheet of OTP. That is why the relative size of OTP's loan portfolio was significantly lower than that of PKO BP. As the figures in Table 5.3 show, the major part of household loans in the loan portfolio of OTP is still housing loans, which explains why household loans appear more important for OTP than for SSB, ČS, or ESB.

6. THE FUTURE STRUCTURE OF BANKING IN CEE AND THE SAVING BANKS

It is increasingly understood by policy makers and bankers in CEE that household savings will play an important role in providing finance, in particular medium- to long-term finance for the other sectors in the economy. Moreover, SBs in CEE are increasingly regarded as the major retail banking institutions that will have a paramount role in providing retail products and services. However, the implications of these changes on the role of SBs and the nature of financial intermediation by SBs will be different in the different phases of development of financial systems in CEE. This also means that the policy implications for countries being in different phases of development will be different.

In the first phase of development of retail banking[18] in CEE – characterized by high levels of market concentration and, thus, by the lack of competitive pressure on SBs, in particular by the lack of foreign competition for collecting and investing household (retail) savings – the major tasks for SBs are to mobilize household (retail) savings and to provide safe and adequate return to them. That is, in this phase, safety and stability are the issues of absolute importance.

Therefore, the most important questions policy makers (will) have to address in this phase are the following ones: What should be the nature of financial intermediation by SBs in order to fulfill the above task? Put differently, what should the typical asset and liability structures of an SB look like? What should (could) be the clientele of SBs in CEE?

Obviously, households are and will be the most important group of clients or customers. While product innovation, already taking place in many CEE countries[19] will to a certain extent decrease the importance of the branch network, for quite a while SBs will maintain their dominant positions in servicing households. But households are not the only group of costumers that require a branch network. The nature of financial services and products small businesses and municipalities need also requires a strong local presence. Moreover, lending by SBs should also have a strong local focus.

Besides local presence, one of the most obvious ways of making lending to these groups of costumers a low risk business is to use mortgage backed (in general collateralized) loan products.[20] SBs, due to the fact that they will remain the major providers of housing loans, at least in this phase, will have a comparative advantage in providing this type of products to small business clients and municipalities. That is, SBs should and could play a central role in providing finance to municipalities, 'de novo' private firms in the early phase of their life cycles, and small, typically unincorporated enterprises. This (potential) role of SBs is also very important and largely neglected so far.

The major question in this regard is to what extent and in what form SBs should finance the corporate sector. The experiences of some of the SBs in CEE, but also those of SBs in more developed countries (most notably the S&Ls in the US) call the attention to the dangers involved in relatively unsophisticated banks acquiring large portfolios of corporate loans. That is, standard corporate loans should not typically be the business of SBs in CEE. However, this does not mean that certain types of corporate loans should be excluded from the assets of SBs. For example, enterprises in the lead countries in CEE are increasingly borrowing directly from foreign banks. These loans are denominated in forex and provide mainly blue chip companies with cheaper funds than the domestic currency denominated loans domestic banks can offer to them. OTP in Hungary and PEKAO SA in Poland have large surplus funds in forex that they could lend (and are increasingly lending) to corporate costumers. As long as this lending is confined to blue chip companies (or the sister companies of large international blue chip companies) and to a relatively small number of large loans that can be handled centrally, this kind of lending fits nicely into the strategy of low-risk lending desirable for SBs in the region.[21]

Besides mobilizing savings, SBs will have a major role in providing financial services and cash substitutes to retail costumers, in particular money transfer and payment services, already in the first phase of development. Cash holding in CEE, though rapidly declining in the lead countries,[22] is still very high when compared to developed countries. Product and technological innovation, in particular card-based products and new types of current accounts[23] play an essential role in reducing cash holding. This role, that is, to providing efficient and low cost payment services to retail customers, will become an increasingly important function of SBs (retail banks) in the second phase of development.

The second phase of development of retail banking in CEE will be characterized by a significantly increased degree of competition for household (retail) savings, in particular for those with longer maturities. Competition will not only or necessarily be among an increased number of retail banks (especially not SBs), but more likely between retail banks (SBs), on the one hand, and commercial banks and non-bank financial institutions, such as investment and pension funds or life insurance companies, on the other hand. As the degree of foreign competition is already higher in these segments of the financial system, and it can be expected to further increase, this second phase of development will also be characterized by increased foreign competition in collecting and investing household (retail) savings, in particular those with longer maturities.

The increase in the degree of competition will come from changes influencing both the demand and supply sides. On the demand side, the increase in the aggregate amount of real net financial wealth of households (retail customers), as well as the increase in the inequalities in income, and more importantly in net (financial) wealth, will increase the number of sophisticated costumers with significant amounts of net financial wealth demanding higher yield, and, thus of course, higher risk products. Another important change influencing demand for financial (saving) products is the increasing importance of private pension schemes.[24]

As far as payment services are concerned, the major product SBs will most likely offer to households and small businesses is a new type of current account. This product offers (will offer) an automatic transfer (direct depositing) of salary and other incomes (such as pension, social security) and a direct payment facility for regular bills and loan payments, access to the account over the telephone, cash and payment (debit) cards, a flexible facility for time deposits linked to the account, and a flexible facility to purchase securities (CDs, T-bills and government bonds, and so on). That is, SBs will most likely become a one-stop financial service center for households and small businesses. Through this, they will have an important role in distributing mainly government securities and providing access to stock exchanges for households. However, in this respect, competition can be expected to become fierce already by the end of the first phase of development.

As far as lending is concerned, SBs should mainly aim at low-risk, mainly collateralized (mortgage) loan products, especially in the first phase of development. Residential housing finance is one of the traditional forms of collateralized loans, which has historically played a central role in integrating households, in particular less wealthy ones, into the financial system. As we pointed out earlier, at present SBs in the region provide very little housing finance, even in countries where they had traditionally played an important role in this regard (Poland and Hungary). This is mainly due to the lack of the necessary legal regulation (on repossessing and eviction) and infrastructure (land and property registers), the high and uncertain rate of inflation, the decline in real incomes of households, and the lack of long-term savings. Nonetheless, housing (mortgage) finance is traditionally the most important form of lending for savings institutions, and revitalizing housing finance in CEE may play an important role in bringing about an extended period of recovery in the region. Investment into housing is an important component of domestic demand in every country, and undoubtedly mostly domestic firms will benefit from an upsurge in housing investment. At present, the levels of housing investments in CEE countries are well below their long-term natural levels, thus the potential in this area is enormous. The task for policy makers is to provide the lacking preconditions for this type of lending.

The other major investment families make is the purchase of new cars. The level of new car purchases in the region is also well below what can be expected in the future. The preconditions for a fast growth in this type of lending are similar to those for housing finance: providing the necessary legal regulations and infrastructure for fast and cheap repossession and getting inflation down. Once these preconditions are created, new car loans will be the kind of safe loans SBs need.

Consumer loans are another natural market for SBs, though at present the amount of this kind of loan provided by SBs is minimal.[25] However, any extension of this type of lending should be preceded by the acquisition of the skills and infrastructure necessary to judge and control the credit risk involved.

In the second phase of development, as longer-term loanable funds are gradually attracted away from SBs (retail banks), these banks will be forced to resell a significant proportion of their assets (loans), mainly those with longer maturities, to avoid maturity mismatch. As the recent development in developed market economies in this regard indicates, this can take several different forms, repackaging and securitization being the most important ones. This will create new products and markets and, thus, demand for new forms of (prudential) regulations.

7. POLICY MEASURES

Policy measures on SBs should first of all fit into a vision for the future of the banking sector (the financial sector in general). Moreover, if we accept the fact that the different phases of development of retail banking have different characteristics, then, obviously, policy measures in the different phases should also be characteristically different.

The fundamental question policy makers face in the first phase of development is whether there should be a separate savings sector providing safe products for households (such as, for example, postal savings institutions), or whether a relatively small number of retail banks with universal banking license should provide these products. Except in Bulgaria, this issue is settled in the countries in our sample. SBs in these countries are actually not savings banks in the legal sense any more, as they have been given universal banking license. Moreover, deposit insurance schemes have been (or are about to be) established that cover every domestic bank licensed to collect retail deposits. In the second-wave transition economies, however, this question should be addressed before major reform steps involving SBs are taken.

In the first phase of the development of the retail banking sector, the stability of the SBs is of overwhelming importance. A major crisis of SBs (á la S&L) would be unmanageable for banking authorities and governments in CEE.

The most important precondition for the safe operation of banks, including SBs, is a stable and enabling environment. This includes, in the first place, macroeconomic stability, in particular low inflation. High inflation front-loads the real costs of loan repayment to an extent that the majority of the population cannot service any larger loan.[26] Moreover, volatile inflation induces currency substitution and a shift away from banking products, in particular long-term products. Besides macroeconomic stability, the environment that enables product and technological innovation includes a very limited use of the financial system to channel (guided loans) or finance subsidies (cross-financing). In the optimal case, the latter is not present at all. Proper accounting standards, prudential and other regulations and legal infrastructure are also vital elements. Stability is of great importance in this respect, too. Finally, effective banking supervision is also an important component of an enabling environment. Naturally, a stable and enabling environment is important not only because of the safe functioning of banks, but also to promote economic growth. However, the consequences of the lack of this are perhaps the most devastating in the banking industry.

The stability of SBs should be of paramount importance to governments and banking authorities in CEE. The sheer size of SBs is a good enough reason to do everything in their capacity to avoid a major SB crisis in these countries. Due to their large size and importance, the stability of SBs is inevitably a political issue. That is, problems and measures related to this issue tend to become overpoliticized.

Even in countries where a deposit insurance scheme has not yet been introduced, there is a full government guarantee on deposits in SBs. In countries where such schemes have been introduced (for example, Hungary and the Czech Republic) an overwhelming share of deposits in Savings banks would be covered by the scheme.[27] Due to the dominant positions of SBs in retail deposit markets in CEE, no deposit insurance scheme would be able to cover any significant proportion of deposits in SBs. Actually, it seems inconceivable to let an SB in CEE fail and thus use the deposit insurance scheme to cover some of the costs involved. SBs in CEE are no doubt 'too big to fail'. They are just too near to the payment system and private deposits to fail. Any major financial difficulties experienced by SBs in CEE would immediately require massive public funds.[28] Anything else would be politically untenable.

Therefore, policy measures that can reduce the likelihood of such problems should be taken as soon as possible.

As we discussed in Section 4, there are several sensible strategies that SBs can follow in order to keep the credit risk they assume sufficiently low. The question is how to make (force) SBs to stay within these limits, and exercise the kind of self-limiting attitude in the development of new business that is required. The best line of defense is a prudent management with integrity combined with strong ownership supervision and a relatively rapid institutional development.

The agony of SBs in the early phase of economic transformation in CEE was to a large extent due to the incompetence of incumbent management and a virtually complete lack of ownership supervision (by the government). That is, policy makers (governments and banking authorities) in CEE should give high priority to making sure that the managements of SBs are competent, and if this is not the case, they should replace them without delay. Managements of SBs should have a strong commitment to (and proper incentives to carry out) institutional development programs to improve the management information system, accounting standards and internal auditing procedures, information systems and data analysis aimed at assessing and monitoring credit risk for individual clients. Moreover, governments (banking authorities) should use their power to exercise strong ownership control over SBs' managements so that damage can be controlled efficiently. Though prudential regulations and banking supervision have important role in preserving the financial stabilities of SBs (banks in general), they cannot be substitutes for the first line of defence described above. They should rather be regarded as a second line of defence.

In countries where SBs are still majority state-owned (such as Bulgaria and Poland) or where the state has a controlling package of shares (such as the Czech Republic) replacing management (if necessary) and exercising strong ownership control seems relatively easy to achieve. But even there, the government body representing the state as an owner should clearly be identified and frequent changes in this respect should be avoided.[29] Moreover, no government body with an overwhelming interest in extracting resources from SBs (banks in general) should be chosen to represent the state as an owner.

In countries where the state is only a minority owner (having no controlling share), that is in countries where privatization of SBs (divesting of state holding) is complete[30] this is a much more complicated task. This leads to the issue of acceptable (desirable) post-privatization ownership structure of SBs. Privatization *per se* is not the subject of this chapter (see Chapter 2), but the impact of different possible post-privatization ownership structures on the financial stability and efficiency (competitiveness) of SBs is. In the section on Hungary below, we shall voice our concern with the possible dangers involved in a dispersed ownership structure (involving pseudo-private owners, such as social security funds) and the lack of a strategic investor in the case of an SB in CEE.

Legal restrictions on the assets SBs can hold is another way of ensuring the safe operation of SBs. Such restrictions are present in many countries for certain types of SBs.[32] However, in most CEE countries, SBs are already granted a full commercial banking license, and given the likely direction of future development, this will be the case generally. Thus, the likely model most SBs will (should) follow is a retail commercial bank with a limited range of business activities, which is the typical model in many developed countries. Business lines will (should) be determined not by legal restrictions (on, for example, the kind of assets SBs can hold) but more by the comparative advantages these banks have over other banks (CBs).

Another very important precondition for a prudent lending policy of SBs is an enabling environment facilitating low risk products SBs are supposed to sell. In particular, the necessary legal environment for mortgage (collateralized) lending and the necessary infrastructure to collect and analyze information on individual and unincorporated business clients discussed above are of importance. Legislation is a classical public good, but the information infrastructure also possesses certain characteristics of public goods.[33] Therefore, measures aimed at these elements should form a central component of policies supporting the prudent management of SBs. They should include legislation on property rights, foreclosure and eviction (allowing the quick removal of defaulting borrowers and non-paying tenants) and on condominiums and housing cooperatives, the necessary infrastructure (courts) to enforce these laws at low cost and within a reasonable time frame, and an effectively functioning land and (residential) property registration.

This paramount interest in stability should, however, be balanced with the commitment to increase the degree of competition in retail banking (financial) markets and the competitiveness of retail banks (SBs) already in the first phase. As we saw in Section 5 above on market structures and competition in retail markets, at present retail banking is perhaps the least competitive segment of banking systems in CEE. That is, policy makers should seriously consider policy options that can increase competitive pressure on SBs in CEE. Competitive pressure is essential in forcing SBs to improve their efficiency and the quality, price and choice of products and services they offer to retail customers. Besides external competitive pressure, internal institutional development is also instrumental in achieving these goals. Thus, finally, policy measures should be designed to induce and facilitate this process.

The longer run cost of weak competition in retail banking though are typically much less visible than that of financial instability of SBs, can also be sizeable.

As we pointed out earlier, there are several impediments to competition in retail banking. While existing SBs possess wide branch network, other banks, including large (SO)CBs, have very limited branch networks and very little free resources to rapidly expand them. Foreign or joint venture banks, at least so far, typically operate out of a single office located in the capital cities. Besides the costs of expanding the branch network, the high administrative costs of maintaining retail accounts and the lack of adequate collateral are also important factors in explaining why the degree of competition is so low in retail banking in CEE.

However, on the other hand, at least in countries that successfully stabilized the economy, households are by far the largest net savers. For commercial banks the only potential source of new loanable funds, in particular longer-term ones, is the retail sector. That is, CBs are in a sense pushed in this direction. This is even more so in countries where the government is heavily borrowing in domestic markets (such as Hungary). The natural direction for CBs, as it is for joint venture and foreign banks, is to target the upper end of the retail market by offering quality service for large depositors, mainly in the areas where their existing offices are located. The upper end of the retail market in larger towns will become (is becoming) more competitive, earlier.[34] Increasing the degree of competitiveness in other segments of the market however needs some policy support.

The most important way of increasing competition and decreasing the extremely high degree of concentration in retail banking in transition economies is product innovation. While in the markets for traditional retail banking products SBs have and most likely will for a long time have a dominant position even in the lead countries, the same is not true for most of the new products, such plastic cards. With the upgrading of the telecommunication and payment system, the room for new, innovative products and services is increasing rapidly, and so technological and product innovation is perhaps the most important way of increasing competition in retail banking in CEE. Moreover, this contributes to a decrease in cash holding, which is very high in CEE, creating further sources for banks.

Creating the necessary legal framework and incentives for the kind of financial institutions that in other countries are the typical competitors of SBs in retail market is another important element of a policy aimed at increasing competition. Savings and loan cooperatives (building societies) play a very important role in developing countries and should be promoted in CEE, too.[35]

The second phase of development of retail banking will be characterized by a product and technological innovation-based competition for providing payment (and other) services, on the one hand, and for household (retail) savings with longer maturities, on the other. This change in the environment will have strong impact on the traditional retail banks (SBs). Their cheap deposit base and best customers (upper end of the market) will to an increasing extent be attracted away by other banks and non-bank financial institutions, while their cost base will remain high, unless they undergo restructuring.

Moreover, increased competition for longer-term savings will most likely push up yield (deposit rates), thus squeezing the profit margins of traditional retail banks. That is, what was (or might have been) a competitive advantage in the first phase (a well developed branch network) may turn into a source of problem. Moreover, the higher cost of loanable funds may force retail banks to move into higher risk areas, thus increasing the risk they assume. The loss of longer-term deposits may also create a problem with the maturity structure of their assets.

The task for policy makers in this phase will be to help the traditional retail banks (SBs) through this period, that is, to help them with the necessary restructuring. Traditional retail banks will have to increase the service components of their products in order to enhance their capacity to earn fees to compensate for the losses in (net) interest earnings. Moreover, they will have to increase the quality of their services in order to meet the standards set by the other (partly foreign) competitors.

Increased competition will also mean that household savings become more mobile, moving easily and quickly not only between different products and different kinds of financial institutions within the country, but also across borders, of course depending on the degree of liberalization (convertibility). That is, not only a part of foreign capital will be 'hot money', but also an increasing proportion of domestic capital. Naturally, this will have implications for monetary, fiscal and exchange rate policies.

8. RETAIL BANKING IN THE CZECH REPUBLIC

Economic transformation in the Czech Republic has had several fairly unique characteristics. Most relevant to our present discussion is the net position of the government sector (*vis-à-vis* other income holders, including foreign ones) and the consequent macroeconomic stability, in particular price stability[36] As Table 5.4 indicates, net credit to the government is practically zero.[38] Thus, unlike for example in Hungary, net household savings financed the corporate sector in full and not the government sector. Not surprisingly, net credit to the corporate sector remained fairly stable after 1992 as measured in either real terms or in forex (USD). This is in sharp contrast with even Hungary,[38] where the corporate sector (see Table 5.7) got crowded out of domestic credit markets to a large extent.

Table 5.4 Net Credits to Households, Corporate Sector, and Government

	Households	Households and small businesses	Corporate Net sector[a]	Government[b]
1992	-231.3	-226.0	310.1	28.5
1993	-290.2	-269.0	345.5	18.4
1994	-338.7	-310.7	378.8	6.6

Notes: a) All forex loans are included in corporate loans.
b) Net credit to government and National Property Fund combined.
Net credit is credit (CSK/CZK + forex) minus deposit (CZK/CSK + forex).
End of period data in bus of CSK/CZK.

Source: Authors' own calculations based on Monetary Survey data published in Czech National Bank Annual Report 1994, Tables II, III, and V pp. 75–82.

The net position of the government is the major factor explaining the relative price stability and the rather favourable net external position of the country. Net foreign debt has been much smaller than in Bulgaria, Hungary and Poland.

Another very important characteristic highly relevant to our topic is the – by Eastern European standards – very high level of net household savings (see Table 5.4) Though, unlike in Hungary and Poland, housing was not typically financed by bank loans,[39] total net household savings expressed in USD were more than twice as much in the Czech Republic as in Hungary, even after 1992 (the year in which a major part of old housing loans of Hungarian households was written down). That is, the available pool of primary savings, or the potential source for financial intermediation, was much larger in the Czech Republic than in any other CEE economy.

A further very important characteristic is the much stronger financial position of the corporate sector. Even though household savings have been high and rather stable in real terms (rapidly increasing in USD terms), the relative importance of retail markets declined significantly (see Table 5.5).[40]

Until 1993, the absolute level and the size and direction of change in the share of household deposits in total deposits were remarkably similar to those observed in Hungary. The same is not true for credit markets. The share of household credits has been much smaller in the Czech Republic than in Hungary, mainly due to the differences in housing finance between the two countries mentioned above. On the other hand, though the share of household credits declined somewhat, the decline was much less dramatic than in Hungary (see Table 5.8). Residential housing (mortgage) loans are virtually non-existent in the Czech Republic, and other household loans (consumer and unsecured loans) are also very limited. That is, the dominant direction of financial intermediation is from households (savers) to enterprises (borrowers). As we shall discuss in more detail later, Česká Spořitelna (ČS) had a virtual monopoly in the retail deposit market and consequently collected a major part of deposits (44.3 percent at the end of 1993)[41] and made a roadway into corporate lending only to a limited extent. Thus, financial intermediation was in major part through interbank markets.

Table 5.5 The Shares of Retail Deposits and Credits in the Czech Republic

Deposits

	CSK/CZK deposits: Households/total	Forex deposits: Households/total	CSK/CZK+Forex deposits: Households/total	CSK/CZK+Forex deposits: Households +small bus. total
1990	60.0			
1991	50.8	62.7	51.8	
1992	46.3	67.8	48.3	52.0
1993	44.6	79.6	47.5	51.0
1994	44.4	69.6	46.3	50.3

Credits

	Households/ total	Households/ corporate	Households/ + small bus./total	Households + small bus./corporate	Net[c] gov't total
1991	6.9	7.8[b]			5.4
1992	7.6	9.1	11.9	14.2	4.7
1993	6.5	7.7	12.9	15.3	2.6
1994	5.6	6.6	13.1	15.2	0.8

Notes: Shares are expressed in percent and are based on data for stocks. End of period data. Total credits refer to domestic credit stock.
a) All forex loans are included in corporate loans.
b) Includes credit to small business.
c) Net credit to government and National Property Fund combined.

Source: Authors' own calculations based on Monetary Survey data from Czech National Bank Annual Report, 1994, Tables II, III, and V pp. 75–82.

Table 5.6 Maturity Structures of Credits and Deposits

	Bank Credits					**Bank Deposits**		
	06/91	1991	1992	1993	1994	1992	1993	1994
short term	36.4	39.5	37.4	41.8	40.7	71.9	72.1	72.0
medium term	17.4	18.2	26.7	28.3	30.1	20.5	21.0	22.6
long term	46.2	42.3	35.9	29.9	29.2	7.6	6.9	5.4

Notes:	Shares are expressed in percent and are based on data for stocks. End of period data. Short term is maturity up to one year. Medium term is maturity between 1 and 4 years. Long term is maturity over 4 years.
Source:	Authors' own calculations based on Monetary Survey Czech National Bank Annual Report, 1994, Tables III and V pp. 77–82.

Price stability and the strong domestic currency also explains the much lower level of currency substitution than the ones observed in Bulgaria, Hungary, or Poland (see Table 5.2). That is, domestic currency denominated instruments played a much more important role than in other countries.

Finally, economic transformation in the Czech Republic is characterized by 'short-termism' to a much lesser extent than in any other CEE country. The share of long(er)-term financial instruments is significantly higher than in other CEE countries and remained relatively stable. As Table 5.6 shows, the shares of credits with maturity over one year was 59.3 at the end of 1994, down from 63.6 in June 1991 and 60.5 in December 1991. Within this group, the share of credits with maturities over 4 years was 29.2, down from 46.2 in June 1991. Though the share of short-term credits within newly granted credits remained above 70 percent throughout 1994, the share of long(er)-term credits are still much higher and stable than even in Hungary. The share of long(er)-term deposits was significantly lower, 28 percent at the end of 1994, but it remained unchanged since 1992 (when it was 28.1 percent at the end of the year). That is, another very important characteristic of financial intermediation in the Czech Republic is that financial contracts are much more long-term than in other CEE countries.

From the policy viewpoint, the important finding is that Czech policy makers achieved macroeconomic stability – the most important precondition for the safe operation of the financial system in general and that of the banking system in particular – early in the process of economic transformation.

Banking markets are still rather concentrated in CEE, but in the Czech Republic they have been highly concentrated even by CEE standards. The four large banks (KB,ČS, IB and ČSOB) had 61.1 percent of credit markets and 91.6 percent of deposit markets at the end of 1993; and within this, KB and ČS were the two banks dominating retail and corporate markets respectively, having combined market shares of 40.6 and 73.1 in these two markets.

9. RETAIL BANKING IN ESTONIA

Estonia has a number of special characteristics that make Estonian financial markets in general, and retail and interbank markets in particular rather different from financial markets in other CEE countries. First, the openness of the economy in general and that of the financial system in particular. This makes cross-border banking a real option for a relatively large number of Estonian bank customers (retail and corporate ones), thus making domestic market structure less important than in other CEE countries. Second, individual (household) savings are small and an unusually high proportion of net financial wealth of households is kept in cash.[42] Therefore, the share of individuals' (households) deposits in total deposits in the banking system is much smaller than in other former centrally planned economies[43] and the position of the Estonian Savings Bank (ESB) is far from being 'dominant' in general,[44] though it still has the highest market shares among banks in retail deposits and loans markets.[45] In discussing the Hansabank–ESB marriage, we shall touch upon this issue in more detail.

The second very important feature of the Estonian financial markets is the very short maturity of financial assets. As mentioned earlier, cash holding in the economy is very high in general.[46] Regarding bank deposits, the share of demand deposits is overwhelming: in May 1995 this share was 82 percent. Individuals (households) were somewhat more willing to hold time and saving deposits, the share of demand deposits in this group was thus somewhat lower but still very high, 76.2 percent (in May 1995). Therefore, the domestic supply of medium to long-term loanable funds is extremely limited. Not surprisingly, most of the medium- to long-term loans are backed by foreign (mostly official) funds. That is, intermediation between domestic savers and borrowers will for quite some time be of secondary importance, at least as far as absolute numbers (levels) are concerned.

The third important feature of the Estonian financial markets is the fairly high, and presently rapidly increasing concentration in banking. The combined overall market share (based on balance sheet total) of the four largest banks – Hansabank, Union Bank of Estonia, ESB, and North Estonian Bank – was 68.4 percent in May 1995.[47] The bank crisis in 1992, and more recently the collapse of the Social Bank in 1994, further speeded up this process, as part of the assets and liabilities of this bank was taken over by banks in this group. Another factor that is expected to further increase the degree of concentration is the increased minimum capital requirement.[48]

A special aspect of concentration within the banking system is the cross-holding between Hansabank, the largest bank, and ESB, the third largest bank and the largest retail (household) bank. The combined overall market share of these two banks was 39.5 percent in May 1995, very high and rapidly increasing.[49]

Hansabank is the largest bank in Estonia with an overall market share of 23.4 percent (in May 1995, based on balance sheet total). In the corporate deposit market its share was 35.1 percent in May 1995 (40 percent among private enterprises), in the corporate loan market its share was 19.4 percent (19.5 percent among private enterprises). While Hansabank is still mainly a commercial bank, it is gradually increasing its market shares in retail markets, mainly through product innovation. Its respective market shares in retail deposits and loans were 11.5 and 9.4 percent, making it the second largest in the retail deposit market and the fourth largest in the retail loan market. Hansabank's product innovation relies on its superiority over other banks in banking technology (electronic transfer and computerization). The major forms of product innovation are direct deposit salary account (current account combined with cash card and electronic transfer of salaries) for employees of large enterprises,[50] and card based products (cash and payment, debit, and credit cards). An important element of the strategy is to substitute branch network for technology (ATM, phone based services) and thereby reducing the need for heavy up-front investment.[51] At present, Hansabank is by far the most profitable bank in Estonia: it produced 64.8 percent of the total profits of the Estonian banking system in the first quarter of 1995.

Estonian Savings Bank (ESB) is the third-largest bank in Estonia, with an overall market share of 16.1 percent in May 1995,[52] and the largest retail bank, with market shares of 43.2 and 34.7 percent in retail deposits and loans in May 1995, respectively. After the recent increase in share capital subscribed by EBRD[53] and Hansabank, Hansabank holds 30.1 percent of ESB's share capital, with EBRD holding another 30.1, the management holding 5.4 percent and the rest held by the Bank of Estonia (BoE). Even though, at present, Hansabank appears to act as an institutional investor, potentially an ownership structure of this kind provides Hansabank with complete control over ESB.[55] Just to remind the reader, the combined overall market share of the two banks was 39.4 percent in May 1995, and in the retail deposit and loan markets the respective figures were 54.7 and 44.1 percent. In the first quarter of 1995, these two banks produced 85.5 percent of the total profit in the Estonian banking system.

The interesting thing about this marriage is that it was arranged by BoE. While in other countries central authorities try to do their best to reduce the degree of concentration in banking, in Estonia one can witness an opposite direction of development. The ideology is that, in the future, competition will be not so much among Estonian banks, but much more importantly between Estonian and foreign banks. Moreover, the central bank seems to be less concerned with giving the savings bank to the largest and most dynamic, private commercial bank because, as pointed out above, accumulated individual (household) savings at the time of establishing the Estonian banking system were much less important than in any other CEE country and due to the very underdeveloped nature of (retail) banking, the starting position of ESB, or any bank for that matter, was much less of an issue than anywhere else in the region. Finally, ESB was on the verge of collapsing and badly needed a strong partner. BoE was probably afraid of the potential costs and problems involved in assuming full responsibility over ESB. Thus, BoE decided to involve Hansabank and, thus, limit its responsibility. Moreover, Hansabank was private, apparently sound and dynamic bank, characteristics that were all too valuable in a country shaken by a series of bank collapses.

While most of these arguments make a great deal of sense, this development is not without potential danger. Foreign competition is indeed a major threat to Estonian banks, not only in the form of (fully or partly) foreign-owned banks incorporated in Estonia, but also in form of cross-border banking, a development all too obvious in a country liberalized to the extent Estonia is. Creaming off the upper end of the corporate finance (mainly loan) market is something that will inevitably happen, if for no other reason than because of the sheer sizes of the loans these companies will need.[55] But does this justify the policy of BoE? Before answering this question, let us deal with the other arguments.

Household savings are indeed very low and kept in large part in cash, and retail banking was at the beginning very basic. But these things are already changing rapidly, and will do so even more rapidly in the future. It is difficult to imagine that during the fairly long period of rapid growth Estonia is facing the corporate sector will not have a sizeable demand for (net) loans. While foreign finance, through the banking system and directly, will no doubt play an important role in meeting this demand, the role of domestic savings will become much more important than it is at present. Actually, it is safe to say that retail banking will be the most important market for Estonian banks, one that can provide them with room for further growth. Banks which are unable to benefit from this factor will have very little chance to keep up with those which are so. Besides deposit collection, the importance of retail loans (consumer and mortgage) will obviously increase substantially.

Moreover, at least based on the experiences of other countries thus far, foreign banks are rather cautious in entering retail markets,and so new foreign entrants will hardly pose a real threat of competition here. Put differently, the competition here will be between the existing (at present Estonian) banks.

It is also true that individual savings were practically wiped out by hyper-inflation (while still within the ruble zone) and that retail banking was very basic at the beginning of transformation. But still, in spite of all this, the Savings Bank had a very strong market position that provided it with a strong potential to further improve its position. Moreover, due to the very low level of retail loans, ESB is extremely liquid providing it with a sizeable power in interbank markets. Actually, the Hansabank–ESB marriage was also the marriage of the two most liquid banks in Estonia, giving them an almost overwhelming (potential) combined market share in interbank markets.

While at present in Estonia, as pointed out above, financial intermediation is based on very short-term instruments, the share of medium- to long-term borrowing and to some extent medium- to long-term investment instruments (mainly deposits) is rapidly increasing. Besides foreign funds, retail banking will obviously be a major source of medium- to long-term loanable funds. Banks that have strong positions in retail markets will be well positioned to benefit from this tendency. Foreign competition in long-term lending is much more realistic, but still domestic sources will be important.

What one can expect to happen is not that new foreign banks will enter the market and crowd out the existing banks, but rather that Hansabank itself will change hands and become foreign-controlled. Helping Hansabank to become the dominant Estonian bank through selling ESB to it did not really increase its potential to compete with foreign banks in areas where it was poised to be weak in the first place, but rather created the potential problem of excessive market power in markets where foreign competition is not a real alternative. Moreover, it created the potential for a foreign takeover of a bank that occupies some 40 percent of the Estonian banking market.

10. RETAIL BANKING IN HUNGARY

Hungary was the first to reform its financial system in 1987[56] and for quite a while it was the lead reforming country as far as financial reforms were concerned.[57] This leading role has been gradually eroded, especially towards the end of the period under investigation here. The same tendency was observable in retail banking.

Hungary was also the first to start to integrate the retail and commercial segments of the banking market. The National Savings Bank (OTP) was established in 1949 and throughout central planning it functioned as a separate legal entity. In 1989, it received a full commercial banking license. Shortly afterward commercial banks were also allowed to enter retail markets (Székely, 1990).

Table 5.7 Net Credits to Households, Corporate Sector, and Government

	Households and small business[a]	Net Credits to Corporate sector[a]	General government[b]	Net credits to general gov't plus valuation changes[c]	Net foreign liabilities
1989	35.0	295.3	742.9	1203.6	1019.4
1990	13.5	316.6	752.3	1271.5	1024.3
1991	-225.8	381.0	875.4	1653.3	1134.5
1992	-358.9	300.0	1054.6	1943.5	1109.8
1993	-466.8	176.5	1319.6	2501.6	1346.6
1994	-540.0	262.7	1566.7	3007.2	1774.4

Notes: The group of income holders in this table is not complete, the Hungarian Banking Survey data also carry data on non-profit organizations. As the assets and liabilities *vis-à-vis* this group are very small and this group is not relevant from the viewpoint ofour present analysis, this group is left out. Figures on 'Banknotes and coins outside banks', 'Bonds and savings notes', 'other' within 'other deposits', 'Credits to financial institutions' (liabilities side) and 'Other assets' other than 'Valuation changes'(assets side) are not shown or used in calculating net categories shown the table above.Therefore, the basic identity between assets and liabilities cannot be calculated from the figures shown here.

a) Net credit is credit (HUF + forex) minus deposit (HUF + forex).

b) Net credits to general government is 'Net credits to general government' (from the asset side of the Banking Survey, NBH, 1995, p. 14f0) + 'Credits to local governments' (asset side, source is same as before) 'local governments deposits' (liabilities side, source as before, p. 143)

c) The logic behind adding up these two categories is that 'Valuation changes' is an asset (of NBH) which is (formally) not a liability of any of the income holders. However, from the viewpoint of our present analysis, it can be regarded as a liability of the government. That is why we added this category to net (general) government redits.

Source: Authors' own calculations based on Banking Survey data in National Bank of Hungary, Monthly Report, 3/1995, pp. 140–143.

1. The relative importance and characteristics of retail banking markets

The relative importance of retail banking markets[58] depends on two major factors: the size and distribution of net (financial) wealth within the country (the net positions of the different sectors), and the portfolio structures of households and other retail costumers.[59] These two factors determine to a large extent the direction of capital flows and the share of intermediated finance (channelled by banks) versus direct finance.[60]

Table 5.7 shows the overall direction of net credit flows in Hungary during the period 1989–1994. The not-too-surprising finding is that the most important direction is towards the general government. This direction of net credit flows is even more pronounced if we add up net credit to (general) government and what is called 'valuation changes'.[61] The net lenders are, again not surprisingly, households (and small business) and foreign lenders. While the absolute size of net foreign liabilities is much larger than that of net lending by households (and small business), the rapid increase in the latter is a major finding for our analysis. To a rapidly growing extent retail customers financed domestic net borrowers. The other important finding is that net borrowing by the corporate sector (especially in real terms) rapidly declined until the end of 1993 and gradually increased only afterwards. That is, net lenders mainly financed the government.

Table 5.8 shows the relative importance of retail costumers from another angle. It gives the shares of retail customers in the deposit and credit markets in Hungary over the period 1989–1994. Since currency substitution is very strong in Hungary, as it is in any of the CEE countries, we make distinction between forint (HUF) and forex deposits.[62] In the bank deposit market, there was a major drop in the share of retail deposits in 1990, which was obviously due to the fact that the number of corporate units increased radically while the average (typical) size of corporate costumers decreased substantially. This clearly created an enormous demand for corporate accounts. After 1990, however, the shares of the different kinds of retail deposits increased rapidly, by 1994 surpassing the level observed in 1989. That is, the importance of retail deposits increased rapidly, especially in the market for forex deposits. By 1994, the share of retail deposits was well above one-half and above two-thirds in the case of forex deposits, the latter being the most rapidly increasing segment of the retail market.[63] The importance of small business in this respect is fairly limited, the share of small business deposits declined rapidly after 1992.[64]

The picture is quite different for the bank credit market. By 1994, household credit was less than 10 percent of the market, slowly declining since 1991.[65] The overall shares of household credits are however somewhat misleading because of the continuous and rather strong crowding out of

Table 5.8 The Shares of Retail Deposits and Credits in Hungary

Deposits

	HUF deposits: Households/ total	Forex deposits: Households/ total	HUF+Forex deposits: Households/ total	HUF+Forex deposits: Households + small bus./total
1989	51.3	59.8	51.9	56.4
1990	44.4	55.8	46.3	51.5
1991	42.4	66.3	47.5	53.9
1992	45.5	70.7	50.2	55.6
1993	46.4	62.1	50.2	52.6
1994	49.1	72.4	55.1	57.1

Credits

	Households/ total	Households/ corporate	Households + small bus./ total	Households + small bus./ corporate	General gov't. /total
1989	20.2	66.0	21.4	69.9	46.7
1990	19.2	55.5	21.7	62.9	42.4
1991	11.0	28.7	14.3	37.4	46.2
1992	10.3	30.1	14.0	41.0	50.9
1993	10.0	35.4	13.5	48.1	57.1
1994	9.8	35.0	13.0	46.3	56.7

Notes: Shares are expressed in percent and are based on data for stocks. End of period data. Total deposits equal to broad money grand total banknotes and coins outside banks. Total credits refer to domestic credit stock.

Source: Authors' own calculations based on Banking Survey data of National Bank of Hungary, Monthly Report, 3/1995, pp. 140–143.

Table 5.9 Household Savings and Portfolio Structures in Hungary

Portfolio structure (in percent)

	cash	HUF deposits	Forex deposits	Total deposits	Financial institutional securities	other securities	total securities	insurance
1990	27.1	39.0	10.7	49.7	11.8	6.9	18.7	4.6
1991	23.1	34.1	14.6	48.6	16.3	7.8	24.1	4.2
1992	23.0	36.7	13.0	49.7	16.3	7.4	23.7	3.5
1993	23.4	35.7	14.9	50.5	14.6	7.7	22.3	3.8
1994	21.0	33.5	17.0	50.5	13.2	11.8	25.0	3.4

Change in real savings[a]

	Real gross savings	Real net savings[b]
1990	100.0	100.0
1991	100.3	162.6
1992	108.7	189.9
1993	105.7	187.0
1994	109.3	198.5

Notes: Shares are expressed in percent and are based on data for stocks. End of period data.
Total for portfolio structure refers to the stock of total gross household savings.
a) Nominal figures on financial wealth (stocks) deflated by CPI. December 1990
equals 100.
b) Net of household loans.

Source: Authors' own calculations based on data on net financial savings of households
published in NBH (1995), pp. 116–117.

non-government costumers. If we compare the household sector to the corpo-rate sector, the picture is somewhat different. This comparison shows that corporate customers were crowded out by the government faster and at a larger scale than households.[66] The share of small business credits remained relatively stable.

Table 5.9 shows the portfolio structure for households.[67] The noteworthy tendency is the rapid decline of cash holding. While the decline in 1991 can mainly be attributed to the increase in opportunity costs (inflation), the further sizeable decline in 1994 is most likely to be a result of product innovation (card based products) offering cheap and convenient cash substitutes. Though the decline over the period under investigation here is sizeable (over 6 percentage points), there is obviously more room for further decline. Banks that can offer the products and services necessary to benefit from this poten-tial will be able to increase their market shares (both in deposits and services attached to these products). The other important tendency is the strong currency substitution, the increase in the share of forex deposits is similar to the size of the decline in cash holding (6.3 percentage points). Obviously, banks with stronger market positions for this product[68] were able to benefit from this shift. However, the share of total (HUF+forex) deposits remained remarkably stable. The other major shift in the portfolio structure of house-holds was towards securities, first towards bank securities (mainly CDs), later non-bank securities. While banks clearly benefited from the decline in cash holding, this was to a large extent offset by the increase in non-bank securi-ties. That is, the net gain was very limited (slightly above 1 percentage point). The gain was much larger from the increase in real, gross, household savings also shown in Table 5.9. While real GDP declined by 15.6 percent between 1990 and 1994, real gross savings increased by 9.3 percent.[69]

To sum up, the relative importance of retail markets increased substan-tially and retail products were instrumental in collecting loanable funds. Besides, product innovation clearly created potential for larger service fee incomes. The (by western standards) still high level of cash holding indicates that there is room for increasing the share of retail banking products. However, on the other hand, non-bank securities clearly pose a sizeable threat to retail banking products. Obviously, the major danger is the government tap-ping directly the retail market by means of retail government securities. While this may very well attract away funds presently kept in deposits (and other securities), (mainly retail) banks can still derive sizeable fee income from the distribution and secondary trade of these products.

Another very interesting characteristic of the changes in the portfolio structures of households is the high yield[70] elasticity of the structure. Shifts between HUF and forex deposits, between bank and non-bank securities, and the first major shift away from cash can to a large extent be attributed to changes in relative yields. These shifts have strong and immediate impact on the market structure, as the market strengths of banks (financial institutions in general) in different markets can (did) differ substantially. That is, price (yield) competition was apparently rather strong in Hungary suggesting that the overall competitiveness of the financial system improved.

As in other CEE economies, currency substitution is very strong in Hungary. Put it differently, a significant proportion of the net financial wealth of households is kept in forex denominated financial instruments in Hungary.[71] As the holding and using of forex deposits got gradually liberalized, practically a parallel market developed for forex denominated retail products and services linked to these products. Thus, the deposit market (including current account like products) and the card (mainly debit payment card) markets have two parallel segments in forex and HUF-denominated products.[72] The market shares of retail banks in these parallel markets, as we shall point this out for OTP below, may and did differ quite significantly. Consequently, any change in the shares of forex denominated financial instruments (so far deposits) in the asset portfolios of households leads to a concomitant change in the market shares of retail banks. As we pointed out above, such changes in household portfolios were sizeable in the past and could be explained by changes in relative yields and in the level of exchange rate and inflation risks.

2. The market position and ownership structure of OTP

OTP is by far the largest bank in Hungary.[73] At the end of 1993, the overall market share of OTP (based on balance sheet total) was 31.6 percent. The second largest bank, the Hungarian Credit Bank (MHB) had a market share of 13.6 and another four banks had market shares between 6 and 9.1 percent. Put it differently, the combined market share of the other five large banks[74] was 43.9 percent (Várhegyi, 1995, p. 6). The market position of OTP is even stronger in retail (household) markets. At the end of 1993, the share of OTP in retail bank products (including securities issued by financial institutions to retail costumers) was 60 percent. The second largest bank, Postabank, had a market share of 15 percent, the combined market shares of Saving Cooperatives (SCs)[75] was 11–13 percent. That is, the combined market share of banks other than the ones mentioned so far was 12-14 percent.

In retail deposits, the market share of OTP was 65 percent at the end of 1993, followed by Postabank with 14 percent market share. In HUF deposits, the market share of OTP was 70 percent, while in forex deposits it was only 55 percent. In the latter market, the main rival of OTP was IBUSZ Bank with a market share of 30 percent. Finally, the market share of OTP in the market of retail securities issued by financial institutions was 28 percent, in CDs 15 percent. In retail housing loans, OTP had an almost complete monopoly, a market share of 90 percent, with a 99 percent market share in the housing loans provided under market conditions (non-concessional housing loans). In consumer (car and lombard) loans, OTP had a market share of 37 percent, but the rest of this market was mainly occupied by non-financial institution lenders (mainly retail traders lending directly to their customers).

That is, the overall market position of OTP is overwhelming. However, it is important to point out that in certain markets, mainly in the non-traditional markets, the market shares of OTP are significantly lower. Moreover, while the overall market share of OTP in retail markets is changing (declining) very slowly, in certain markets changes (the decline) is much faster. For example, the market share of OTP in financial institution issued securities declined from 28 percent in 1993 to 20 percent in June 1994. In CDs, its market share declined from 15 percent at the end of 1993 to 7 percent by the end of 1994. The share of OTP in total ATMs was only 50 percent in May 1995, though it desperately tried to catch up with the others who started to develop their ATM networks earlier. Similarly, OTP was somewhat late in entering the plastic card market, leaving the benefits of being the first one to other banks. That is, as in many other CEE countries, product innovation may play a very important role in changing market structures in Hungary (though so far mainly potentially). Product and technological innovation is probably the only way for the other banks to increase their market shares because of the very high costs of increasing their branch office networks. At present, OTP has 378 branches, five times as many as the nearest competitor. Besides the Saving Cooperatives,[76] the only bank that can to some extent compete with OTP in this regard is Postabank that can to some extent rely on the Post Office branch network.[77]

Though we decided not to treat municipalities as retail customers, it is important to mention that OTP has an overall 97 percent market share in the municipalities deposits and loans markets.

To sum up, OTP is by far the largest retail bank. Its market strength is based on its traditions and its superior branch network. Though its overall market shares over time show a tendency of very slow decline, up to now, it managed to retain its initially very strong market position. OTP is not only the largest retail bank, but it is also the largest bank.

Therefore, not surprisingly, the importance of retail markets for OTP is overwhelming. At the end of 1994, retail (forex+HUF) deposits represented two-thirds of the balance sheet total and 69 percent of total liabilities.[78]

As we mentioned earlier, OTP started off as a fully state-owned bank. In 1994, 20 percent of the (then) share capital was offered to holders of compensation vouchers. Later HUF 5bn of new shares were issued fully subscribed by the Ministry of Finance (MoF). Towards the end of 1994, according to the Transformation Act, 2 percent of the shares was transferred to municipalities (from the then AV Rt). In May 1995, a 20 percent package (of the share capital at that time) was transferred to the two Social Securities Funds.[79] The outcome of this process was the following ownership structure (with voting shares in brackets): ÁPV Rt (State Privatization and Holding Co.) 58.4 (60.9) percent, Social Security Funds 20 (19.9) percent, OTP (shares bought back) 2.8 (2.9), Municipalities 2 (2), Other investors 16.8 (14.2). That is, before the recent privatization, some 41.6 percent of the (present) share capital has been divested. The recent offering involves 28.4 (29.6) percent of the shares plus a 5 (5.2) percent employee offering.[80]

Given the structure of the present offering and the ownership structure before privatization, we can conclude that holdings in OTP will be widely dispersed, with the state (ÁPV Rt.) having 25 (26.1) percent, on the one hand, and the Social Securities Funds having 20 (19.9) percent, on the other hand, having the potential to form a controlling block of shares. The latter combined with the holding of management (employees) (5 percent, 5.2 of votes)[81] will however be large enough to counterbalance the state.[82] Moreover, no private shareholder will have the opportunity to gain control over OTP in the future. This, combined with the market positions of OTP described above and the nature of its channeling of funds from primary savers to borrowers described below will give sizeable influence to the incumbent management.

3. The assets and liabilities structures of OTP

OTP is the largest collector of primary savings in Hungary. In this section, we shall discuss the structures of its liabilities and assets, that is, the way OTP pools and channels primary savings to borrowers and the services OTP provides linked to its assets and liabilities.

OTP, in spite of its name, is a fully licensed commercial bank. It has a large number of business lines, including retail, municipal, commercial, treasury, securities, international and investment businesses. When receiving the commercial banking license, OTP started off as a 100 percent state-owned bank. In the meantime, it established a fairly well-developed banking group, including Garancia Insurance Ltd, OTP-Deutsche Leasing Kft, OTP Mutual Fund Managing Co. Ltd, OTP Confidencia Ltd, OTP Bank Security Ltd. Even though this is an important development that has a strong bearing on the market position of OTP, as well as on its potential to grow, in the remaining part of this section, we shall concentrate on OTP Bank only.

If we analyze the net positions of the major groups of clients (state, households, corporate sector, municipalities) *vis-á-vis* OTP (by comparing Tables 5.10 and 5.11), we find that the only net borrower is the state. That is, the essence of channelling financial resources by OTP is financing the net borrowing requirement of the state. As Table 5.10 shows, at the end of 1994 22.3 percent (25. 3 at the end of 1993) of balance sheet total was government securities (almost entirely bonds), 5.9 percent (2.8 at the end of 1993) loans to municipalities, and 25.3 percent (23.8 percent at the end of 1993) was balances with the NBH, the major part of it representing the reserve requirements (18 percent of deposits). Put differently, only 45 percent[83] of the balance sheet total (total assets) represented liabilities of non-government clients. Though in 1994, as compared to 1993, the net lending to non-government clients increased somewhat it did not change the nature of financial intermediation through OTP.

Another important characteristic of the balance sheet of OTP is the very high share of short-term funds, 80.5 percent at the end of 1994 (82.2 at the end of 1993). The share of long-term assets was significantly higher than that, though mainly due to the large share of government bonds. The share of long-term loans to clients in balance sheet total, 23.8 percent at the end of 1994 (22.2 at the end of 1993, see Table 5.10) was only somewhat higher than the share of long-term funds. Put differently, the major source of maturity mismatch is again the net lending to the government. Any decline in long-term funds would thus almost immediately necessitate a reduction in long-term lending to clients. As the major part of long-term lending to clients is housing loans, such a reduction would mean a much larger than proportional reduction in loans to corporate clients. A major potential source of decline in long-term funds is a shift towards forex deposits, as forex deposits are almost entirely short-term deposits.[84]

Regarding retail customers[86] (households), retail deposits gave 80.8 percent of total deposits and 66.3 percent of balance sheet total at the end of 1994 (80.5 and 64.1 respectively at the end of 1993). A further 2.6 percent (4.0 in 1993) of balance sheet total was CDs issued by OTP mainly to retail customers. That is, as far as collecting loanable funds is concerned, retail markets were of primary importance to OTP, and the share of this component was very stable during the last two years. The importance of retail loans was much smaller, retail loans represented 20.5 percent of the balance sheet total in 1994 (22.9 in 1993), out of which 18 percent of the balance sheet total was housing loans. A major part of these loans is concessional loans, new housing loans provided to customers under market conditions (rate and maturity) is very small.[86] Consumer loans represented only 7 percent of the loan portfolio in 1994 (5.9 in 1993), the increase was mainly due to an increase in new car loans and a special lombard type loan to purchase government securities.[87]

The major product of OTP, occupying a key role in OTP's strategy for retail markets, is its retail current account. This is by Hungarian standards a very advanced product, as it provides a facility for an electronic transfer of salaries,[88] monthly bills (utilities, phone), (OTP) loan payments, and retail

Table 5.10 The Asset Side of the Balance Sheet of OTP

	1993		1994	
	Share within group of liabilities	Balance sheet share (total=100)	Share within group of liabilities	Balance sheet share (total=100)
Loan portfolio	100.0	33.7	100.0	35.9
short-term loans	34.0	11.5	33.6	12.1
retail	17.2	5.8	13.9	5.0
corporate	13.6	4.6	13.7	4.9
municipalities	3.2	1.1	5.9	2.1
long-term loans	66.0	22.2	66.4	23.8
retail	50.6	17.1	43.1	15.5
corporate	10.2	3.4	12.8	4.6
municipalities	5.1	1.7	10.5	3.8
Retail	67.8	22.9	57.1	20.5
housing	61.9	20.9	50.0	18.0
consumer	5.9	2.0	7.1	2.5
municipalities	8.4	2.8	16.4	5.9
Investments	100.0	25.8	100.0	23.1
equity	1.8	0.5	3.0	0.7
debt	98.2	25.3	97.0	22.4
government bonds	98.0	25.2	96.8	22.3
Cash		2.3		1.4
Balances with NBH		23.8		25.3
Placements				
with other banks	100.0	3.9	100.0	3.4
short-term	94.1	3.7	89.9	3.0
long-term	5.9	0.2	10.1	0.4
Trading securities		4.8		4.0
Treasury securities				1.5

Note: Selected items of the asset side of the balance sheet.

Table 5.11   The Liability Side of the Balance Sheet of OTP

	1993		1994	
	Share within group of liabilities	Balance sheet share (total=100)	Share within group of liabilities	Balance sheet share (total=100)
Deposits from				
consumers	100.0	79.7	100.0	82.1
short-term	89.1	71.0	89.7	73.6
long-term	10.9	8.7	10.3	8.5
HUF	79.9	63.7	76.2	62.5
Forex	20.1	16.0	23.8	19.6
Retail	80.5	64.1	80.8	66.3
short-term	70.4	56.1	71.1	58.3
long-term	10.1	8.0	9.7	8.0
HUF	60.8	48.4	57.6	47.3
Forex	19.7	15.7	23.2	19.0
Corporate	11.7	9.3	13.3	10.9
Municipalities	7.8	6.2	5.9	4.8
Issued securities	100.0	4.2	100.0	2.6
CDs	94.8	4.0	99.8	2.6
Bonds	5.2	0.2	0.2	0.0
short-term	17.4	0.7	18.1	0.5
long-term	82.6	3.5	81.9	2.1
Other liabilities		7.2		6.8
Equity		3.5		4.3
Memo items:				
short-term liabilities		82.2		80.5
long-term liabilities		13.8		14.2

Note: Selected items of the liability side of the balance sheet.

customers can choose among a number of different types of cards linked to this type of account. These cards are basic client cards (check guarantee card plus ATM cash card), ATM cash card, junior card (for young people with no income or with limited income, mainly scholarships), and HUF-based EC/MC debit cards. OTP is planning to introduce forex-based EC/MC, Visa, and Cirrus Maestro cards, and HUF-based Visa card.[89] OTP had 200 ATMs and 1000 POSs at the end of May, the former representing 50 percent of all ATMs in Hungary, the latter some 20 percent of total POSs.[90] OTP also offers a range of very flexible term deposits linked to current accounts and overdraft facilities.[91] OTP customers can also access their accounts over the phone. The number of retail current accounts reached 1.1 milion,[92] the number of cards issued reached 225,000 by the end of 1994. The total ATM turnover increased from HUF 7.1 bilion in 1993 to HUF 17 bilion in 1994.

The retail current account and the cards and services attached to this account is the major field of product innovation for banks in Hungary, and thus providing such an account is the major way for banks to increase their market shares in retail banking. Besides OTP, a large number of banks offer such an account (and the attached cards and services) to retail customers. Postabank, the number two retail bank, started to offer retail current accounts in 1992. By mid-1994, Postabank had 40,000 accounts (compared to 1.04 milion in OTP at that time). The characteristics of the product are becoming rather similar to those of OTP, though the number of ATMs accessible for Postabank customers is much smaller than that of ATMs accessible for OTP customers. Saving Cooperatives, as a group being number three in retail markets, though offer retail current accounts, their product is much less sophisticated than those of the formers. BB, Dunabank and K&H also offer retail current accounts rather similar to those by OTP and Postabank, but at present their market shares are rather small.

NOTES

1. For an overview of the first phase of financial reforms in CEE, see Bonin and Székely, 1994, and Caprio et al., 1994.
2. Minimum capital requirements have been tightened in several countries in the course of economic transformation. In Estonia, where initial requirement was perhaps the lowest, the latest stage of the increase of minimum capital requirement will take place on 1 January 1996 when it will be increased to EEK 50 milion (appr. US$4.5 million up from EEK 15 million).
3. Most notably in Bulgaria, Estonia and Poland in our sample, but to some extent in Hungary too.
4. Through close collaboration with and using the advice given by international financial/development institutions.

5. In the sections discussing the characteristics of the specific countries, we present available information on the size and structure of household portfolios and on the net positions of households and other retail customers (for example small unincorporated businesses).

6. For a detailed discussion of the issue for transition economies and estimates for Hungary, see Ábel and Székely, 1993.

7. The competitive pressure from insurance companies is also rather limited at present.

8. The corresponding exchange rates for CSK/CZK and HUF (end of period) for 1991–1994 are 27.84, 28.90, 29.955, 28.049 and 75.62, 83.97, 100.7, 110.69. Using these rates, the net positions of Czech households in 1992–1994 were US$8.0, 9.7, and 12.1 billion, while for Hungary the corresponding figures were US$4.3, 4.6, and 4.9 billion.

9. There were subsidized housing loans in Poland too, but those were typically granted to housing cooperatives, thus they show up in other parts of the balance sheet of PKO BP.

10. These figures underestimate the true extent of currency substitutions for two reasons. First, they do not reflect forex cash holding, in many countries the most important forex denominated financial asset. Second, they do not contain direct forex loans of enterprises from abroad, which is quite substantial at least in Hungary and the Czech Republic.

11. In Estonia, a large proportion of formally EEK-denominated loans are in practice denominated in DM because there is a special clause in them allowing for a revaluation of the principal should the EEK be devalued against DM. This is so in spite of the fact that there is a law pegging EEK to DM and banks are free to have as large an open position in DM as they want.

12. Actually, OTP has realized this situation and started to promote forex lending to blue chip companies (and the treasury).

13. In some countries, such as Hungary for example, it was a separate legal entity, while in other countries it was a part of the central bank, like PKO BP after 1975 in Poland. Whether or not the Savings Bank had a separate legal status had some significance after the introduction of reform measures aimed at establishing a two-tier banking system, but under the monobank system this was an insignificant detail.

14. It is important to point out that this implies net financial wealth. That is, if households had direct or implicit liabilities of similar characteristics, such as for example housing loans, they also benefitted from the transfer of wealth involved in this process. Among the countries under investigation, this was important in Poland (housing loans to coops) and Hungary (individual housing loans) where households held direct or indirect fixed rate liabilities.

15. It is important to point out that in Hungary loans were granted to individuals (families), while in Poland, to Housing Cooperatives. Thus, the nature of the problem was somewhat different in the two countries. In Hungary, these loans were not dubious or bad loans in the technical sense as, at least at that time, the default rate on these loans was very low. The problem in Hungary was with the low (0–3 percent) and fixed interest rate on these loans which were well below the market rate or the rates OTP had to pay to depositors. Put differently, the market values of these loans were well below their face values, but the cash flow was secure and predictable. In Poland, on the other hand, a large number of Housing Coops, especially those that could not finish new housing projects, got into financial distress and technically defaulted on their loans. That is, a considerable proportion of the loan portfolio of PKO BP became dubious or bad.

16. For a further discussion of this issue, see the section on Estonia.

17. Unlike in other countries, most of the foreign loans are on the book of this bank. Moreover, Bulgaria has one of the highest per capita foreign debts in the region.

18. We distinguish different phases of the development of financial systems and those of retail banking in CEE in the paper. These phases should be interpreted as logical categories, rather than actual, consecutive time periods. These categories (phases) are defined and used in order to discuss certain characteristics of development, rather than to describe actual development in a particular country. In some countries, certain characteristics attributed to a particular phase may emerge earlier, or later than in others, that is, actual development we can observe

may very well blur the lines dividing these phases. Nonetheless, we regard these categories as useful ones to our discussion of issues and problems. Moreover, the two phases of the development of retail banking defined in this section do not necessarily correspond to the two phases of the development of financial systems in CEE discussed earlier in the paper

19. Bulgaria being the only exception in this respect in our sample of countries.
20. For small, start-up business, the residential property of the owner is the natural collateral.
21. Actually, many of the parent companies have better ratings than these countries as sovereign borrowers.
22. For details on this point on Hungary, see the section on Hungary below.
23. The expression of 'checking account' is somewhat inadequate for the region as these countries have practically skipped the phase of check-based payments and introduced different types of plastic cards immediately. Though, in many countries, there were checks introduced for households, the check never became the major form of payment. With the rapid introduction of cards and related information technologies (ATMs and POSs), cards are rapidly becoming the typical means of payment. On the other hand, direct transfer of household (utility) bill payments and salaries (mainly for large enterprises) made checks unnecessary in a relatively early phase for many of the typical forms of payments (money transfer) for households.
24. For a discussion of the importance of retirement (pension) savings in the process of financial liberalization, see McKinnon and Pill (1995).
25. In the kind of liberalized environment CEE countries are and will have to operate, it is difficult to imagine that the level of consumer loans (including new car loans) can be regulated by administrative instruments. If increasing net household savings is a policy target for a government in CEE, as it should be, it should use other policy tools to achieve this target. Therefore, when discussing the desirable forms of assets for SBs, we shall assume that no such administrative tools are used and that it is not a task for an SB to limit the supply of consumer loans, but rather its task is to fully meet the existing demand for such loans, because it is a natural form of lending where SBs have comparative advantages, and where they can judge and control the credit risk.
26. Just to illustrate this point, let us consider a numerical example. The average size of an apartment in Hungary is around 60 square meters. Assuming that the average cost of building one square meter is around HUF 40,000 (roughly correct number), the total costs of such a dwelling is around HUF2.4m. Assuming a 50 percent mortgage and an interest rate of 35 percent (repo rate is still above 30 percent at present) just the interest payment (that is assuming that no principal is repaid) would amount to HUF 420,000 a year, or HUF 35,000 a month. This compares to the average net salary of 23,473 (first quarter 1995). Not surprisingly, while the number of newly built residential units declined dramatically since 1989, the size and value of them increased rapidly. Obviously, these units are not built by or for people with an average income nor are they typically financed by mortgage loans from SBs.
27. Deposit insurance schemes are typically designed to protect 'small investors', the dominant group among the clients of SBs. The usual limits on amounts covered by such schemes are well above the average size of deposits in SBs.
28. For illustrative purposes, let's take the example of OTP. The balance sheet total of OTP at the end of 1994 was HUF939.9 bn. Taking the typical share of dubious (problem) loans observed in CBs in the region (20-25 percent), the potential amount of losses comes to HUF 190 to 235bn (US$1.70 to 2.10bn). This amount would no doubt be a major blow to the Hungarian budget (the amount of public money involved in the two bank consolidation schemes in Hungary was around US$1 and 3bn). What is even worse is that, as the recent experience of Hungarian SOCBs shows, if proper measures are not taken, banks can very quickly accumulate new problem loans after a balance sheet clean-up.
29. The Hungarian experience in this respect is a very striking one. The far too frequent shifts in the control over the state holding in banks among the Ministry of Finance, the State Property Agency and the State Holding Company made it almost impossible to exercise a strong own-

ership supervision over banks. The frictions among these agencies and the lack of ability of any of them to gain a full control over the state holding in banks created an undesirably large room for manoeuvering for incumbent bank managements.

30. Or has reached the level where the state has lost its control over SBs as an owner.

31. The Japanese postal banking system being the best known example.

32. Most notably, strong positive externalities. Though exclusion is relatively easy, the potential saving in avoiding parallel systems and the potential costs involved in non-cooperation among parallel systems makes coordination a lucrative option.

33. There are already clear signs of such a development in Hungary. The new state-of-the-art branch of Citibank in the heart of Budapest, offering exactly the same kind and quality of service as the branch on Fifth Avenue, is just one example to support this statement.

34. In the Czech Republic, the necessary legislation has been passed and the first licenses have already been granted.

35. Though inflation in 1991 was rather high, 56.7 percent in terms of CPI and 70.4 percent in terms of PPI, this was widely perceived as a one-time adjustment in price level and relative prices, rather than usual inflation, as most changes concentrated in the first quarter of the year and inflation afterwards remained at a much lower level. Consumer prices shot up again in 1993, though to a much lesser extent, by 21.5 percent, but this was again mainly due to a one-time change, namely the introduction of VAT. The perception of (relative) price stability was further created by the strong domestic currency.

36. See the section on Hungary below, and Table 5.7 in particular.

37. The only other country in CEE that could maintain a relative macroeconomic stability throughout the entire process of economic transformation, at least so far.

38. Granted to either directly to families, as was the case in Hungary, or to housing cooperatives, as in Poland.

39. This true even for the period after 1991, though the decline in this period is much less than the one from 1990 to 1991.

40. 55.7, 51.2 and 44.3 percent in 1991, 1992, and 1993 respectively, that is somewhat more than the shares of household deposits in these years.

41. In January 1995 (the latest available data), cash holding of households equalled their holding of bank deposits. The same ratio between cash and deposits in Hungary was 1:2.4 (also in January 1995).

42. The share of deposits held by individuals among total deposits in commercial banks was 24.9 percent at the end of May 1995. The same share for Hungarian banks was 55.1 percent in December 1994.

43. Based on the balance sheet total, the market share of ESB was 16.1 percent at the end of March 1995. The increase in the balance sheet total of ESB over the 12 month ending in March 1995 was 89.5 percent, slightly above the average increase for the four large banks. In Hungary, the overall market share of OTP was some 31 percent at the end of 1994.

44. The market share of ESB in individuals' deposit market was 43.2 percent in May 1995. The combined market share of the other four large players – Hansabank, Tallin Bank, Union Bank of Estonia, and North-Estonian Bank – was 36.4 percent.

45. The ratio between cash and non-government, domestic currency denominated deposits in banks was roughly 1:2 in May 1995. The same ratio in Hungary was 1:3.5 (in January 1995). The ratio is probably even higher in Hungary if foreign currency denominated deposits and foreign cash are taken into account. However, figures on the latter (foreign cash) are not available.

46. The combined market share of this group was 55.2 percent in March 1994, 62.1 percent in December 1994, and 66.4 percent in March 1995.

47. By 1 January 1996, that is within a short period after the previous increase in minimum capital requirement in April 1995, banks' own funds should reach EEK50 m (US$4.5m, up from EEK 15m).

48. Their combined market share was 29.7 percent in March 1994, and 37.4 percent in March 1995.
49. Mainly due to the introduction of this product, the bank clientele increased rapidly, over 3.5 times, and for the first time, the number of retail customers (13,800) surpassed the number of legal entities (10,000) (Hansabank, 1994, p. 17).
50. In 1994, Hansabank invested EEK 16m into a state-of-art computer systems network. The before-tax net income was EEK 71.2m in 1994. The number of on-line terminals increased by almost 50 percent and reached 450, out of which 200 are used for customer service. In 1994, the number of branch offices increased from 6 to 13 (out of which 7 were in Tallin). The number of cards increased to over 4000 by the end of 1994. The average monthly ATM turnover increased (from practically zero) to over EEK 15m (Hansabank, 1994, pp. 17–19.)
51. The respective figures in March 1994 and March 1995 were 13.2 and 16.1 percent.
52. In addition to subscribing part of the new share issue, EBRD provided ESB with a credit line of DM 13m (EEK 104m, some 18 percent of the total loan portfolio at the end of 1994) providing medium-term funding for lending to small- and medium-sized enterprises. The value of the equity investment was US$3m (some 28 percent of the equity at the end of 1994).
53. Based on the experience with previous EBRD investments into CEE banks, EBRD can be expected to exercise very weak control, if any, over ESB.
54. At present, the largest amount of syndicated loan Hansabank, ESB and the Estonian Investment Bank, the three largest credit institutions, can offer to a single borrower (group of jointly owned firms) is EEK 120m, US$10.9m. The largest investment project in Estonia is the Port of Tallin project with a total investment of US$600 m, but even a recent loan to a cement factory was in the range of US$40m, almost four times as large as the combined lending capacity of these banks.
55. For further details of the development until the beginning of economic transformation, see Székely (1990) and Balassa (1992).
56. For reviews of the overall development of the Hungarian financial system, see, for example, Bonin and Székely (1994), Estrin, Hare, and Surányi (1992), Piper, Ábel, and Király (1994), Székely (1994), and Várhegyi (1994, 1995). For an analysis of the possible directions of future development in this respect, see Király (1993).
57. Under central planning, retail banking was highly monopolized and the financial system was designed in a way to make sure that a change in the net financial position of households did not have a direct (immediate) impact on that of the corporate sector. However, as empirical analysis suggests, this segmentation was not perfect in Hungary (see Ábel and Székely, 1992).
58. In the present analysis, we shall take households (individual financial investors, or non-corporate, non-government, non-profit institutions) and small enterprises as retail customers. Enterprises (other than small ones) are clearly customers for merchandise (commercial) banks. Central government, though it can bank with any large bank in principle, obviously cannot be regarded as a retail customer. Municipalities are a border case, as the kinds of products and services they demand are very similar in nature to those offered to traditional retail customers. This segment of the market, as we shall see, is indeed important for OTP, though more so potentially than at present. Nonetheless, mainly due to the fact that similar figures are not easily (or at all) available for the other countries, we shall not regard municipalities as retail customers.
59. This distinction is not necessarily the same as the one between deposits and securities, as a major part of securities is issued by banks (most importantly CDs) and held by retail customers.
60. The latter is a very strange asset (in the balance sheet of NBH) as it is not a liability of anyone at least not formally. However, we can say that 'at the end of the day' this is a liability of the government, even though it is not paying interest on it, at least not yet. If policy (law) makers will ever decide to remove this asset from the balance sheet of NBH, the only conceivable technique is to substitute this item for government bonds or credits (with positive

yield). That is why we are convinced that in our analysis this item should be treated as a government liability.

61. We do not make the same distinction on the credit side, as retail customers, at least so far, have not been allowed to take out credits denominated in foreign currencies. The same is not true for enterprises, but this is not relevant in the present context.

62. This situation may well change as the restrictions on the holding of forex deposits by corporate units have been partly removed recently. This change may result in an increase in the share of corporate forex deposits.

63. This is however partly due to changes in the methodology used in compiling these data.

64. The major decline from 1990 to 1991 was the result of a special scheme for concessional housing loans. It was basically a one-time transfer of liabilities from households to government. For further details of this scheme, see Sagari and Chiquier (1992).

65. This is explained mainly by the nature of the loans households had, the bulk of what was left was the remainder of housing loans.

66. In the present analysis, we concentrate on financial assets and the factors determining the relative importance of them within household portfolios. However, the substitution between financial and non-financial assets is also an important aspect of the issue under investigation here, in particular in the case of former CPEs. For a detailed analysis on this aspect for Hungary, see Ábel and Székely (1993).

67. Most notably IBUSZ Bank, as we will see below when we analyze the market position of OTP.

68. The difference is probably even larger in reality as the increase in CPI, used in deflating savings, was higher than the increase in the implicit GDP price deflator. The very rapid increase in real net savings is somewhat misleading as it was mainly due to the transfer of liabilities from households to government mentioned earlier. Nonetheless, the decline in real household credit is also an important characteristic of the development, as we pointed out earlier.

69. Risk-adjusted relative yield.

70. At the end of 1994, one-third of the total amount of household deposits was in forex denominated deposits. No data is available on forex cash holding of households.

71. So far, no such parallel markets evolved for loans and bank securities, mainly because of the still remaining restrictions. If and when the restrictions are removed, these parallel segments will no doubt evolve. The two segments are sometimes linked, as forex deposits have been frequently used as collateral to HUF denominated retail loans. A special repo window by the NBH supported this construction.

72. In the present analysis, we focus on the market position of OTP. For more general analyses of market structures and competitiveness of the Hungarian banking sector see Vittas and Neal (1992) and Abel and Székely (1994).

73. MHB (13.6 percent), Hungarian Foreign Trade Bank (MKB, 9.1 percent), Hungarian Commerce and Credit Bank (K&H, 8.8 percent), Postabank (6.4 percent) and Budapest Bank (BB, 6 percent).

74. At that time there were 259 Saving Cooperatives.

75. Though the number of SCs (and Credit Cooperatives) is large, there is hardly any competition between OTP and them. SCs are mainly present in places where there is no OTP branch office, and individually, they are very small and provide only basic services.

76. Postabank clients can withdraw money from their passbook at any Post Office branch.

77. Lines 64+79, liabilities other than Accrued interest payables, Provisions and Equity. CDs represented another 3 percent of balance sheet total.

78. According to the Privatization Act, the MoF's holding of 5 m shares was transferred to APV, the State Privatization and Holding company in June 1995.

79. The privatization of OTP, that is, the present offering of shares mentioned above, is a topic to be discussed by the issue paper on bank privatization. From our viewpoint, the only important aspect of this change in the ownership structure of OTP is the final structure of holdings and the likely impact of this on the future behaviour of OTP.

80. The 2.8 percent bought back from the market (from those who swapped their compensation vouchers for OTP shares) will eventually end up in the hands of the management.
81. The recent events at the share holders' meeting showed that such an alliance is not at all only a theoretical possibility.
82. This number also includes the treasury securities in the trading securities portfolio of OTP. Though municipalities represent only a small part of OTP business, it is important to point out that municipalities as a group was a net lender both in 1993 and 1994.
83. As Table 5.11 shows, there was such a shift between 1993 and 1994, but so far it has been offset by an increase in the share of long-term HUF funds.
84. In the balance sheet of OTP, small businesses are treated as corporate (commercial) clients. Thus, in this section, we shall follow this classification, that is, retail customers will mean households.
85. The share of housing loans granted after 1993 in total housing loans was 7.4 percent in 1994.
86. The purchased government securities served as collateral. The purpose of the purchase was to become eligible for tax deduction.
87. Mainly for large enterprises. The increase in the number of such accounts is attributable to this facility, as several large enterprises signed up with OTP in order to be able to abandon cash payment of salaries.
88. All these cards are debit cards, no credit card is planned.
89. OTP paired up with BB and MKB to unify their ATM networks by mutually accepting the EC/MC cards they issue. The competing group consists of NBH, MHB, Postabank, K&H, IBUSZ Bank, Creditanstalt and Agrobank having a total of 97 ATMs. The total number of ATMs was 400 at the end of May 1995.
90. Recently OTP started to offer a flexible security investments scheme also linked to this type of account, though the security customers may purchase this way is not issued by OTP but a separate finance firm.
91. The number of households in Hungary is 3.4 m, that is roughly every third household has a retail current account with OTP.

References

Newspapers articles and data sources are referenced in the text or footnotes as they appear. This reference list includes books and articles that are referenced in the text by author and year of publication.

Aarle, van B. and Budina, N. (1995), 'Currency Substitution in Eastern Europe,' Tenth Annual Congress of the European Economic Association, Prague, September.

Ábel, I. and Bonin, J.P. (1994), 'Financial Sector Reform in the Economies in Transition: On the Way To Privatizing Commercial Banks,' in Bonin, J. and Székely, I.P.(eds).

Ábel, I. and Székely, I.P. (1992), 'Monetary Policy and Separated Monetary Circuits in a Modified Centrally Planned Economy: The Case of Hungary,' *Acta Oeconomica* 44(3–4), pp.393–428.

Ábel, I. and Székely, I.P. (1993), 'Changing Structure of Household Portfolios in Emerging Market Economies: The Case of Hungary, 1970–1989,' in Székely, I.P. and Newbery, D.M.G. (eds), *Hungary: An Economy in Transition*, Cambridge, Cambridge University Press, pp.163–80.

Ábel, I. and Székely, I.P. (1994), 'Market Structures and Competition in the Hungarian Banking System,' in Bonin, J.and Székely, I.P.(eds), pp.272–92.

Ábel, I. and Székely, I.P. (1995), 'The Economic Environment for Enterprise Restructuring: Financial Sector Reforms,' ACE Conference on Corporate Adjustment, Market Failures and Industrial Policy in the Transition, Prague, May.

Ambrus L. (1995), 'Large Monetary Institutions and Monetary Policy during Transition: Ramifications of the Lender of Last Resort Function' (Manuscript).

Balassa, Á. (1992), 'The Transformation and Development of the Hungarian Banking System,' in Kemme, D.M. and Rudka, A.(eds), *Monetary and Banking Reform in the Postcommunist Economies,* New York, Institute for EastWest Studies.

The Banking System in Poland, 1992–93: A Guide to the Polish Banks and the Banking Sector, Ministry of Finance and Polish Development Bank, Warsaw.

Barnea, E. and Goldberg, L. (1995), 'Absence of Foreign Banks In Israel: An Industrial Organization Theory of Foreign Banking,' Bank of Israel Working Paper, August.

Begg, D. and Portes, R. (1992), 'Enterprise Debt and Economic Transformation: Financial Restructuring in the State Sector in Central and Eastern Europe,' Discussion Paper Series No.695, Centre for Economic Policy Research, London.

Belka, M. (1995), 'Financial Restructuring of Banks and Enterprises: The Polish Solution,' in *Bad Enterprise Debts in Central and Eastern Europe*, Mizsei, K. and Székely, I.P. (eds), Institute for EastWest Studies.

Benston, G.J. et al. (1986), *Perspectives on Safe and Sound Banking: Past, Present and Future.* MIT Press, Cambridge, Massachusetts and London, England.

Bisignano, J. (1992), 'Banking in the European Community: Structure, Competition and Public Policy, in *'Banking Structures in Major Countries,'* George Kaufman (eds), Kluwer Publishers.

Bonin, J.P. and Leven, B. (1995), 'Polish Banks Prepare for the Foreign Invasion: Consolidation – Orchestrated or Market Driven?' August.

Bonin, J.P. and Leven, B. (1996), 'Polish Bank Consolidation and Foreign Competition: Creating a Market–Oriented Banking Sector,' *Journal of Comparative Economics,* 23(1),August, pp.52–73.

Bonin, J.P. and Wachtel, P. (1996), 'Towards Market–Oriented Banking in the Economies in Transition,' Second Dubrovnik Conference on Transition Economies, June.

Bonin, J.P. and Székely, I.P. (eds) (1994), *The Development and Reform of Financial Systems in Central and Eastern Europe,* London, Edward Elgar.

Brealey, R.A. and Kaplanis, E. (1994), 'The Growth and Structure of International Banking,' The City Research Project Subject Report, London Business School, July.

Capek, A. (1995), 'The Bad Loans and the Commercial Banks Policies in the Czech Republic,' Institute of Economics, Czech National Bank, May.

Caprio, G., Folkerts–Landau, D., and Lane, T.D. (eds) (1994), *Building Sound Finance in Emerging Market Economies,'* Washington, D.C., International Monetary Fund and World Bank.

De Juan, A. (1995a), 'The Roots of Banking Crisis: Microeconomic Issues and Issues of Supervision and Regulation,' (Manuscript).

De Juan, A. (1995b), 'False Friends in Banking Reform,' (Manuscript).

Dobrinsky, R. (1994), 'The Problem of Bad Loans and Enterprise Indebtedness in Bulgaria,' MOST, 4:37–58.

Estrin, S., Hare, P. and Suranyi, M. (1992), 'Banking in Transition: Development and Current Problems in Hungary,' *Soviet Studies*, 44(5).

The Financial System in Poland, 1993–1994: A Guide to the Polish Financial Sector, Polish Development Bank with association of Ministry of Finance, Warsaw.

Flannery, M.J. (1995), 'Prudential Regulation for Banks,' in Sawamoto, K., Nakajima, Z. and Taguchi, H.(eds).

Gardner, Edward P.M. and Molyneux, P. (1990), *Changes in Western European Banking*, London: Unwin Hyman.

Goodhart, C.A.E. (1995), *The Central Bank and the Financial System*, MacMillan Press, London.

Hansson, A. (1994), 'Reforming the Banking System in Estonia,' Paper prepared for the LSE/IEWS conference on Banking Reform in FSU and Eastern Europe: Lessons from Central Europe.'

Hirvensalo, I. (1994), 'Banking Reform in Estonia,' in *Review of Economics in Transition*, No.8, Bank of Finland and Baltic Economies in Transition, Bank of Finland.

Hoschka, T. (1993), *Cross–Border Entry in European Retail Financial Services*, New York: St.Martin's Press.

IEWS (1994), *Policy Recommendations on Banks, Capital Markets and Enterprise Restructuring.* Prepared by the Drafting Committee of the Comparative Privatization Project, December 9.

International Monetary Fund (1995), 'International Capital Markets: Developments, Prospects and Policy Issues,' August.

Kaufman, G. (1995), 'The US Banking Debacle: An Overview and Lessons,' *The Financier,* 2(2), May.

Király, J. (1993), 'A pénzügyi szektor fejlödése 1993–2005' (The Development of the Financial Sector 1993–2005), (mimeo), International Training Center for Bankers, Budapest.

Konings, J. Lehmann, H. and Schaffer, M.A. (1995), 'Employment Growth, Job Creation and Job Destruction in Polish Industry: 1988–91', (mimeo).

Kormendi, R.C. and Schatterly, K. (1996), 'Bank Privatization in Hungary and the Magyar Kulkereskedelmi Bank Transaction,' William Davidson Institute, University of Michigan, March.

McKinnon, R.I., and Pill, H. (1995), 'Credible Liberalizations and International Capital Flows: The Over–borrowing Syndrome,' Stanford University, (mimeo).

Mejstrk, M. (1995), 'The Banking Sector and the Non–Financial Sector: Their Roles in Privatization of the Economy and of the Banks Themselves,' June.

Mizsei, K.and Székely, I.P. (eds) (1995), 'Bad Enterprise Debts in Central and Eastern Europe,' New York, Institute for EastWest Studies.

Petkova, I. (1995), 'Bank Privatization in Bulgaria,' Conference on The Role of the Banking System in the Economic Transformation of Central European Economies, Warsaw, May.

Pierce, J.L. (1991), *The Future of Banking,* Yale University Press, New Haven, London.

Piper, R.P., Ábel, I. and Király, J. (1994), 'Transformation at a Cross–roads: Financial Sector Reform in Hungary,' Policy Study No.5, The Joint Hungarian–International Blue Ribbon Commission.

Rojas–Suarez, L. and Weisbrod, S.R. (1995), 'Resolving the Banking Crises of the 1990s in Latin America,' *The Brown Journal of World Affairs,* Summer.

Sagari, S.B. and Chiquier, L. (1992), 'Coping with the Legacies of Subsidized Mortgage Credit in Hungary,' WPS 847, The World Bank, Washington, D.C.

Salsman, R.M. (1993), 'Bankers as Scapegoats for Government–Created Banking Crises in US History' in White, L.H. (ed.).

Savela, J. and Herrala, R. (1992), 'Foreign–owned Banks in Finland,' *Bank of Finland Bulletin,* 66(4), April.

Sawamoto, K., Nakajima, Z. and Taguchi, H. (eds) (1995), *Financial Stability in a Changing Environment,* St.Martin's Press, New York.

Shibayama, T. (1994), 'A Comparison of Proposals for Structural Reform of Prudential Policy for the Financial System,' Washington, DC: The Brookings Institution, 1994.

Smith, R.C. (1994), *Comeback: The Restoration of American Banking Power in the New World Economy.* Harvard Business School Press.

Sundararajan, V. and Balino, T.J.T. (eds.) (1991),*Banking Crises: Cases and Issues,* International Monetary Fund.

Székely, I.P (1994), 'Economic Transformation and the Reform of the Financial System in Central and Eastern Europe' in Agabegyan, A. and Bogomolov, E. (eds.), *Economics in a Changing World,* Vol.1, 1994, MacMillan, pp.260–91.

Székely, I.P. (1990), 'The Reform of the Hungarian Financial System,' *European Economy* No.43, March.

Talley, S.H. (1993), 'Are Failproof Banking Systems Feasible? Desirable?' The World Bank Working Papers Series 1095.

Talley, S.H. (1995), 'Protecting Bank Depositors.'

Talley, S.H. and Mas, I. (1990), *Deposit Insurance in Developing Countries,* World Bank Working Paper, November.

Udell, G.F. and Wachtel, P. (1995), 'Financial System Design for Formerly Planned Economies: Defining the Issues,' *Financial Markets, Institutions and Instruments,* 4(2).

US Treasury (1991), *Modernizing the Financial System: Recommendations for Safe, More Competitive Banks.*

Várhegyi, É. (1995), 'A magyar bankpiac állapota és fejlödése' (The Hungarian banking market and its development, in Hungarian), (mimeo).

Várhegyi, É. (1994), 'The "Second" Reform of the Hungarian Banking System,' in Bonin, J.P. and Székely, I.P. (1994), pp.293–308.

Vittas, D. and Neal, C. (1992), 'Competition and Efficiency in Hungarian Banking,' (mimeo), The World Bank, Washington, D.C.

White, L.H., ed. (1993), *The Crisis in American Banking,* New York University Press, New York and London.

Wijnbergen, S.van (1994), 'On the Role of Banks in Enterprise Restructuring: The Polish Example,' Discussion Paper Series No.898, Centre for Economic Policy Research, London.

World Bank (1989), *World Development Report: Financial Systems and Development,* Washington.

Zank, N.S, Mathieson, J.A., Nieder, F.T., Vickland, K.D., and Ivey, R.J. (1991), *Reforming Financial Systems: Policy Change and Privatization,* Greenwood Press, New York, Westport, Connecticut and London.

Index

ABN-AMRO 30, 140
accounting standard 15, 71, 116, 158
Agro Bank (Hungary) 86, 116, 132, 136
Agrobanka (Czech) 41, 88, 90
AIB — *see* Allied Irish Banks
Allied Irish Banks (AIB) 5, 18, 26, 36, 49, 52, 78, 80
American Baltic Bank 94
American depository receipts 32, 55
auditing 5, 71, 158

Baltija Bank 104, 105, 124, 125
Bank Austria 88
Bank Biochim 119
Bank Consolidation Company (Bulgaria) 20, 92, 119
Bank Depozytowo-Kredytowy (BDK) 32, 33
Bank Gdanski (BG) 18, 29, 31, 32
Bank Gospodarki Zywnosciowej (BGZ) 33, 48, 103, 120
Bank Handlowy 6, 18, 33, 148
Bank Inicjatyw Gospodarczych (BIG) 18, 32
Bank of Estonia (BoE) 20, 121-3, 166-7
Bank of Latvia 125
Bank of New York 32
Bank Polska Kasa Opieki SA (PeKaO SA) 33, 148, 154
Bank Rozwoju Exportu (BRE) 27, 54

Bank Slaski (BSK) 5, 18, 26-31, 44, 48-50, 52, 54, 77-8, 81, 98, 103
Bank Slaski affair 29-30, 49
Bank Zachodni (BZ) 32
Banque Paribas 26
Barings 36, 111
Basel minimum capital standards 15, 16, 123
Bayerische Landesbank Girozentrale Bank (BLB) 34-5, 51-2, 82
BB — *see* Budapest Bank
Bekesi, Laszlo 36
BG — *see* Bank Gdanski
BGZ — *see* Bank Gospodarki Zywnosciowej
BHF 88, 92
BIG — *see* Bank Inicjatyw Gospodarczych
BLB — *see* Bayerische Landesbank Girozentrale Bank
BNP — Dresdner Bank 100
BoE — *see* Bank of Estonia
Bojanczyk, Miroslaw 26
Bokros, Lajos 36
Borowski, Marek 29
BPH 6, 7, 18, 26, 30, 31, 44, 48, 50, 52
BRE — *see* Bank Rozwoju Exportu
BSK — *see* Bank Slaski
Budapest Bank (BB) 35-7, 39, 52, 65, 73, 82-3, 96, 98, 117, 180

Budapest Stock Exchange 64
budget constraint 106, 111, 112
Budgoski Bank 80
Bulgarian Brady Bonds 22
Bulgarian National Bank 20, 92,
    94
BZ — *see* Bank Zachodni

capital requirements 8, 58, 63, 64,
    82, 88, 94, 98, 107, 108, 116,
    125, 127, 133, 142, 166
central bank (*see also* National
    Bank of Hungary, National
    Bank of Poland, Czech
    National Bank etc.) 13-16,
    18-19, 70, 72, 95, 108-109,
    123,127-8, 130, 132, 136, 148
Central-European International
    Bank Ltd. (CIB) 45
Česka Pojistovná 43
Česka Spořitelna 19, 39-42, 51, 90,
    100, 152, 153, 163, 165
Československá Obchodní Banka
    (ČSOB) 40, 41, 42, 51, 55, 165
CIB — *see* Central-European
    International Bank Ltd.
Citibank 37, 45, 63, 73, 76, 78, 80,
    81, 84, 87-8, 91-2, 98
ČNB — *see* Czech National Bank
COMECON 118
competition 1, 8, 10, 11, 17, 21,
    40, 45-6, 53-4, 59-60, 62, 65,
    68,74, 99, 101, 107, 111, 112,
    116, 129, 141, 143, 149, 154-
    5, 159-161, 168, 174
concentration of ownership 42, 43,
    59, 62, 64, 69, 73, 88, 96, 98,
    109, 111, 150, 153, 160, 165
consolidation 6, 11, 32-3, 45-7,
    53, 69, 73, 80, 85, 93-4, 111,
    116, 128
Consolidation Bank (Konsolidačni

Banka) 88, 120
consumer confidence 112, 131
consumption 66
contractualism 101
Cosmo 108
Credit Agricole 36
Credit Lyonnais 110
Credit Suisse First Boston (CSFB)
    30, 36-7, 52, 61, 80, 83
Creditanstalt 37, 41, 61, 64, 80, 84,
    85, 87, 98
cross-border activities 57-9, 62,
    143, 165, 167
ČS — *see* Ceska Spořitelna
CSFB — *see* Credit Suisse First
    Boston
ČSOB — *see* Československá
    Obchodní Banka
currency substitution 147-9, 157,
    164, 170, 173-4
Czech National Bank (ČNB)
    40, 55, 121
Czech Savings Bank — *see* Česka
    Spořitelna
Czechoslovak Savings Bank 19
Czechoslovak State Bank 19

Daewoo Corp. 33
Daiwa Europe Ltd. 31-2, 50
Deloitte and Touche 30
deposit insurance 13-16, 69, 87,
    104, 105, 107, 111-114, 126,
    129-31, 134-9, 149, 157
deregulation 107-110, 113, 115, 121
Deutsche Bank 61
dividend policy 3, 4
Duna Bank 84, 180

EBRD — *see* European Bank for
    Reconstruction and
    Development Economic Bank
    118

efficiency 7, 68-9, 73, 91, 101,
103, 112, 116, 134, 142, 159,
174
Erdely, Gabor 35
Espebebe 31
Estonian Investment Bank 94-5,
184
Estonian Savings Bank 126, 148,
152-3, 165-8, 183-4
EU — *see* European Union
European Bank for Reconstruction
and Development (EBRD) 7,
25-6, 31, 34, 35, 37, 49-52,
78, 80, 82, 84, 93, 94, 103,
166, 184
European Union 15, 46, 53, 61,
71, 106, 110, 121, 125, 138

Federal Deposit Insurance Corp.
(FDIC) 106
Fiat 26
First Private Bank of Bulgaria 126
Ford Credit Europe 80, 100
FSM SA 26

GE Capital 37, 65, 83
German Investment and
Development Corp. (GIDC) 35
Glass-Steagall Act 106
global depository receipts 32, 54,90
Gosbank 20

Hansabank 126, 150, 165-8, 184
Harvard Group 41-2
Hebrosbank 103
HSBC Investment Bank Limited 32
Hyogo Bank 108
HYPO Bank 88

IBP 81
IBUSZ Bank 174
IFC — *see* International Finance

Corporation
International Finance Corporation
(IFC) 88, 92
ING 5, 18, 29, 31, 36-7, 44, 49,
50, 52, 77-8, 80-81, 83-4, 93,
98
initial public offerings (IPO) 4, 6,
21, 25, 27, 28, 30-32, 39, 44,
52-3, 76
InterTek 125
Investiční a Poštovní Banka (IPB)
40-43, 51, 165
investment banking 64, 76, 80, 91,
93
IPB — *see* Investiční a Poštovní
Banka
IPO — *see* Initial public offerings

J.P. Morgan 34
James Capel 32
Japanese Deposit Insurance Corp.
(JDIC) 108
Jeantet et Associes 26
joint ventures 58

K&H — *see* Kereskedelmi Bank
Kavanek, Pavel 40
Kawalek, Stefan 29
Kereskedelmi Bank (K&H) 39,
124, 180
Kizu 108
Klapal, Jaroslav 40
Komercni Banka (KB) 39, 41-2,
51, 65, 73, 90, 92, 100, 104,
165
Kožený, Viktor 41-2
Kredo Bank 126
Kredyt Bank 32

Latvian Banka Baltija 126
Latvian Deposit Bank 126
Latvian Savings Bank 124

Lerner, A.H. 35
London Club 94, 100

Magyar Hitel Bank 39, 84
Magyar Kulkereskedelmi Bank
   (MKB) 34, 35, 37, 51-2, 82
maturity mismatch 156
Mellinger, P. 35
Mexican economic crisis 66-7
MHB 124, 140, 174
Midland Bank 88
Mineralbank 118, 119
MKB — *see* Magyar
   Kulkereskedelmi Bank
Morgan Grenfell 33

National Bank of Poland (NBP)
   19, 32, 77-8, 120
National Bank of Hungary (NBH)
   19, 33, 35, 45, 81, 84, 123, 177
National Property Fund (Czech
   Republic) 88, 100
nationalism 66
NBH — *see* National Bank of
   Hungary
NBP — *see* National Bank of
   Poland
non-performing loans 4, 58, 65,
   66, 73, 78, 91, 92, 94, 98, 102-
   104,108-110, 117-120, 127-8,
   132-4, 142
North Estonian Bank 122, 165

Orszagos Takarekpenztar es
   Kereskedelmi Bank (OTP) 37-
   9, 44, 51, 63, 83, 84, 148, 150,
   152-4, 168, 174-7, 180, 183,
   186
OTP — *see* Orszagos
   Takarekpenztar es
   Kereskedelmi Bank

Pawlak, Waldemar 29
PBG — see Powszechny Bank
   Gospodarczy
PBK — *see* Powszechny Bank
   Kredytowy
PBKS — *see* Pomorski Bank
   Kredytowy
PBR 33
PeKaO SA — *see* Bank Polska
   Kasa Opieki SA
personnel issues 9, 73, 84, 86, 98,
   104, 124, 132, 158
PKO BP — *see* Powszechny Kasa
   Oszczednosci-Bank
   Panstwowy
Polgari (Civic) Bank 117
Polish Development Bank 78
Pomorski Bank Kredytowy
   (PBKS) 32-3
Postabank 174-5, 178
Powszechny Bank Gospodarczy
   (PBG) 32, 33
Powszechny Bank Kredytowy
   (PBK) 32
Powszechny Kasa Oszczednosci-
   Bank Panstwowy (PKO-BP)
   33, 120, 148, 152-3, 181
product innovation 11, 46, 73, 75,
   85, 92, 134, 144, 153-6, 159-
   61,166, 173-4, 177, 180
provisioning 4, 92, 116, 133, 139
První Investični AS (PIAS) 43

Quandt, Janusz 30, 31

Raiffeisen 78
Rajczyk, Marian 29
recapitalization 9, 12, 15, 17, 69,
   83, 94, 103, 120, 123
regulatory structure 1-3, 12-17, 47,
   52-4, 57-8, 63, 72, 86, 108,
   116, 131, 139, 156-8

Repse, Einars 125
Restitution Investment Fund (RIF)
   42-3

Salzmann, Richard 42, 90
Sberbank 124, 148
Schroders 37
Sczurek, Stan 77
Simor, Andras 85-6
Slovak Savings Bank 19
Social Bank 166
Solidarnosc Chase Bank 83
Sopot Bank 31
Soros, George 38, 83
state savings banks (*see also* Česka
   Spořitelna, OTP, etc.) 11-12,
   19-20, 24, 33, 46-7, 53, 119,
   131, 139, 141-3, 147-161
State Savings Bank (Bulgaria)
   152-3
subordinated debt 138-9
Swoboda, Karel 91-2

Takarebank 84
Tarafas, Imre 84
Tartu Commercial Bank 94, 122
tax policy 3-4, 11, 46, 70-71, 80,
   133, 137
Templeton Worldwide 48

Tolwinski, Edmund 31
Tourist-Sport Bank 126
Uher, Thomas 64
Union Baltic Bank 122
Union Bank of Estonia 165
United Bulgarian Bank 103, 119

Vneshekonombank 122
voucher distribution 4, 6, 21, 39,
   41, 43, 52-3, 76, 87-8, 91-2,
   95-6
Všeobečna Uvěrová Banka 41-2

Warsaw Stock Exchange (WSE)
   18, 25-9, 31-2, 48, 50-52, 54, 80
WBK — see Wielkopolski Bank
   Kredytowy
Westdeutsches Landesbank 88, 100
Wielkopolski Bank Kredytowy
   (WBK) 4, 7, 18, 25-8, 31, 47-
   9, 52, 54, 78, 80, 104
World Bank 104, 113
Wroblewski, Andrzej 50-51
WSE — *see* Warsaw Stock
   Exchange

Ybl 117

Živnostenská Banka 88, 92